About Island Press

Island Press is the only nonprofit organization in the United States whose principal purpose is the publication of books on environmental issues and natural resource management. We provide solutions-oriented information to professionals, public officials, business and community leaders, and concerned citizens who are shaping responses to environmental problems.

In 1994, Island Press celebrated its tenth anniversary as the leading provider of timely and practical books that take a multidisciplinary approach to critical environmental concerns. Our growing list of titles reflects our commitment to bringing the best of an expanding body of literature to the environmental community throughout North America and the world.

Support for Island Press is provided by Apple Computer, Inc., The Bullitt Foundation, The Geraldine R. Dodge Foundation, The Energy Foundation, The Ford Foundation, The W. Alton Jones Foundation, The Lyndhurst Foundation, The John D. and Catherine T. MacArthur Foundation, The Andrew W. Mellon Foundation, The Joyce Mertz-Gilmore Foundation, The National Fish and Wildlife Foundation, The Pew Charitable Trusts, The Pew Global Stewardship Initiative, The Rockefeller Philanthropic Collaborative, Inc., and individual donors.

About Defenders of Wildlife

Defenders of Wildlife is a national, nonprofit membership organization headquartered in Washington, D.C., with field offices in Alaska, Arizona, Florida, Montana, New Mexico, and Oregon. Founded in 1947, Defenders has nearly half a century of leadership in educating and advocating for the protection, restoration, and enhancement of all species of wild animals and plants in their natural communities.

Defenders' staff of wildlife professionals works to shape policy and programs at the state and federal levels through numerous partnership efforts with public agencies. Through conferences and publications, including the award-winning magazine *Defenders* and membership newsletter *Wildlife Advocate,* the organization works to educate people across the nation on a wide range of biodiversity-related issues.

Defenders gratefully acknowledges the support of more than 120,000 members, corporations, foundations, and a national network of devoted conservation activists.

BIODIVERSITY AND THE LAW

And I brought you into a plentiful country,
to eat the fruit thereof and the goodness thereof:
but when ye entered,
ye defiled my land,
and made mine heritage an abomination.
—BOOK OF JEREMIAH 2:7

BIODIVERSITY AND THE LAW

EDITED BY

WILLIAM J. SNAPE III

FOREWORD BY

OLIVER A. HOUCK

DEFENDERS OF WILDLIFE

ISLAND PRESS

WASHINGTON, D.C. ■ COVELO, CALIFORNIA

Library of Congress Cataloging-in-Publication Data

Biodiversity and the law / edited and written by William J. Snape, III.
        p.   cm.
    Includes bibliographical references and index.
    ISBN 1-55963-394-8. — ISBN 1-55963-395-6 (pbk.)
    1. Biological diversity conservation—Law and legislation.
    2. Biological diversity conservation. 3. Biological diversity.
    I. Snape, William J., III.
    K3478.B56   1996
    346.04'695—dc20
    [342.64695]   95-9317
                                                              CIP

Printed on recycled, acid-free paper ⊛

Manufactured in the United States of America

10 9   8   7   6   5   4   3   2   1

To Tony S. Norton

CONTENTS

Foreword by Oliver A. Houck   xi

Preface   xv

Acknowledgments   xvii

Introduction   xix

PART I
BIODIVERSITY LAW: WHERE SCIENCE AND POLICY MEET
1

1. Biodiversity Policy and Ecosystem Management   11
   Mollie Beattie

2. Biodiversity as a Basis for Conservation Efforts   16
   Donald M. Waller

PART II
BIODIVERSITY'S SAFETY NET: SAVING ENDANGERED SPECIES
33

3. Biodiversity, Ecosystems, and Endangered Species   43
   Jason Patlis
4. Conservation Planning Under the ESA: A New Paradigm   59
   Lindell L. Marsh
5. Biodiversity and Private Property: Conflict or Opportunity?   67
   Todd G. Olson

PART III
INTERNATIONAL PROTECTION: BEYOND HUMAN BOUNDARIES
81

6. Using Trade Measures to Protect Biodiversity   93
    Leesteffy Jenkins

7. Harmful Exotics in the United States   105
    Peter Jenkins

8. Protecting Global Marine Biodiversity   120
    Suzanne Iudicello

9. Biodiversity Conservation and International Instruments   131
    Scott Hajost and Curtis Fish

PART IV
WHO OWNS WHAT? A PUBLIC TRUST FOR BIODIVERSITY
145

10. Can the Public Trust Doctrine Prevent Extinctions?   157
     Ralph W. Johnson with William C. Galloway

11. Rediscovering Old Tools   165
     John A. Pendergrass

12. The Promise of NEPA   178
     Dinah Bear

13. Wildlife's Burden   189
     Walter Kuhlmann

14. Global Trade, Local Economies, and the
     Biodiversity Convention   202
     David R. Downes

Conclusion   217

*Epilogue: The Argument for a Constitutional
Amendment to Protect Living Nature*   221
Rodger Schlickeisen

About the Contributors   243

Index   247

FOREWORD

Every once in a while an idea comes along that changes the way we think about ourselves. The great religions are enduring examples, but nearly as powerful have been the secular teachings of Gandhi, Darwin, and Freud. Here at the end of the twentieth century we find ourselves at the doorsill of another new teaching. It has been preceded by a handful of prophets—Aldo Leopold and Rachael Carson for openers—who have demonstrated the interconnectedness of living things. It has been resisted by the followers of other prophets who see in this interconnectedness a threat to the supremacy of the master species, humankind. The emerging idea is not yet crystal clear, but what the writings of E. O. Wilson, Michael Scott, Reed Noss, and other scientist-preachers of the field of conservation biology are outlining is a new organizing principle for life on earth: biological diversity.

This book is a first response to the idea of biological diversity. It is an unfinished response. Indeed, it is a variety of partial responses by over a dozen experts in the biological sciences, social sciences, and law who are asking themselves the question: If biological diversity is an imperative, then how do we get there from here? The writings offered here are as informative in the composite as they are individually. Taken together they indicate ways in which human institutions may, and should, change. Change is, of course, what is so threatening about environmental principles in general and about the idea of biological diversity. If the diversity of life is indeed necessary for the future of life on earth and human institutions must indeed change to accommodate it, then the maintenance of biological diversity sets a new bottom line for human activity—one higher than that currently set even for the protection of endangered species. Suddenly we are talking about Major Accommodation of nature. If you dislike environmental protection, if you thought endangered species protection was faintly hysterical, then biological diversity will send you up the wall.

These worries remain, however, largely premature. Biological diversity, with the exception of a few federal natural resources programs, has not yet risen to bite any human activity on the ankle or steer any use of the earth and its resources in a new direction. At least three obstacles stand in its way. The first obstacle is the lack of precision on exactly what biological diversity *is*. The second is the lack of public awareness of biological diversity and a reason to maintain it. The third is the paucity of mechanisms for incorporating the idea—however it is defined and accepted—into human institutions so that life on earth remains, in fact, diverse. The magnitude of these tasks should not be underestimated.

The threshold challenge to biological diversity, the first obstacle, is the ease with which the term is spoken and the difficulty by which it is interpreted and applied. More than half a century ago, Aldo Leopold wrote that the first order of intelligent tinkering is to save every cog and wheel—which seems a perfectly sensible statement in the context of, say, the Atom Bomb but becomes more problematic when we come to mowing the lawn or building a new road through town. The fact is that nearly all human development impinges on the resilience of the earth and its biota.

The challenge, then, is to draw the line in an objective, scientifically supportable fashion so that human beings can understand and be guided by it. Setting these thresholds, however, has proved no small task even for discrete parts of our ecosystem, such as water and air quality, and great debates continue to rage over "acceptable levels" of dioxin in the environment, of particulates, and even the exhaustively studied DDT. The task has not proved much easier in setting thresholds for the endangerment of discrete species whose histories may be little known and whose distinction from related subspecies and populations are . . . subtle, to put the matter generously. The conservation of biological diversity requires us to go beyond even these difficulties to address water, air, soil, and living things, endangered and nonendangered, as a whole. The task is daunting. I have had the good fortune to participate with some of the best minds in conservation biology at several meetings addressed to this task. My conclusion: the science may be close, but it has not yet arrived.

The second obstacle facing biological diversity is its low resonance with the American people as an idea or a threat. E. O. Wilson's magnificent statement of the idea in *The Diversity of Life* may have sounded the alarm bell, but not many of us have looked outside to see what was going on. A 1993 poll conducted by Defenders of Wildlife, a Washington-based environmental organization, showed that, as an issue, biological diversity rated dead last in public awareness on a list of environmental issues ranging from endangered species to global warming. We have come to the point that while we, many Americans at least, appreciate the pieces, we do not yet take in the whole. We will move mountains to save baby seals, wolves, and stranded whales. But in a world rife with streetshootings, grinding inequity, and ethnic wars of extermination, it is hard to get worked up over "ecosystems." The idea lacks the cachet of a best-seller, and an idea that can't be easily sold these days is in trouble.

The third obstacle facing biological diversity is the scarcity of mechanisms to implement it—whether for major federal activities or on a local, private level. As was the case with the term "environment" thirty years ago, few federal statutes today even contain the word "diversity." The one federal agency with an explicit diversity mandate, the U.S. Forest Service, has a checkered record of interpreting its meaning. Several forest plans, some described later in this book by Walter Kuhlmann, defend the continued fragmentation of forest ecosystems through extensive clearcutting as actually promoting "diversity" by the introduction of habitat for deer, rabbit, and other species that are widespread, if not epidemic, in the nation at large. Newer forest plans, on the other hand, such as that developed for the immense Tongass forest of Alaska, start with the long-term needs of rare species to then determine what other uses, including timber harvest, remain. The Forest Service has, in effect, become the laboratory for the concept of biological diversity at the federal level.

Two-thirds of America is privately owned, however, and the states with the greatest numbers of vanishing species and ecosystems are those that have been subject to the most rapid private development: Florida, California, and Hawaii. Mechanisms to preserve biological diversity on private lands include conservation easements, tax reductions, and endangered lands purchase programs, but in their aggregate they remain dwarfed by the pace of private land development itself. Few adult Americans raised outside of cities can even recognize the landscapes around their home towns, and no one could predict anything but even more rapid development in the years to come. The one startling innovation on the nonfederal side of land development—habitat conservation planning—has been prompted by the Endangered Species Act. It is the state of California that is serving as the laboratory here, and California habitat conservation plans have become impressively ambitious, covering acreage as vast as several states, numerous species and ecosystems, and a mix of zoning, tax, and property right trading mechanisms. This planning process may well be the last best hope of saving at least some cogs and wheels of our natural world.

And saving ourselves? As I've said, that case is not yet firmly established. The link between biodiversity and human welfare is certainly supported by medical and scientific uses of little-known and lower-form biota, but it has not yet been proved as linear. Less Yet is this link accepted as a fact of life by the American public, for an increasing number of whom life in a city or a well-tended suburb is about all there needs to be. Still fewer are mechanisms in place for either public or private development that are even in the same ballpark as the soaring rate of development and the crash of life systems on earth. The first is a job for science; the second, for educators; and the third, for lawyers like me. I have no confidence that these jobs can be done. I only know that the situation seems too critical not to try.

OLIVER A. HOUCK
NEW ORLEANS, LOUISIANA

Oliver A. Houck is professor of law at Tulane Law School, where he teaches several environmental law courses and serves as faculty advisor for The Tulane Environmental Law Journal. *He is a past chairman of the Defenders of Wildlife Board of Directors' Program Policy Committee and a member of the board's Litigation Committee. He is also former general counsel of the National Wildlife Federation, specializing in endangered species and wetlands protection, and a former prosecutor with the U.S. Attorney's Office in Washington, D.C.*

PREFACE

In March 1994, Defenders of Wildlife held what we believe is the first legally accredited conference on biological diversity. There had already been several informal workshops and a handful of publications on the subject, but no one had attempted to pull all the various aspects together in a comprehensive manner. Our conference speakers reflected the diversity of those committed to advancing the protection of biodiversity, from policymakers and scholars to advocates and entrepreneurs.

We are indebted to these biodiversity professionals, who made impressive presentations at the conference and then spent considerable time working on the chapters that appear here. Their charge, and my goal, was to explain the legal tenets of biodiversity in a way that is not only intellectually credible but also understandable to a broad spectrum of nonlawyers and scientific laypeople.

Part I of the book lays the scientific and policy foundations for the broad topic of biodiversity and the law. U.S. domestic efforts to establish an effective endangered species protection regime is the topic of Part II, which reveals the considerable creativity now necessary for effective 1990s conservation regulation. Part III takes an international look at biodiversity protection, which is driven by a number of multilateral agreements and institutions that are integrally related to powerful global economic forces. Examining biodiversity as a genuinely public entity is the theme of Part IV, where a vision of the law's future begins to emerge. Finally, Rodger Schlickeisen's Epilogue makes a bold proposal to change the very basis of biodiversity law by amending the U.S. Constitution to include sustainable ecological values.

In no way is this book meant to be an encyclopedia of biodiversity law. Such a task may not be possible for a legal discipline with so many facets and, at this early stage of development, could easily lose even the most experienced lawyer or policy advocate. Instead, this book is a description of biodiversity's basic legal threads and themes. Its aim is to explain the importance of biodiversity law to those inside and outside the conservation profession, to educate people on the major scientific and legal angles to biodiversity, and to relate biodiversity law to all aspects of everyday human life.

I was drawn to the environmental movement by an inherent belief that the human quality of life is directly linked to the health of the natural world around us. This is not an issue of different political parties, religions, or lifestyles. It is an issue of humanity. The U.S. Congress and various state legislatures that are now actively considering the roll back of environmental protection must understand the gravity of their actions.

This book argues that biodiversity, which by definition includes all species of life on earth, will eventually be seen as the major tenet of environmental law and policy. In addition to its emphasis on traditional species protection efforts, as well as pollution concerns like clean air and water, biodiversity ultimately addresses the human relationship with the greater natural world. Inevitably, the relationship is based on personal experience and attachment to place. You can only conserve, protect, and defend what you know. For me, this means an affinity for the Pine Barrens of New Jersey with its particular smells, brush, and people. What is universal, however, are certain fundamental elements of all these peculiar relationships, which this book describes in factual and legal detail. In simple terms, if we each took care of our home and treated others' as we would our own, then the world would undoubtedly be a better place.

This book, therefore, is also a call to action. Its contents do not seek to impose an agenda on reluctant officials or citizens, but merely to preserve a way of life for those who care and for those not yet born. As one who has spent the bulk of his life following and studying society's rules, I am losing patience with business as usual. I know I am not alone. The rules must be changed to protect what we now call biodiversity.

W.J.S. III

ACKNOWLEDGMENTS

To bring a book to fruition is to fully understand the meaning of an acknowledgments page. I could not have completed this book without the assistance of a number of people: Rodger Schlickeisen, who has been a driving force behind the process of examining biodiversity and the law; Elizabeth Saxton, who contributed in countless ways; Tracey Bohn, who graciously volunteered her time to edit a number of the chapters; Nina Fascione, without whom I would have certainly lost my sanity during the last days of manuscript preparation; Charles Beretz, who was almost always able to crack a tough research question; and Lisa Osborn, who served as a fantastic reality check on my chapters and contributed substantial editing on others.

Others who made significant contributions to the final product were Ted Illston, Dennis Hughes, Matt Royer, John Perrine, Elizabeth Hammond, Rob Peters, and literally the rest of the Defenders of Wildlife staff. Thanks are also in order to Karin Sheldon, John Fitzgerald, and Oliver Houck, who served as moderators for the conference that sprung this book. In addition, Barbara Dean, Barbara Youngblood, and Christine McGowan at Island Press provided invaluable editorial expertise, and this entire exercise would not have been possible without the support of both The Bydale Foundation and The Florence and John Schumann Foundation.

Above all I want to acknowledge my family, friends, and colleagues whose ideas and support are sprinkled throughout the pages that follow. And, finally, to Deb, who reminds me to live and learn a diversity of ideas every day.

INTRODUCTION

Without a diversity of people we cannot maintain a diversity of anything else. By a diversity of people I do not mean a diversity of specialists, but a diversity of people elegantly suited to live in their places and to bring them to their best use, whether the use is that of uselessness, as in a place left wild, or that of the highest sustainable productivity.

—WENDELL BERRY

The immediate challenge for a book on biodiversity and the law is defining "biodiversity." The term intimidates. To the layperson, it sounds big and detached, vaguely like a difficult high school science question. To the wildlife conservationist, it represents an exciting but almost overwhelming opportunity. To many in the business world, it signifies nefarious government regulation.

But biodiversity, short for biological diversity, is not an extraordinarily complicated concept. Nor should it be controversial. It is a term that possesses familiar Greek (*bio*) and Latin (*diversitas*) roots and describes a reality far older than our own species. At its most literal level, biodiversity represents the variability of all natural life forms. On a slightly more sophisticated level, it is the sum of all genes, species, habitats, and natural processes that constitute the very essence of existence on earth. In short, biodiversity is life.

For its part "the law" may be generically more comprehensible than biodiversity, but its workings can be just as complex and unpredictable. We know, for example, that the law tells us not to speed when driving an automobile and to pay our taxes every April 15. Yet the average citizen does not readily understand the details of the latest congressional bill on farm spending or the recent Supreme Court decision relating to interstate commerce. Despite its frequent contortions, the law has always reflected human values. Such was the case in tribal Africa, dynastic China, ancient Greece, and feudal Europe, where those who governed could not rule for long without the rudimentary consent of the masses. Even Machiavelli acknowledged the importance of the "friendship of the people" and "good laws."[1] Today, throughout a largely democratic world, the law is premised on accepted social norms and customs, whether they relate to free speech, criminal violations, or environmental protection.

Since the explosion of industrial capitalism several hundred years ago, the law has been saddled with a new tension over the proper role of government. As citizens gained the power to exchange and collect items of value, national governments inherited the concomitant ability to regulate private transactions in favor of their interpretation of the greater public good. The rationale for governmental intrusion into private exchanges has always been that the free market does not perfectly allocate all societal resources, even if it serves as an indispensable engine of social organization. While Nazi Germany and the communist Soviet Union represent two undesirable extremes of governmental intervention, few credible politicians have ever seriously advocated completely abdicating government's role as society's referee. Nonetheless, government regulations have become the focal point for the basically unresolvable debate between private profit and public obligation. Despite the relatively recent origin of these often fierce ideological disputes, they are now of central relevance to the implementation of almost every social law.

In this context, we arrive at a threshold legal question for biodiversity: is it a human value worthy of government regulation? The assumption in this book is that biodiversity, and lots of it, should be conserved and preserved by law. The reasons are as varied as they are compelling: scientific, technological, economic, philosophical, ethical, aesthetic, and emotional. The challenge is to build a comprehensive biodiversity policy from a variety of other legal disciplines that read almost like a Rolodex: administrative, clean air and water, endangered species, federal, game, international, natural resources, patent, property, state, toxics, trade, water, and zoning. Essential to such a massive synthesis will be broad political support and concerted public education.

As Oliver Houck notes in the Foreword, Aldo Leopold's admonition, "To keep every cog and wheel is the first precaution of intelligent tinkering,"[2] is perhaps the ultimate reason to support biodiversity protection. Without biodiversity, we humans would deny ourselves the myriad scientific treasures offered by nature and the very resources on which we depend for survival. If Leopold was correct, as most scientists now believe, current data indicate that we have a grave problem. Species are declining at a rate hundreds, if not thousands, of times faster than in any other era of human history. Cogs and wheels are vanishing not only in the well-publicized rain forests of Brazil, but in almost every other corner of the world as well.

Though barely out of its infancy, the science of conservation biology is taking its first steps toward a comprehension of biodiversity. It is able to identify species that are indicators or keystones for an entire ecosystem. It understands many ecological processes and their functional roles. It can offer a crude measure for the overall health of the earth. For when the natural variety of species in a habitat area declines, it is highly likely that the associated condition of the land, air, water, and food chain in that location is also declining. The necessity of a healthy environment, therefore, is helplessly intertwined with the importance of natural species diversity. Only life possesses both the ability and the liability to reflect fundamental environmental change. This is why biodiversity law will inevitably become the central tenet of environmental law.

The fruits of biodiversity are, in fact, already producing tangible human benefits. Wildlife species yield a steady flow of pest and disease-resistant food varieties, as well as new medications that have led to cancer cures and could hold the key to solving the AIDS crisis.[3] Biodiversity science helps to formulate sustainable harvest levels and state-of-the-art management models for living natural resources like trees and fish, both of which are rapidly dwindling around the globe. Biodiversity applications have even been used in directly advancing the law, as when the microbe *Thermus aquaticus* was used in a blood analysis test alleged to have linked O.J. Simpson to a double-murder.

For all its good, though, biodiversity is not without its controversies. Genetically engineered foodstuffs now engender fierce arguments over the appropriate level of government regulation. The political battle between biodiversity protection and private property rights rages at all levels of government. And the debate about the necessity of only utilitarian justifications for Mother Earth's life forms continues to hover over many philosophical and religious deliberations. But regardless of one's views on any of these issues, it is naive to believe that humans will decline to take part in the "contest between intelligence, which presses forward, and an unworthy, timid ignorance obstructing our progress."[4] The potential of biodiversity science beckons our innately curious species, even as we debate definitions of "intelligence" and "progress."

The science of biodiversity, like all sciences, is laden with unavoidable human judgments. Science after all is no more than reality through a human lens. It leads but does not tell. Sound scientific public policy, therefore, demands a forthright examination of biodiversity's value and importance:

> There are occasions when we will run the risk of the possibility of the extinction of species. Because we think that whatever other options we have

are too damaging. And I say run the risk. . . . This is not an excuse for ignoring science. But it is a plea for balance.[5]

Despite his frequent opposition to various biodiversity-related governmental protections, former Senator Robert Packwood (R–OR) has at least framed the key question in the preceding statement: given that species extinction at some rate or other is a natural phenomenon, how many of them should the human species allow or authorize? This is an eminently serious question. Never has one species possessed so much power over life.

Conservationists, who perhaps share more than a prefix with true conservatives, generally want to err on the side of caution when expending natural resources. Instead of asking "Must we save *every* species?" as Packwood did, they ask "Can we afford to lose *any* species?" Being a conservationist means deferring to age-old, relatively stable, evolutionary processes over short-term human actions and desires. It means remembering that extinction is both forever and irreversible.

Still, such sweeping exhortations on behalf of biodiversity go only so far. In the ruthless political arena, which reflexively seeks short-term economic satisfaction, conservationists possess the practical burden of demonstrating the social costs of biodiversity loss. But as one scholar has noted: "The dichotomy that many perceive to have arisen between economics and ecology is false and has persisted because of bad economics."[6] The solution, long a challenge for economists and policymakers alike, is "full-cost internalization." That is, we need mechanisms that will capture the broader social and biodiversity costs not reflected in individual-to-individual transactions. For example, the sale of an endangered tiger pelt might not reflect the public's interest in avoiding extinction of this species, just as the sale of a wetland might not capture socity's ecological interest in water purification and bird habitat, or the sale of widgets might not reflect the effluent pollution and waste generated by manufacturing processes.

While most critics of species protection focus on the economic losses of biodiversity regulation, the shallowness of many of these arguments is becoming increasingly apparent. Strip malls, corporate farming, and mineral exploitation are certainly no more economically important than the entire fishing industry, a booming biotechnology sector, or the multifaceted business of ecotourism. The question is not whether economic development is desirable, but what form of development is sustainable in the long run. If government-sponsored biodiversity protection is inefficient or subject to bureaucratic abuse, then the debate should focus on this problem. Biodiversity is simply too important to leave unprotected or at the total whim of an economic market.

Indeed, from the food we eat to the clothes we wear, all human economic development is ultimately dependent on biodiversity and its associated natural resources. But by its very nature, biodiversity cannot be neatly packaged or contained. Humans cannot behave with reckless abandon and expect natural biodiversity to remain intact. Many scientists already hypothesize, for example, that human health is directly linked to natural diversity.[7] Also compelling are the intergenerational arguments in favor of biodiversity protection, which urge the living not to rob our descendants of essential biological resources.

One cannot escape the profound ethical questions that biodiversity raises. It forces us to ask whether other forms of life possess a right to exist apart from human valuation. It draws into focus the massive consumption habits of many in the developed world. It questions how much more separate from nature we wish to become. At its core, biodiversity asks us who we are.

So who are we? Certain aspects of human existence are virtually irreproachable: survival, family, friends, home. Others, like competition and conflict, seem inescapable. What ultimately ties the human species together is culture, the expression of emotion and reason that adds meaning to life. Nature, in all its diversity, is no less than the setting where life and culture take place.

Culture has reflected symbols and objects of nature—or biodiversity— throughout history. Religions of many societies, past and present, starkly demonstrate this relationship. Contemporary culture is no different, whether it is a story by Wallace Stegner, a poem by Gary Snyder, or a football game between the Eagles and Rams. Metaphorical references to biodiversity now even emerge in popular music,

> *Sell the kids for food*
> *Weather changes moods.*
> *Spring is here again*
> *Reproductive glands.*
> *We can have some more*
> *Nature is a whore.*
> *Bruises on the fruit*
> *Tender age in bloom.*[8]

where the basic elements of life—food, sex, and nature—are sometimes used to symbolize a generational coming of age.

Indeed, there is an uncanny similarity between late-twentiety-century rock music and none other than Henry David Thoreau: "I was surprised to see on the snow over the river a great many birch scales and seeds, though the snow had but recently fallen and there had been but little wind. . . . It suggested how unwearied Nature is in spreading her seeds."[9] Thoreau may have been too erudite to call nature a whore but his description of Nature is certainly no less fecund. And while it may be true that some form of life may indeed endure irrespective of human influence or degradation, what form will it take? What form is right? How will humans know right from wrong? These are fundamental questions of existence grounded in perpetual scientific, ethical, and spiritual inquiry. These are the questions of biodiversity.

As Darwin taught us, life is always evolving. Its coughs and hiccups are nothing compared to its mysterious strength. Although questions about biodiversity now hold a sense of scientific urgency, the human relationship with our wild brethren has been a thread in the social fabric since the origin of human existence itself. And an information-laden, technologically driven, twenty-first century is no more certain to define the optimal relationship than past generations.

Harvard professor E. O. Wilson has coined the term "biophilia"—literally the love of life—to describe the symbiotic concepts of physical survival and emotional satisfaction, which may well be embedded in human genes. Biophilia captures the rush of inhaling crisp air on a grassy mountaintop and the dire necessity of that oxygen for human survival. It describes the awe of seeing a wild grizzly bear, the appreciation of a colorful autumn afternoon, or even the fear of a wasp buzzing around your ears. Stephen Kellert observed: "Philosophers, poets, the rarest of politicians, and even the occasional scientist have at times indulged in the effort to rationalize how human life is enriched by its broadest affiliation with the natural world—and, conversely, how the impoverishment of this relationship with nature could foster a less satisfactory existence."[10] If biodiversity were to vanish, what would it do to human notions of survival, happiness, and wildness?

The law was specifically created by humans to ensure fruitful existence. As an amalgamation of human morality and culture, it is simply incapable of ignoring life. Life, in turn, cannot ignore the concept of survival, without which human law would be meaningless. Biodiversity law, then, is ultimately about meaningful survival. It is about challenging the human mind to face a world it has largely created and to shape inevitable change with intelligence and dignity.

Fortunately the human race possesses the unique capacity for original thought and action. But the present challenge is monumental. The question of this generation may be whether our species perches on the precipice of fundamental change with the surrounding natural world. As the law of life, biodiversity law describes not only the rules imposed upon ourselves as a species, but also the vast and powerful rules thrust upon us by nature. The natural laws of biodiversity await further human discovery. Biodiversity law represents a challenge to understand the full splendor of life and to respond to the social organization it will require.

NOTES

1. Niccolo Machiavelli, *The Prince,* trans. George Bull (New York: Penguin, 1981), pp. 69, 77.

2. *A Sand County Almanac* (New York: Oxford University Press, 1966), p. 190.

3. See *Greenwire,* Dec. 6, 1994, from a story by Philip Shendon in the *New York Times.* The leaves of the Calophyllum tree in the Malaysian forests of Borneo possess a substance that destroys the HIV virus without killing healthy cells. In addition, extracts from a related gum tree in Borneo, a rare vine found in Cameroon, and a shrub native to western Australia have also shown "initial success" against the HIV virus.

4. The credo of *The Economist,* transcribed on each edition's cover page.

5. Senator Packwood's statement before the Senate Environment and Public Works Committee, Subcommittee on Clean Water, Fisheries, and Wildlife, Sept. 29, 1994.

6. Malcolm Gillis, "Mending the Broken Circle for Tropical Forests," in F. H. Bormann and S. Kellert, eds., *Ecology, Economics and Ethics* (New Haven: Yale University Press, 1991), pp. 157–158.

7. See, for example, Eric Chivian, M.D., "Species Extinction and Biodiversity Loss: The Implications for Human Health," in Eric Chivian et al., *Critical Condition* (Cambridge, Mass.: MIT Press, 1993), pp. 193–224.

8. Kurt Cobain, "In Bloom," from Nirvana *Nevermind.*

9. Henry David Thoreau, *Faith in a Seed* (Washington, D.C.: Island Press, 1993), p. 44.

10. Stephen Kellert and Edward Wilson, eds., *The Biophilia Hypothesis* (Washington, D.C.: Island Press, 1993), p. 20.

REFERENCES

Abbey, Edward. 1968. *Desert Solitaire.* New York: Random House.

Ackerman, Jennifer. 1995. *Notes from the Shore.* New York: Viking.

Adams, Lowell. 1994. *Urban Wildlife Habitats.* Minneapolis: University of Minnesota Press.

Armstrong, Karen. 1993. *A History of God.* New York: Ballantine Books.

Berry, Wendell. 1993. *Sex, Economy, Freedom and Community.* New York: Pantheon Books.

Brower, David. 1985. *Let the Mountains Talk, Let the Rivers Run.* San Francisco: Harper Collins West.

Brown, Tom Jr. 1978. *The Tracker.* New York: Berkeley Books.

Brussard, Peter. 1994. Why do we want to conserve biodiversity anyway? *Society for Conservation Biology Newsletter* 1(4) (November).

Burks, David Clarke, ed. 1994. *Place of the Wild.* Washington, D.C.: Island Press.

deTocqueville, Alexis. 1964. Trans. George Lawrence; ed. J. P. Mayer. *Democracy in America*. New York: Anchor Books.

Dowie, Mark. 1995. *Losing Ground: American Environmentalism at the Close of the Twentieth Century*. Cambridge: MIT Press.

Earle, Sylvia. 1995. *Sea Change: A Message of the Oceans*. New York: G.P. Putnam's Sons.

Easterbrook, Gregg. 1995. *A Moment on Earth*. New York: Viking.

Fleming, J.R. and H.A. Gemery. 1994. *Science, Technology and the Environmental Multidisciplinary Perspectives*. Akron: The University of Akron Press.

Friedman, Lawrence. 1985. *A History of American Law*. New York: Simon & Schuster.

Fryfogle, Eric. 1993. *Justice and the Earth*. New York: Macmillan Press.

Galston, William and Karen Baehler. 1995. *Rural Development in the United States*. Washington, D.C.: Island Press.

Garrett, Laurie. 1994. *The Coming Plague*. New York: Farrar, Straus & Giroux.

Gellner, Ernest. 1994. *Conditions of Liberty*. New York: Penguin.

Goddard, Donald. 1995. *Saving Wildlife: A Century of Wildlife Conservation*. New York: Harry Abrams.

Gould, Stephen Jay. 1991. *Bully for Brontosaurus*. New York: Norton.

Grossinger, Richard, ed. 1992. *Ecology and Consciousness*. Berkeley: North Atlantic.

Hardin, Garrett. 1993. *Living Within Limits: Ecology, Economics and Population Taboos*. New York: Oxford University Press.

Hawking, Stephen. 1988. *A Brief History of Time*. New York: Bantam Books.

Hempel, Carl. 1966. *Philosophy of Natural Science*. Englewood Cliffs, N.J.: Prentice-Hall.

Huxley, Aldous. 1932. *Brave New World*. New York: Harper & Row.

Jackson, John B. 1994. *A Sense of Place, a Sense of Time*. New Haven: Yale University Press.

Kim, Ke Chung, and Robert Weaver, eds. 1994. *Biodiversity and Landscape: A Paradox of Humanity*. New York: Cambridge University Press.

Leopold, Aldo. 1933. *Game Management*. New York: Scribner's.

Lewis, Meriwether, and William Clark. 1964. Ed. John Bakeless. *Journals*. New York: Penguin.

Lyon, Thomas, ed. 1989. *This Incomperable Lande*. New York: Penguin.

Masson, Jeffrey Moussaieff, and Susan McCarthy. *When Elephants Weep*. New York: Delacorte Press.

Matthiessen, Peter. 1959. *Wildlife in America*. New York: Viking.

McPhee, John. 1968. *The Pine Barrens*. New York: Farrar, Straus & Giroux.

Morris, Desmond. 1967. *The Naked Ape*. New York: Dell Publishing.

Muir, John. 1911. *My First Summer in the Sierra*. Boston: Houghton Mifflin.

Murphy, Jeffrie, and Jules Coleman. 1990. *The Philosophy of Law*. Boulder: Westview.

Myers, Norman. 1979. *The Sinking Ark*. Oxford: Pergamon.

O'Rourke, P. J. 1994. *All the Trouble in the World: The Lighter Side of Overpopulation, Famine, Ecological Disaster, Ethnic Hatred, Plague and Poverty.* New York: Atlantic Monthly Press.

Payne, Roger. 1995. *Among Whales.* New York: Scribner's.

Peacock, Doug. 1990. *Grizzly Years.* New York: Zebra Books.

Peterson, Roger Tory. 1980. *Eastern Birds.* Boston: Houghton Mifflin.

Peterson, Roger Tory. 1990. *Western Birds.* Boston: Houghton Mifflin.

Plotkin, Mark. 1993. *Tales of a Shaman's Apprentice.* New York: Penguin.

Preston, Richard. 1994. *The Hot Zone.* New York: Random House.

Repetto, Robert, William Magrath, Michael Wells, Christine Beer, and Fabrizio Rossini. 1989. *Wasting Assets: Natural Resources in the National Income Accounts.* Washington, D.C.: World Resources Institute.

Robinson, Kim, ed. 1994. *Future Primitive.* New York: Tom Doherty Associates.

Rockwell, David. 1991. *Giving Voice to Bear.* Toronto: Robert Rinehart International.

Ruse, Michael. 1979. *The Darwinian Revolution.* Chicago: University of Chicago Press.

Schama, Simon. 1995. *Landscape and Memory.* New York: Knopf.

Scheffer, Victor. 1974. *A Voice for Wildlife.* New York: Scribner's.

Seideman, David. 1993. *Showdown at Opal Creek: The Battle for America's Last Wilderness.* New York: Carroll & Graf.

Snyder, Gary. 1990. *The Practice of the Wild.* San Francisco: North Point.

Stegner, Wallace. 1953. *Beyond the Hundredth Meridian.* Boston: Houghton Mifflin.

Stevens, William. 1995. *Miracle Under the Oaks.* New York: Pocket Books.

Stewart, Frank. 1995. *A Natural History of Nature Writing.* Washington, D.C.: Island Press.

Thomas, Lewis. 1974. *Lives of a Cell.* New York: Bantam.

Taylor, C. Barr. 1994. *Shadow of the Salmon.* New York: Tehabi Books.

Toffler, Alvin. 1983. *Previews and Premises.* New York: William Morrow.

Toffler, Alvin and Heidi. 1995. *Creating a New Civilization: The Politics of the Third Wave.* Atlanta: Turner Publishing.

Van Dyke, John. 1903. *The Desert.* New York: Scribner's.

Veblen, Thorstein. 1967. *The Theory of the Leisure Class.* London: Viking Penguin.

Vogel, Virgil. 1970. *American Indian Medicine.* Norman: University of Oklahoma Press.

Weber, Michael and Judith Gradwohl. 1995. *The Wealth of Oceans.* New York: W.W. Norton.

Wilson, Edward O. 1992. *The Diversity of Life.* Cambridge, Mass: Belknap Press.

Wilson, Edward O. 1994. *Naturalist.* Washington, D.C.: Island Press.

Worster, Donald. 1993. *The Wealth of Nature: Environmental History and the Ecological Imagination.* New York: Oxford University Press.

Wright, Robert. 1994. *The Moral Animal.* New York: Pantheon.

PART I

BIODIVERSITY LAW: WHERE SCIENCE AND POLICY MEET

Choices made today can narrow or expand future options.
—LYNTON CALDWELL

If protecting natural biodiversity is a genuine policy goal, both existing law and present interpretations of existing law are clearly inadequate. Biodiversity is plummeting at an alarming rate. Many large mammalian predators, from Asian tigers to Florida panthers, are on the brink of extinction as their habitats shrink and poachers exploit them. A great majority of our planet's bird species are in decline. Amphibians are vanishing mysteriously and precipitously. Countless invertebrates are disappearing before humans even know they exist. Native plant species are being trampled by development or overrun by exotics. Entire fisheries, once plentiful, have collapsed.

The list of depleted and vanishing species is as long as it is depressing. Ideally this problem could be solved by passing national biodiversity protection statutes across the globe that would lead to an instant cure. There are, however, two fundamental difficulties with this approach. First, such a scenario presumes that individual governments possess the political will to take such action. Second, it is far from certain that even committed policymakers know exactly how to stem the loss of biodiversity. Because biodiversity law is essentially about the intersection of broad environmental policy with science-based regulation, it is fitting that Part I features two eminent nonlawyers: U.S. Fish and Wildlife Service director Mollie Beattie and University of Wisconsin–Madison botanist Donald Waller, each of whom discuss the obstacles in establishing an effective biodiversity protection regime.

Director Beattie's challenge is especially daunting. As head of the leading federal wildlife agency, she sits in the hot seat of almost all major U.S. biodiversity policy initiatives and reactions. While environmentalists constantly warn her of the dire straits of America's wildlife species, natural resource industries clamor for job security in a ruthless global marketplace. With endangered species petitions stacked to the roof and management responsibilities of over 90 million acres of national wildlife refuges, Director Beattie must frequently remind people that the choice between jobs and species is a false one. Protecting biodiversity will protect jobs that last beyond tomorrow or next year. If water use from an aquifer, for example, is causing even a small aquatic species to decline, it is logical to conclude that such water depletion will eventually harm humans similarly dependent on that aquifer. It is not coincidence that the terms ecosystem, ecology, and economics all possess the same Greek root (*eco*) meaning "home." Still, too many Americans continue to believe that unfettered natural resource use is possible and indeed desirable. Whether this belief is the result of some innate American optimism or the 1980s-like penchant for a free lunch, Director Beattie and the rest of her colleagues in government often face a tough sell in promoting biodiversity initiatives.

The federal government, in particular, faces numerous challenges in advancing biodiversity protection. Apart from the fact that biodiversity is a relatively long-term public interest, meaning that its injury is likely to be felt most acutely by future generations, federal species protection also inherently intrudes on traditionally nonfederal concerns. Unlike federal pollution prevention or remediation statutes such as the Clean Air Act or Superfund, which largely concentrate their attention on specific industries and sites, ecologically based laws like the Endangered Species Act (ESA) necessarily touch almost every square acre of American soil and water and affect almost every human action.

This type of regulatory supervision is a problem for the federal government in several respects. First, through a tradition dating back to Roman law, state governments have historically managed wildlife.[1] Second, states (and by delegation local governments) possess what are known as "police powers," which are utilized to secure the people's health, safety, and welfare.[2] Third, federal biodiversity protection, authorized by the Constitution's commerce clause among others[3] comes at a time of extreme hostility and frustration toward the federal government. Despite the best efforts of public servants like Beattie, the American electorate has become downright surly toward a federal bureaucracy considered inefficient at best and toward a Congress where the theatrics of Democrat–Republican jousts are carried out at the expense of policies that could benefit Americans as a whole.

Consequently, Beattie manages an agency in the midst of monumental paradigm shifts. The most significant of these institutional changes is the way in which public resource decisions are now being made and implemented. A qualified and conscientious public land professional acting alone is no longer sufficient to manage natural resources, as both the science and politics of biodiversity protection demand that this professional incorporate the sentiments of his or her own interdisciplinary staff, other affected federal agencies, applicable state and local officials, and an increasingly educated public.[4]

From the perspectives of both democracy and biodiversity, the bottom line is *process*—that is, in order to manage the array of natural biotic communities in a given land unit, the government must not only solicit participation from a diverse citizenry but must also understand the complex relationships between and within wildlife species. The government, in other words, should be receptive to new ideas from both human citizens and the greater natural world.

These changing bureaucratic and environmental factors are almost perfectly encapsulated by the recent ascension of "ecosystem management" in conservation circles. On its face, the concept is highly appealing. Instead of focusing on single species and particular patches of habitat, this approach takes a look at the big picture, recognizing Leopold's observation that "the individual is a member of a community of interdependent parts."[5] In theory, the approach should be as effective as it is efficient.

Dig below the surface, however, and unresolved issues percolate rapidly. The biggest problem is definitional. To the environmental professional, ecosystem management means protecting viable populations of all naturally occurring species and their habitat within and between ecosystems. To the livestock, timber, or development industries, ecosystem management is generally considered this generation's version of multiple use/sustained yield (MUSY),[6] which enables them to extract human commodities from a portion of an ecosystem so long as another portion is protected. Each definition and set of policy alternatives possesses significant ramifications for biodiversity.

As might be expected, the government is usually caught between competing views; indeed, different officials and presidential administrations are sympathetic to various points of view. To further complicate matters, there are many definitions of what exactly constitutes an ecosystem. Should it be based on keystone species like grizzly bears or prairie dogs? On vegetation varieties and patterns? On weather or related geophysical characteristics? Other problems with implementing ecosystem management include questions of spatial scale (how ecosystems relate to larger areas), boundaries (who is in charge of what), natural processes (distinguishing between dynamism and stability), temporal change (how long is long), data collection and monitoring (is management working), and, most challenging, the natural role of humans in an ecosystem (consumption, recreation, conservation, preservation). In short, the law pertaining to ecosystem management is still in great flux.

Nonetheless, ecosystem management is beginning to yield some conservation policy gains that surely would not have occurred in the era of single-species regulation. Under the auspices of the Endangered Species Act, for instance, four federal agencies (including the FWS) and the state of California struck a historic deal on water use in late 1994 on the San Francisco Bay and Sacramento–San Joaquin Delta Estuary. This agreement established limits on freshwater diversion for agricultural and municipal uses, protections for the threatened delta smelt and other fish, and measures for valuable wetlands habitat. Officials like Director Beattie and Governor Pete Wilson should receive considerable credit for this complicated but cooperative piece of biodiversity negotiation.[7]

While Professor Waller might enjoy the luxury of examining different notions of ecosystem management outside a political pressure cooker, his scientific understanding of biodiversity only hastens his sense of urgency. For the past several years, Waller has been an integral part of efforts to protect biodiversity in two Wisconsin national forests. As a result of these administrative and judicial tribulations, Waller is now keenly aware of the importance in securing scientifically sound interpretations of sometimes ambiguous environmental law. The U.S. Forest Service's (USFS) reluctance to fully embrace the natural diversity requirements in the National Forest Management Act of 1976,[8] the only U.S. statute with such an explicit mandate, has led Waller and other top conservation biologists to confront the often clumsy interface between science and law.

Waller and Defenders of Wildlife convened a workshop in Madison, Wisconsin, in July 1994 for the purpose of helping the Forest Service and other land management agencies articulate criteria, standards, and procedures essential for effective biodiversity management.[9] The assumption behind the meeting was that, despite the usual professional disagreements on certain cutting-edge questions, the science of conservation biology had greatly matured since a panel of experts convened by the USFS in 1977 stated, "We believe it is impossible to write specific regulations to provide for diversity."[10] The impetus for the Madison workshop was several recent federal cases,[11] which essentially have held that it was inappropriate for the judiciary to question the USFS discretion on land management matters, even if this supposed expertise was leading to decisions antithetical to well-accepted and current scientific understandings of biodiversity. In the Wisconsin cases, for example, national forest managers had ignored the ecological consequences of forest fragmentation, did not include sufficient migration corridors, and purposely created deleterious edge effects with their timber cut rotations.

Such practices are still being repeated across the country. The Madison group's goal, therefore, was not only to enunciate the established tenets of conservation biology but also to demonstrate that the applicable U.S. land agencies were not even remotely following them.

The major breakthrough of the Madison workshop was an identification of the need to develop guidelines for so-called sustainable dynamic areas (SDA).[12] An SDA is the minimum habitat needed for the long-term perpetuation of all ecological processes and community types within a managed unit. It must be large enough to allow fires, blowdowns, and other natural disturbances, which are essential to maintaining all biotic communities and to providing a healthy variety of naturally occurring seral stages. In conjunction with the somewhat traditional minimum viable population (MVP) requirements for all naturally occurring species, the SDA approach would scientifically support the hypothesis that large natural preserves, surrounded by areas of tiered human development, are the surest and perhaps best way to protect native biodiversity.[13]

The large natural preserve approach to biodiversity protection has been advocated by environmental activists in the form of the Wildlands Project[14] and by the U.S. Congress in the form of the Northern Rockies Ecosystem Protection Act (NREPA) bill.[15] NREPA, which would establish a huge network of wilderness and other highly protected federal landholdings, is a fascinating case study of late-twentieth-century biodiversity protection for two major reasons. First, despite cosponsorship by over sixty members of the House of Representatives in 1993, it engendered considerable consternation and anger from many western members of Congress and even created a nasty split within the Sierra Club. Second, if adopted, NREPA would represent an outright rejection of Gifford Pinchot's theory of "wise use"—which, in addition to being bastardized by contemporary antienvironmental extremists, rejected John Muir's ideal of natural preservation in favor of enlightened human manipulation of all natural resources. The second reason for NREPA's significance surely explains the first one. And, more important, it highlights the burning question in contemporary biodiversity policy: who is able to protect nature more effectively, people or nature?

This century-old but evolutionarily young philosophical inquiry, which now presents serious policy ramifications for governments around the world, squarely faces this generation's leaders. In the months ahead, FWS Director Beattie will be the traffic cop for many endangered and threatened species actions and will be forced to determine the compatibility of a number of actions affecting national wildlife refuges. USFS chief and conservation biologist Jack Ward Thomas will begin to chart his vision of forest biodiversity more thoroughly with the mandatory five-year Renewable Resource (RPA) program,[16] as well as his interpretation of the USFS's diversity regulations.

Similarly, leading officials from the National Marine Fisheries Service, the Bureau of Land Management, the Department of Defense, the Bureau of Reclamation, the Army Corps of Engineers, the Environmental Protection Agency, and the Animal and Plant Health Inspection Service will all possess authority to positively or negatively affect the biodiversity on U.S. public and private land. Agencies like the Departments of Transportation, Energy, and Housing and Urban Development, as well as numerous state and local governments and organizations, will each have the opportunity to integrate biodiversity concerns into their daily decision making.

Driving these political processes will be the science of conservation biology. But behind the veneer of both science and politics are committed men and women who believe that biodiversity protection can work for all walks of life. Only the human species possesses the will and the ability to significantly influence natural (or already degraded) ecosystems. Finding the right balance between humans and the rest of biodiversity will be a monumental policy challenge for years to come.

NOTES

1. See, for example, *Geer v. Connecticut* 161 U.S. 519 (1896).

2. See Dan Tarlock, "Local Government Protection of Biodiversity: What Is Its Niche?" *University of Chicago Law Review* 60 (1993):555. Tarlock argues that biodiversity protection itself is a logical extension of traditional police powers, but that it takes such powers to line of nonanthropocentric theories of law.

3. U.S. Const. art. I, §8. This authority has been interpreted by the U.S. Supreme Court to cover a wide variety of social legislation by virtue of the board reach of interstate commerce. See, for example, *Andrus v. Allard,* 444 U.S. (1979). See also U.S. Const. art. IV, §3 (property clause); U.S. Const. art. VI (treaty-making and supremacy clause).

4. See, for example, Tim Clark, "Practicing Natural Resource Management with a Policy Orientation," *Environmental Management* 16 (1992):423.

5. *A Sand County Almanac* (New York: Oxford University Press, 1966), p. 239.

6. See the Multiple Use Sustained Yield Act of 1960, 16 USC §§528–531, which has been supplemented but not entirely repealed by later forest and range legislation.

7. See 59 *Fed. Reg.* 810 (Jan. 6, 1994) (proposed rule for water quality standards for surface waters of the Sacramento River, San Joaquin River, and San Francisco Bay and Delta for the State of California); see also Gary Lee, "U.S., State Issue Plan to Aid Northern California's Environment," *Washington Post,* Dec. 16, 1994, p. A20.

8. National Forest Management Act (NFMA) of 1976, 16 USC §1601 et seq. NFMA specifically requires that forest plans "provide for diversity of plant and animal communities," 16 USC §1604(g)(3)(B), which is further elaborated upon in the Forest Service's implementing regulations, 36 CFR §§219.26, 219.27(g).

9. In attendance were Waller, Dennis Murphy, Barry Noon, Ross Kiester, Russell Lande, Steward Pickett, Thomas Givnish, Joel Cracraft, Rob Peters, Walter Kuhlmann, Oliver Houck, Curt Meine, Cara Nelson, and William Snape.

10. 44 *Fed. Reg.* 26609 (1979).

11. See, for example, *Sierra Club v. Marita,* 845 F. Supp. 1317 (E.D. Wis. 1994).

12. SDA is an extension of the minimum dynamic area (MDA) concept developed over the past decade, which examines broad ecological processes as opposed to species-specific events. See S.T.A. Pickett and J. N. Thompson, "Patch Dynamics and the Design of Nature Reserves," *Biological Conservation* 13 (1978):27.

13. See, for example, The Wilderness Act, 16 USC §§1131–1136; Alaska National Interest Lands and Conservation Act (ANILCA), 16 USC §§410bb, 410hh–410hh-5; Wild and Scenic Rivers Act, 16 USC §§1271–1287. While these pieces of legislation all have considerable conservation value because they limit most human development, they were not promulgated for explicit biodiversity purposes. But see the Tongass Timber Reform Act, 16 USC §§472a, 539d; R. Kiester, et al., *Review of Wildlife Management and Conservation Biology on the Tongass National Forest* (March 1994).

14. The Wildlands Project would establish a continental network of nature preserves. See Dave Foreman, "NREPA and the Evolving Wilderness Area Model," *Wild Earth* 3(4) (Winter 1993-1994); Marcia Carey and Rod Mordt, "The Wildlands Project Update," Ibid.

15. H.R. 2638 (103rd Cong.); see also S. 2543 (103rd Cong.) (a bill to "strengthen the protection of native biodiversity" and "to designate special areas where extractive logging is prohibited" on public lands).

16. See NFMA, 16 USC §1602.

REFERENCES

Alverson, W., W. Kuhlmann, and D. Waller. 1994. *Wild Forests: Conservation Biology and Public Policy.* Washington, D.C.: Island Press.

Blaustein, Andrew and David Wake. (1995) The puzzle of declining amphibian populations. *Scientific American* April, pp. 52–57.

Botkin, D. 1990. *Discordant Harmonies: A New Ecology for the Twenty-First Century.* New York: Oxford University Press.

Brooks, Daniel and E.O. Wiley. 1988. *Evolution as Entropy.* Chicago: University of Chicago Press.

Burton, John, and Bruce Pearson. 1987. *Rare Mammals of the World.* London: Collins.

Commoner, Barry. 1990. *Making Peace with the Planet.* New York: Pantheon.

Cooperrider, Allen, Raymond Boyd, and Hanson Stuart. 1986. *Inventorying and Monitoring of Wildlife Habitat.* Washington, D.C.: Government Printing Office.

Crow, Thomas, Alan Haney, and Donald Waller. 1993. *Report of the Scientific Roundtable on Biological Diversity: Chequamegon and Nicolet National Forests.* Washington, D.C.: USDA Forest Service.

Diamond, Jared, and Ted Case. 1986. *Community Ecology.* New York: Harper & Row.

Foreman, Dave, and H. Wolke. 1989. *The Big Outside.* Tucson: Ned Ludd Books.

Fox, S. R. 1981. *John Muir and His Legacy: The American Conservation Movement.* Boston: Little, Brown.

Francione, Gary. 1995. *Animals, Property and the Law.* Philadelphia: Temple University Press.

Futrell, J. William. 1994. *The Transition to Sustainable Development Law.* Washington, D.C.: Environmental Law Institute.

General Accounting Office. 1994. *Ecosystem Management: Additional Actions Needed to Adequately Test a Promising Approach.* Washington,D.C.: Government Printing Office.

Gotelli, Nicholas. 1995. *A Primer of Ecology.* Sunderland, MA: Sinauer Associates.

Gray, Gary. 1993. *Wildlife and People.* Urbana: University of Illinois Press.

Gross, Paul, and Norman Levitt. 1994. *Higher Superstition: The Academic Left and Its Quarrels with Science.* Baltimore: Johns Hopkins University Press.

Grumbine, R. Edward. 1992. *Ghost Bears: Exploring the Biodiversity Crisis.* Washington, D.C.: Island Press.

Grumbine, R. Edward, ed. 1994. *Environmental Policy and Biodiversity.* Washington, D.C.: Island Press.

Keystone Center. 1991. *Final Consensus Report of the Keystone Policy Dialogue on Biological Diversity on Federal Lands.* Keystone, Colo.: Keystone Center.

MacArthur, R. H., and E. O. Wilson. 1967. *The Theory of Island Biogeography.* Princeton: Princeton University Press.

Martell, Luke. 1994. *Ecology and Society: An Introduction.* Amherst: University of Massachusetts Press.

Meffe, Gary, and C. Ronald Carroll. *Principles of Conservation Biology.* Sunderland, Mass.: Sinauer.

Murphy, Dennis, and Barry Noon. 1991. Coping with uncertainty in wildlife biology. *Journal of Wildlife Management* 55(4):773.

Musgrave, Ruth and Mary Anne Stein. 1993. *State Wildlife Laws Handbook.* Rockville, MD: Government Institutes.

Nabhan, Gary Paul. 1995. The dangers of reductionism in biodiversity conservation. *Conservation Biology* 9(3):479.

National Fish and Wildlife Foundation. 1994. *FY 1995 Fisheries and Wildlife Assessment.* Washington, D.C.: NFWF.

National Research Council. 1990. *Decline of the Sea Turtles.* Washington, D.C.: National Academy Press.

Noon, B., and K. Young. 1991. Evidence of continuing worldwide declines in bird populations. *Conservation Biology* 5(2):141.

Noss, Reed, and Allen Cooperrider. 1994. *Saving Nature's Legacy.* Washington, D.C.: Defenders of Wildlife/Island Press.

Odum Eugene. 1993. *Ecology and Our Endangered Life-Support Systems.* Sunderland, MA: Sinauer Associates.

Peters, Robert. 1990. Forests and Climate Change. *Forest Ecology and Management* 35:13–33.

Peters, Robert, and Thomas Lovejoy, eds. 1992. *Biological Diversity and Global Climate Change.* New Haven: Yale University Press.

Primack, Richard. 1993. *Essentials of Conservation Biology.* Sunderland, Mass: Sinauer.

Robison, Wade. 1994. *Decisions in Doubt: The Environment and Public Policy.* Hanover, N.H.: The University Press of New England.

Ruggiero, Leonard, Keith Aubrey, Steven Buskirk, L. Jack Lyon, and William Zielinski. 1994. *American Marten, Fisher, Lynx and Wolverine in the Western United States.* Fort Collins, Colo.: USDA Forest Service.

Ruttan, Vernon, ed. 1994. *Health and Sustainable Agricultural Development: Perspectives on Growth and Constraints.* Boulder: Westview Press.

Sample, V. Alaric, ed. 1994. *Remote Sensing and GIS in Ecosystem Management.* Washington, D.C.: Island Press.

Simon, J. L. 1981. *The Ultimate Resource.* Princeton: Princeton University Press.

Thomas, Jack Ward, E. D. Forsman, J. B. Lint, E. C. Meslow, B. R. Noon, and J. Verner. 1990. *A Conservation Strategy for the Northern Spotted Owl.* Portland, Ore.: USDA Forest Service, USDI Bureau of Land Management, USDI Fish and Wildlife Service, USDI National Park Service.

Thomas, J. W., M. G. Raphael, R. G. Anthony, E. D. Forsman, A. G. Gunderson, R. S. Holthausen, B. G. Marcot, G. H. Reeves, J. R. Sedell, and D. M. Solis. 1993. *Viability Assessments and Management Considerations for Species Associated with Late-Successional and Old-Growth Forests of the Pacific Northwest.* Washington, D.C.: USDA Forest Service.

USDA Forest Service. 1994. *Western Forest Health Initiative.* Washington, D.C.: USDA Forest Service.

U.S. Fish and Wildlife Service. 1994. *Ecosystem Approach to Fish and Wildlife Conservation: An Approach to More Effectively Conserve the Nation's Biodiversity.* Washington, D.C.: USFWS.

Western, David, and R. Michael Wright, eds. 1994. *Natural Connections: Perspectives in Community-Based Conservation.* Washington, D.C.: Island Press.

Yoffe, Emily. 1992. Silence of the frogs. *New York Times Magazine,* December 13, p. 36.

Chapter 1

BIODIVERSITY POLICY AND ECOSYSTEM MANAGEMENT

Mollie Beattie

One of my first actions as director of the U.S. Fish and Wildlife Service was to announce that the service would shift to an ecosystem approach to managing our fish and wildlife resources. This announcement caused a stir both inside and outside the agency.

The idea of an ecosystem approach is not new. The service has been moving toward implementing this approach for some time. My announcement was more a confirmation of what has already begun rather than the launching something new—an evolution rather than a revolution.

Aldo Leopold first conceived the concept of an ecosystem approach a half century ago. In his earlier writings, recently published in a book called *The River of the Mother of God,* the evolution of Leopold's thinking can be traced from being fully in favor of predator control and vermin elimination (as well as maximum production of those species that humans find entertaining) to recognition that we cannot manage for any one piece of the system and expect to save the rest. His final work, *A Sand County Almanac,* embodies a resounding testament to an ecosystem approach. Wildlife managers are finally catching up to him fifty years later.

TOWARD AN ECOSYSTEM APPROACH

The concept of an ecosystem approach is easier for people to understand than the concept of biodiversity. Additionally, the ecosystem approach is taking on a broader meaning in the federal government. Here it is frequently used to refer to interagency cooperation, expanding the definition to include the administrative end of conservation programs. Nevertheless, the underlying premise remains unchanged—that there are many uses people make of ecosystems and if we do not take an ecosystem approach to conserving biodiversity, none of them will be long lived.

We are making the ecosystem approach an important element in the management of the National Wildlife Refuge System. This does not mean that traditional uses such as hunting, fishing, and bird watching will be excluded. Rather, it means that we want to use the refuges as anchor points for maintaining biodiversity and as keystones to demonstrate the success of the ecosystem approach. Because ecosystems rarely stop at the border of refuges, we will seek to work in partnership with all those outside refuges, such as neighboring landowners.

People who oppose the ecosystem approach interpret it to mean the Fish and Wildlife Service is going to encroach on their right to manage their lands and programs. Nothing could be further from the truth. In fact, the ecosystem approach entails exactly the opposite. The service recognizes that its statutory mandates are rather narrow: only a few categories of species are its direct responsibility. We cannot do a good job with these species unless we work with everybody who manages the habitat upon which they depend and the programs that affect them. This is why we think refuges should serve as anchors from which our biologists can involve other landowners, through voluntary, mutually beneficial partnerships, in the proper management of ecosystems.

The ecosystem approach will also help us direct our increasingly limited resources within the refuge system. It was once the norm for refuges to be far-flung pieces of land with minimal surrounding development pressure. This is no longer the case. And as development pressures have increased around refuges, management costs have gone through the ceiling. The ecosystem approach will help us to think about which ecosystems are the most threatened and which are the most recoverable. In short, it will help focus our resources to get the most bang for our buck.

Among the national resource management agencies, only the Forest Service and the Fish and Wildlife Service have the authority to work on private land. In fact, our private lands program is becoming more and more central to our efforts. Through this program we talk to private landowners and implement wildlife improvement efforts on their land in exchange for long-term agreements that the landowners will protect these improvements. To date, our private lands program has restored more than 240,000 acres of valuable wildlife habitat.

We recognize that no mandate from Washington is going to solve our nation's ecological problems. Progress will need to be forged acre by acre, wetland by wetland, in communities across this country. This effort must involve the willing partnership of the people who own and live on the land.

USING THE ESA TO PROTECT BIODIVERSITY

The Fish and Wildlife Service's administration of the Endangered Species Act (ESA) will be significantly affected by this new emphasis on an ecosystem approach to fish and wildlife conservation. Up to now, the ESA has largely been administered on a single-species basis. It has been driven by petitions to list individual species, and it has become for many a tool of choice in dictating the future of land use. In other words, if you can find a listed species, or species that may need listing, you can stop development. In many regards, this has given a good law a bad name. Regardless of how the ESA has been used in the past, we intend to use it to support and conserve biodiversity and ecosystems.

One of the complaints heard most frequently about the ESA is that it has a huge negative impact on the economy. But in fact, its historical impact has been extremely minor. There is a lot of smoke and not much fire. Under the ESA, for example, all federal agencies are required to consult with the Fish and Wildlife Service or the National Marine Fisheries Service before conducting an activity, issuing a permit, or funding an activity on federal land that might affect a threatened or endangered species. By the outcry, you would think these consultations have a major economic impact. In fact, the opposite is true. Of the 118,000 informal and formal consultations required of other federal agencies under the ESA from 1979 to 1991, only 33 development projects were halted. That is one project halted for every 3,578 consultations. The majority of the rest went forward with just minor modifications or none at all.

The ESA has built-in flexibility to accommodate both species protection and sustainable economic development. We find that it is precisely in those places where economic activity is not sustainable, whether because of overharvesting of timber or overdrawing of an aquifer, that ecosystems are in trouble. Coincidentally, a growing number of threatened and endangered species, as well as candidate species, are found in these places. The presence of these threatened and endangered species is an early warning sign of a crisis. We must address problems in these ecosystems before they become intractable and harm not only wildlife, but also humans.

The Fish and Wildlife Service's shift to an ecosystem approach will not eliminate support for some of the successful single-species programs that are moving these species toward delisting. It is important to show that the ESA is not a one-way street. Furthermore, where you have declines of large keystone species—the kind that the public pays attention to—you usually have an ecosystem in trouble as well. The grizzly bear and Mexican wolf are good examples, and their habitats are places we would want to focus our energy anyway.

Although the service has at times been criticized for focusing too much on some of these "charismatic" species, the biggest challenge we face involves obscure, noncharismatic species, such as mussels, snails, and lichen. It is often hard to explain to people why it is desirable, much less necessary, to save these species. After all, people might ask, what difference does it make whether we have any freshwater mussels in our river bottoms?

Of course, these species are merely indicators of bigger ecological problems that people should care about. There is a snail in Idaho that is one of my favorite parables on this point. This snail is found in an isolated series of hot springs in a single valley. It is being pushed to extinction by overpumping of the aquifer; the springs are disappearing as the groundwater levels are lowering. Opponents have done a thorough job of painting the issue in terms of "jobs versus snails." But the real issue is whether we are going to continue this unsustainable use of an aquifer until ultimately no water remains for either humans or snails.

There are numerous cases like this in which a little slimy species with an inelegant name serves as nature's smoke alarm. Disconnecting the alarm does not make the fire go out. Ignoring these species, as some opponents of the ESA would have us do, will not eliminate the ecological crisis.

Again, the Fish and Wildlife Service is going to focus the greatest attention on areas where there are multiple endangered and threatened species or multiple candidate species. We provided Interior Secretary Babbitt with a map of the United States showing the concentrations of candidate species. He is interested in getting out in front of the ESA and avoiding what he terms "train wrecks." If we start to see a buildup of candidate species somewhere, he wants the service to get ahead of the curve and avoid having to invoke the ESA at all. Prelisting conservation will be crucial in achieving this objective.

We are often driven so hard by the listing petitions of the ESA that putting together the staffing and funding resources to get out in front of the curve is one of our ever-growing challenges. Again, we need to combine our resources with our many partners to be effective.

In any event, in 25 years the Endangered Species Act has helped prevent extinction of over 200 species. Most important, the Act has given warning of ecological crisis while time still remained to take action. The increasing frequency with which these warnings are sounding today does not mean that something is wrong with the alarm. It signals unsustainable use of natural resources—over-harvesting timber, pollution, destruction of wetlands and other habitats vital to both wildlife and and human health.

Until we change our ways, such problems will exist whether or not we have an Endangered Species Act. Congress may change the act, but it cannot repeal the laws of nature.

PREPARING FOR A NEW ERA

The Fish and Wildlife Service is still in the early stages of implementing the ecosystem approach. We recently distributed a final draft of our concept to our employees and our partners in the states and elsewhere. This document includes the most current map of the United States showing how we delineate ecosystems. This will allow us, in consultation with our partners, to organize our regulatory activities as well as our programs along boundaries that make sense from a biological perspective as opposed to a political, jurisdictional perspective.

We anticipate that the National Biological Service (NBS) will assist us in improving the inventory and monitoring of biotic resources. Additionally, we expect the NBS to carry on the work previously conducted by the Fish and Wildlife Service's research arm—those dirt-under-the-fingernails kinds of things.

The initial inventory and monitoring priority will be to assess what we know and to find out what additional data are needed to round out this knowledge. This will entail identifying data banks currently available around the United States and developing mechanisms to integrate them in a useful manner.

In the end, conservation in the future will weave together a broad tapestry of conservation techniques applied across the landscape at all levels, public and private. Federal acquisition, land trusts, and state, local, and city efforts will need to be interwoven into a new kind of wildlife ethic. We need to see progress toward preemptive conservation in places where no crisis is yet evident.

The U.S. Fish and Wildlife Service is preparing itself for this new era. The twenty-first century is going to demand that the service be flexible, proactive, and able to work with diverse partners to respond to increasingly complex conservation challenges. We are convinced that the ecosystem approach is the best way to meet these challenges.

Chapter 2

Biodiversity as a Basis for Conservation Efforts

Donald M. Waller

When I ran into a friend a year ago he asked what I was up to. I answered that I was writing a book on biodiversity and forest management.[1] He responded by asking, "And what will you do after this environmental fad passes?"

Was the Earth Summit in Rio a flash in the pan? Will new graduate programs in conservation biology, such as the one at the University of Wisconsin, wither from lack of interest? Are journals like *Conservation Biology* destined to decline as rapidly as they have grown in the last few years? Here I evaluate the lasting value of biodiversity as a basis and criterion for conservation. How well does biodiversity serve as an umbrella, or overall goal, for conservation efforts? How suitable and effective is biodiversity as a standard for advancing conservation? Why haven't earlier laws, such as the Endangered Species Act, sufficed to protect biodiversity? As a scientist relatively familiar with the law and the courts, I also want to ask: what dangers are associated with embracing biodiversity as a criterion for conservation? Biodiversity has and will be misinterpreted, sometimes unknowingly or accidentally, out of ignorance, but often willfully. Even when diversity is not willfully misinterpreted, the variety of meanings ascribed to it make the use of biodiversity in policy difficult and challenging. This means we must be careful in interpreting and applying this concept and should accept the need for more scientific, as well as legal and policy, expertise.

Today, federal agencies are publicly embracing a group of concepts termed "ecosystem management." The pitfalls outlined here suggest that we will need to be cautious in inserting our concerns for biodiversity into ecosystem management and must be vigilant in monitoring how our government applies these concepts. I therefore conclude this chapter with a challenge to environmentalists, scientists, and agency personnel to work together to accomplish the important goal of sustaining our biodiversity into the twenty-first century.

WHAT THREATENS DIVERSITY?

Our main tools for conserving diversity historically have been fish and game laws such as the Lacey Act of 1900 and the Migratory Bird Hunting Stamp Act of 1934. These laws were created to counter the specific threats posed by overharvesting certain fish, mammal, and bird species. At the time they were enacted, it was obvious to all that many of these species were declining in direct response to human depredation. Such laws effectively curtailed the excessive hunting and fishing that were decimating wildlife populations and, moreover, effectively reversed declines in many of these species (often in the nick of time). Wildlife populations have rebounded in many states, species have been successfully reintroduced into areas where they were extirpated, and income from the sale of ammunition, hunting and fishing licenses, and similar programs fund conservation programs in all states.

This is the success story that state conservation programs justifiably feel proud of. Yet duck populations remain perilously low, anadromous fish stocks have crashed in the Northwest, wolves have yet to reoccupy more than a fraction of their previous range, and neotropical migratory songbirds continue steep declines across eastern North America. Why, if we have protected these species from overharvesting, do they continue to decline? Why are we adding species to the threatened and endangered lists so much faster than species are recovering?

The answer, in most cases, is that habitats continue to be lost, fragmented, and otherwise degraded. While the historic threats to biodiversity revolved around the conspicuous and direct threats of overharvesting, today we are confronted with different kinds of environmental change. We see pervasive changes in our landscapes that collectively alter the ecological context under which our species evolved. These changes are usually incremental, masking their effect, yet the changes they bring are profound and insidious. Most species in decline now are suffering the indirect and often subtle effects of changes in ecological processes, such as patterns of disturbance. These changes are difficult to reverse, and often they pose unexpected threats to inconspicuous species. They also have tended to favor a different class of species, the weedy invaders and exotics, that themselves further threaten and displace native species. Because species losses generally lag behind these environmental changes, losses already imminent will take many years to play themselves out, further masking their cause and full scope. Although subtle and slow to our eyes, these changes ultimately pose greater threats to far more species than the direct threats of yesterday.

As we approach the twenty-first century, conservationists must take a broad view to encompass concerns for the cumulative losses of the habitat and changes in ecological processes that now represent the principal threats to biological diversity. Such habitat concerns have already come to the fore in the Northwest as initial concern for the spotted owl has broadened to include the marbled murrelet, salmonid fishes, and an assortment of other vertebrate and invertebrate species. To conserve these species, we have learned that we must also conserve community and landscape structure and processes, including coarse woody debris, habitat contiguity, and wildlife corridors.

WHY ISN'T THE ESA PROTECTING DIVERSITY?

By the 1960s, it was apparent to all that fish and game conservation laws alone were not sufficient to protect our biological diversity. To more directly protect species sliding toward extinction, Congress passed the Endangered Species Act (ESA) in 1973. How well has it protected the species dependent on it? We know that it has protected many species and contributed to the recovery of several others. Everyone is aware at least of the bald eagle and the spotted owl. They are aware of the spotted owl because protecting each pair necessarily involved allocating old-growth forests in the Pacific Northwest worth millions of dollars.[2] Legal protection for this (and now other) species has curbed the aggressive overcutting of old-growth forests that was occurring during the 1980s. It has also polarized and politicized public concern for protecting species diversity. Because they served as such conspicuous symbols of the cost of protecting the environment, the snail darter, Furbish's lousewort, and the spotted owl became the butt of crude jokes. In the end, politics dominated the legally protected status of the darter and the lousewort so the dams they threatened were authorized. Thus one conspicuous problem with the ESA has been that, by focusing protection on individual species, it has sometimes vilified them and increased polarization over the value of diversity.

A more serious problem stems from how the ESA typically works. Despite successes in protecting certain species, the ESA has conspicuously failed to stem the slide of many more species toward endangerment, as well as the cumulative losses of habitat and ecological functions that diversity depends upon.[3] In many respects, it tends to perpetuate the species-by-species approaches adopted by fish and game laws. Recovery efforts have often focused on elaborate and usually expensive attempts to captively propagate and reintroduce populations rather than protect habitat at a point before endangerment. Many species have languished while awaiting listing. Scandalously, recovery targets for many endangered species have been set at population levels lower than existed when the species was first listed. The median total population sizes for endangered vertebrates, invertebrates, and plants are only 1,075, 999, and 120, respectively.[4] Clearly this act does too little too late, even for the conspicuous species most likely to be listed.

In addition to these problems, the ESA has also tended to overemphasize the furry and feathery charismatic megafauna—those species that catch the public's attention and imagination—while underfunding and ignoring the inconspicuous and unglamorous majority of endangered species. People play favorites with endangered species. The law has effectively protected our national symbol, the bald eagle, and popular fish and wildlife species such as trout. Yet when you move down toward the crocodile, or snakes, approval slips below a simple majority, and when you get all the way to plants, or to the wolf spider, you are dealing with a minority concern.[5] Not surprisingly, funding within the Fish and Wildlife Service and state agencies to protect and recover species reflects this bias.

I happened to work for several years on one of the least glamorous federally endangered species: Furbish's lousewort. I can tell you many interesting details about its sex life and habitat preferences, several of which turn out to be critical for evaluating recovery potential. Here, working in the narrow field of plant population biology, I quickly learned how inadequate simple population approaches are that ignore species' dependencies on community and landscape processes. I also discovered that a wide array of threatened plant species live up and down the St. John River valley in northern Maine, all of which depend on that river to the same degree that the northern spotted owl and marbled murrelet depend on ancient forests in the Northwest. Interestingly, logging appears to threaten both sets of species. Increases in clearcutting in the watershed on both the Canadian and the U.S. sides have steadily increased the intensity of spring floods on the St. John. Any attempt to conserve these riverine plant habitats that ignores the wider landscape and community processes is myopic and doomed to failure. Here we see the conspicuous failure of traditional incremental species-by-species approaches.

Even when we know the historic disturbance regimes, we may run into significant policy problems. Take the endangered Kirtland's warbler, for example. This neotropical migrant songbird depends critically on recurrent fire disturbances in the jackpine communities of north central Michigan for summer nesting habitat. Because its range is so limited, the Fish and Wildlife Service has attempted to provide more habitat for this bird. However, a controlled burn several years ago got out of control and burned a huge area that included many people's houses. Again, we see how backlashes can occur against conservation efforts generally and this endangered warbler in particular.

Is the ESA a failure? No, I will not argue that at all. The Endangered Species Act is vitally important—and woefully underfunded. The act desperately needs reinforcement and extension, particularly with respect to its authority to designate critical habitat for endangered species. But we should also recognize its limitations. Both the nature of the threats and especially our understanding of them have changed over the years since the ESA first passed.

Diversity as a Goal

Conservation biologists and ecologists began to champion biological diversity as an inclusive and appropriate goal for conservation efforts more than a decade ago. It certainly extends far beyond our historical preoccupation with fish and game species and individual species on the brink of extinction. Most environmentalists have now accepted this point of view and, at least since Rio, embrace biodiversity as an overarching goal to encompass many conservation concerns. Federal agencies have followed suit by developing a number of comprehensive conservation programs often collectively labeled "ecosystem management." Does biodiversity deserve its rapid popularity? Can biodiversity serve as an appropriate, effective, and inclusive standard for conserving our species, habitats, and ecosystems?

I will argue that biodiversity serves very well indeed as an appropriate goal for widening conservation efforts beyond protecting a handful of species on the brink of extinction. Concerns for biodiversity values extend naturally to include ecological processes and landscape context, as well as the majority of species and habitats, many of which are not adequately protected under fish and game laws and the Endangered Species Act. In particular, biodiversity allows land managers to combine multiple concerns regarding the lands they oversee instead of favoring certain species or habitats over others. It also holds promise for bringing environmentalists and conservation agencies closer together by serving as a common goal for conservation activities.

Another important advantage of the diversity concept is that it efficiently captures many of the goals which conservationists embrace. By emphasizing habitats and processes, concerns for overall diversity automatically protect far more of nature than the handful of flagship species such as the bald eagle protected under the ESA (and which may themselves be better protected by more comprehensive approaches). Much, perhaps most, of diversity consists of less conspicuous, somewhat more common, often obscure and ugly species. While these almost never have the flash or appeal of the birds and mammals that garner most of the attention (and funding) under endangered species programs, they may ultimately play larger roles in sustaining food webs and ecosystem function.[6] By protecting areas and processes, even completely unknown species can be protected, usually before they reach the point of being threatened or endangered.

Another point rarely stressed is that managing our lands to conserve diversity serves not only as a useful and appropriate approach, but also as a more *stringent* standard. As protecting individual endangered species has proved insufficient, maintaining ecological processes has proved to be essential. Landscape approaches have legitimately become the focus of ecosystem management for both federal agencies and many research conservation biologists. These approaches lead frequently to the conclusion that, to be effective, programs to protect diversity need to protect large areas. We now know that setting aside small reserves, although essential for specialized habitats, does not suffice to maintain and perpetuate species that depend on large home ranges, extensive natural landscapes, and intact natural processes of disturbance. While national parks and wilderness areas do tend to cover large areas, they were designated primarily for recreation and are often placed in areas—such as at high altitudes in the mountains—that serve poorly to protect biodiversity. It is gratifying to see the recent move among both private concerns such as The Nature Conservancy and federal agencies to make larger areas the focus of conservation efforts.

HAZARDS IN APPLYING THE CONCEPTS

You have heard the good news about diversity. The bad news is that biodiversity is a complex and slippery concept that has already been abused and is likely to be more seriously abused in coming years. Here I will try to give you a glimpse of what these assaults may consist of, progressing from the simpler issues regarding definitions to more problematic issues.

The Question of Definitions

Many still equate "wildlife" diversity with the number of large bird and mammal species present in a given area. Such a limited definition excludes many species, however, and completely avoids the wider context. To conserve diversity effectively and over the long term means that we must necessarily conserve rare habitats, natural environmental gradients, and the disturbances and ecological processes that play such a key role in the life cycles of many species. Most elements of diversity are rare and the "lower forms" of life such as arthropods and soil fungi play critical roles in providing ecosystem "services." This makes it both logical and necessary to encompass concerns for these species within our overall concern for biodiversity regardless of their ugliness or obscurity.

Attempting to manage lands for one or a few favored species is more than inappropriate. In several circumstances, it can also produce pernicious effects. For example, actively managing for game species (such as ruffed grouse and white-tailed deer) throughout a region leads naturally to converting as many habitats as possible to the preferred habitat for these species (young aspen stands intermixed with grassy openings in the upper Midwest). By converting much of the landscape to these cover types, and intensively maintaining them via repeated mowing and clearcuts, we directly and significantly threaten many other elements of diversity, including those dependent on old-growth forests (such as pileated woodpeckers) or undisturbed soil conditions (many herbaceous plants). Once the goal of increasing the populations of game species is reached, their abundance may itself represent a further threat to sensitive species (such as lilies, orchids, and conifer seedlings susceptible to overbrowsing by deer).

Such restricted approaches to conserving "wildlife" or boosting quite local ("alpha") diversity have led us to chop up many managed landscapes into small fragments of habitat with abundant edge. Perversely, such management prescriptions applied across a landscape have had the effect of directly and dramatically reducing overall ("gamma") diversity. This process occurs via several separate, but often mutually reinforcing, mechanisms. For example, several neotropical migrant songbird species subject to losing their precious reproductive investment to opportunistic nest predators and nest parasites have declined in inverse proportion to the increase in scattered openings and associated edge habitat. As habitats have become increasingly fragmented, species such as wolves or bobcats that need broader areas or less disturbed habitats have also declined. The result is that habitat fragments, as well as the landscape as a whole, have become homogenized. Deleterious edge effects have become pervasive. Edge-, area-, and isolation-sensitive species have correspondingly declined, reducing overall diversity.

The Question of Implementation

As we turn to questions of implementation, we face further issues regarding the meaning of diversity and our levels of scientific confidence in the effects of our management activities. Some argue that diversity is too vague or variable a concept to be used in the laws and regulations that govern management. Others argue that relationships determining levels of diversity are not yet fully tested, or only apply in some areas and not elsewhere, making it inappropriate to base management policy on diversity concerns. Finally, some interpret the unpredictability and vagaries present in nature to imply that diversity goals are arbitrary and unreachable. Let us examine each of these propositions in turn.

To begin with, the diversity concept has sometimes been deliberately interpreted to favor certain forms of intensive management. For example, in confronting the diversity provision of the 1976 National Forest Management Act during its planning efforts in the mid-1980s, the U.S. Forest Service developed the idea that an important component of forest diversity concerned the number of age classes represented within each area of the forest (which they termed "age-class" diversity). This notion had the perverse (and perhaps intentional) effect of promoting clearcutting as a means to promote a variety of early age classes. In the Chequamegon and Nicolet National Forests in Wisconsin, the Forest Service explicitly defended high rates of clearcutting in their plans as a technique to enhance the 0–10- and 0–20-year-old age classes of various forest types. This policy is sadly ironic, as clearcuts in this area produce young aspen, a forest type already abundant in the surrounding landscape and one that is usually not allowed to mature into older and more diverse mixed forest. Selective cutting, particularly the harvest of individual trees, works far better to regenerate the mixed hardwood forest that once dominated northern Wisconsin, as demonstrated by forestry practices on the nearby Menominee Indian reservation.

For these reasons, it is inappropriate to favor any single community type to the exclusion of others, even when the favored community has higher local diversity. This danger of relying on local (alpha) diversity as a criterion for conservation is evident in a comparison of the plant diversity among ten woodlands of varying size in northern Ireland.[7] The two sites with the lowest local diversity turn out to be nature reserves chosen for their characteristic vegetation.

While one might expect that by 1995 we would all agree on how to define diversity and concur that sustaining overall (gamma) diversity is our goal, recent events suggest that we are still some distance even from this modest goal. In a 1993 legal decision, a federal district court sided with the Forest Service against a group of scientists and environmentalists on the key legal issue of how to define and interpret the diversity provision of the 1976 National Forest Management Act.[8] In arguing on behalf of the Forest Service, the Justice Department maintained that since scientists themselves disagree over the nature of biological diversity and how it is affected by various management actions, the courts are obliged to defer to agency expertise. This decision was upheld on appeal to the Seventh Circuit Court of Appeals in a ruling with potentially far-reaching implications. In response to the claim that the Forest Service had not used adequate or appropriate science in completing its plans and environmental impact statement, the court ruled that:

"conservation biology is not a necessary element of diversity analysis insofar as the regulations do not dictate that the service analyze diversity in any specific way.[9]" Instead, the Court ruled that conventional species-by-species approaches embodied in the choice and monitoring of particular indicator species sufficed to address the diversity provision of the NFMA. (Ironically, the Chief of the Forest Service had himself already ruled in 1990 that these single species approaches were defective in the particular cases being appealed.) This is a worrisome legal situation, as it allows agencies to justify any conceivable style of management as compatible with any arbitrary definition of diversity that can be devised to fit it. Despite this victory, the Forest Service moved in April 1995 to further restrict interpretation of the diversity language in the NFMA via a proposed change in the relevant federal regulations.[10]

Working Toward Agreement

These cases raise the specter that agencies and scientists might drift further apart on defining what diversity means and interpreting how to implement concerns for diversity in terms of land management. Indeed, diversity will remain just an abstract concept until agencies and scientists (and hopefully courts) can agree on a common and scientifically credible definition for diversity and reach general agreement on what the likely consequences of various management actions will be on this diversity. Unfortunately, minor scholarly disagreements over how diversity responds to the distribution of reserves and what techniques might prove most effective have been misconstrued to imply uncertainty over how diversity responds to management or even a lack of consensus on the general importance of conserving diversity. In fact, these controversies concern technical points of limited scope. Conservation scientists generally agree on what they mean by biodiversity and the major mechanisms that threaten it. Many are also willing to work with policymakers and attorneys to incorporate scientifically sound concepts into regulations or law.

There remains, however, the question of what levels of diversity should be maintained (or its converse: what losses should be considered excessive). This is, of course, a societal decision. Nevertheless, scientists can ably describe the various types of community present in a region and explain how species diversity within each community type typically increases with increases in area (Figure 2.1). Such descriptions make clear and quantitative predictions regarding how losses of habitat area are likely to cause characteristic declines in species diversity. It is further possible in many cases to predict which species are likely to be lost. Ecologists have noted that certain species often require areas of a certain minimum size ("incidence func-

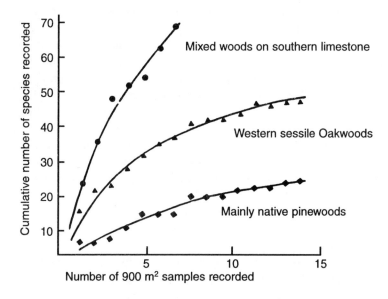

FIGURE 2.1

As areas of increasing size are sampled, more and more species are generally found, yet the rates of these increases depend on the community being sampled. These species/area curves depict increases in diversity of successive 900 m² samples of three types of woodland in Britain. Redrawn from G. F. Peterken, *Woodland Conservation and Management* (London: Chapman & Hall, 1981).

tions")[11] and that smaller or more isolated patches of habitat often contain nested subsets of the species contained in larger or more continuous habitats.[12]

Because each type of community tends to contain species that are at least somewhat unique, efforts to conserve overall species diversity begin by seeking to maintain representatives of all communities originally present. Moreover, it is obviously essential that each community be present in units of sufficient size. Thus conserving diversity demands not only a representative set of habitats but also areas of sufficient size (or connectedness) to sustain populations of its constituent species indefinitely.

HOW RELEVANT IS THEORY?

The area of ecology that deals with how species are distributed among habitats and regions is termed biogeography. Thirty years ago, Robert MacArthur and E. O. Wilson developed a dynamic theory they termed island biogeography to account for species/area relationships in terms of the opposing processes of immigration and extinction.[13] This simple and elegant theory makes a surprisingly wide set of predictions regarding equilibria to be expected in habitat patches of various size as well as extinction dynamics. These predictions have now been tested in hundreds of studies ranging from birds on oceanic islands in the South Pacific to algae colonizing microscope slides in ponds and rivers. Despite this body of accepted theory, decades of empirical work, and the fact that Larry Harris wrote an entire book dedicated to applying island biogeography to forest management, there has been great reluctance to accept the relevance of these ideas. In fact, thirteen county boards in northern Wisconsin passed resolutions against the theory of island biogeography in the mid-1980s when they perceived this previously arcane area of ecological research to be a substantial threat to conventional modes of forest management.

Some also argue that maintaining diversity is inappropriate or impractical. This is sometimes a trivial and sometimes a substantial argument. There are those who argue that because species have always gone extinct, extinction is a natural process. Rare and endangered species should be allowed to go extinct; protecting them would interfere with this natural process. The Blue Ribbon and Wise Use coalitions go even farther to label such species "unadapted" and deserving of extinction. Such claims ignore the fact that the present extinction rate is thousands of times faster than the natural background rate of extinction.[14]

On a more substantial level, we sometimes hear the argument that those concerned with diversity are strict preservationists seeking to recreate an artificial and static world. This may be an idea they have taken inappropriately out of Daniel Botkin's book, *Discordant Harmonies*.[15] Botkin argues convincingly that ecological systems have always been subject to secular change and that notions of equilibria which have played such a large role in the history of ecology occur more often in theoretical models than in nature. Unfortunately, these reasonable ideas have been bent by some to argue that concerns with conserving large areas, or old growth, are anachronistic since all communities must be viewed as dynamic and humans are as "natural" as any other species. Thus they attempt to portray those seeking to protect biodiversity as out of touch with the new ecology, wedded instead to the notion of an unattainable static "climax" stage of succession. According to this line of reasoning, any attempt to recreate old-growth forest or any other set of conditions is inappropriate and impractical.

These arguments display a critical misunderstanding of how species actually depend on ecological processes. One can embrace the need for disturbance and nonequilibrium dynamics, yet come to completely different conclusions. It is critical to understand the thousands of generations and millions of years implicit in the precise adaptations observed in all species. Species have always, of course, adjusted to change in their environments, but they do so only within the tight constraints imposed by their evolutionary history. While species appear remarkably resilient to many types of disturbance, they can also be peculiarly sensitive to novel sources of environmental change. To expect that we can superimpose a starkly different landscape pattern and new set of anthropogenic disturbances and still retain the full set of species, most of which are adapted rather precisely to the conditions that prevailed during their evolution, is naive and dangerous. Even when we know what those preexisting conditions were, we may not be able to re-create them as regional or global changes continue, creating new environmental conditions.

On this point, I think it essential that scientists and land managers seek to know as much as we can about presettlement conditions. This history matters because species can be expected to be adapted to those conditions that were historically most prevalent. The ages and size classes of communities and the patterns of contiguity and disturbance that dominated presettlement landscapes provide context and habitat for the species that evolved in these areas. We also need to know as much as we can about how these patterns changed through time. Whenever conditions deviate significantly from those that prevailed historically, we can expect diversity to decline as those species adapted to historical conditions begin to suffer and sometimes go extinct. If history matters in this way, it behooves us not to radically alter conditions that have existed for eons, as they provide the evolutionary setting for species adaptations.

An interesting example is the intertidal zone. The intertidal zone is one of the most diverse and productive ecosystems on earth. Tens of thousands of species are well adapted to it. If you go to an exactly analogous zone in a freshwater river below a pumped storage power plant, you see mudflats—a biological desert. Diversity is depleted to the vanishing point. The difference is not the regularity or nature of the water's fluctuations. Rather, the crucial difference is that marine tides have washed our shores for over four billion years whereas freshwater pumped-storage "tides" arose only "yesterday." No amount of wishful thinking can dismiss the importance of this evolutionary history.

Nevertheless, Botkin is right to criticize management that blindly seeks to maintain a single or static environmental condition. Rather than attempt to reestablish a particular set of conditions, we should seek to maintain ecosystem functions. It is less politically charged. It is not a red flag. It is not naive. Managing for ecological function puts the emphasis where it should be—on the processes that generate and maintain diversity. We will never know enough to recognize all the dependencies that are out there. But if we can maintain some semblance of how fire, floods, and natural gap-phase dynamics within the forest originally dominated the landscape, we can generally assume that most of the species that have adapted to those disturbances will also persist.

THE IMPORTANCE OF SCALE

A final set of perils we face in applying biodiversity as a basis for conservation stems from these same dynamic processes. To conserve many species, it will be necessary to restore the disturbance regimes, ecological processes, and landscape conditions to which these species are adapted. But, significantly, management becomes increasingly frustrated the smaller the area is because we cannot easily re-create large-scale dynamics in small reserves. Anyone trying to restore a prairie or savanna via fire, or an old-growth forest with its dependence on gap-phase dynamics, faces many obstacles of this kind. We must first know what those conditions were and how they were maintained before we can re-create them on smaller areas or fragmented landscapes.

Thus, to conserve effectively, we should start at larger scales, with gamma diversity, landscapes, and communities. Prairies and oak savannas in the Midwest have been reduced to much less than 1 percent of what they once were. While we obviously need to start by maintaining whatever remnant patches we have of such severely threatened communities, we must soon begin the more arduous and less certain task of restoring them. In some cases, we are discovering that this effort requires that we actively manage conserved lands, sometimes intensively.[16] Ultimately, genetic diversity within species should be evaluated to ensure that genetic exchange and metapopulation dynamics are being maintained. Such management will require us to expand and connect these remnants of habitat via active restoration efforts. These efforts must include concern for natural patterns of disturbance and population dynamics if they are to succeed.

In the long run, it will be far cheaper and more ecologically effective to prevent endangerment via habitat protection than to save single species via "mitigation" or intensive captive breeding efforts. Yet some mitigation is obviously needed. Because we do not have biologically intact landscapes in the northeastern, midwestern, or southern United States, we must seek to restore habitats and communities. Mitigation practices will often be necessary, and we have to acknowledge that development will occur in some places. Farming and silviculture will continue to dominate much of our landscape. What is important is that conservation and development be coordinated in an intelligent way. To accomplish this, people from different agencies and private landowners will need to cooperate to redesign landscapes to include an ecologically viable network of habitats.

THE QUESTION OF UNCERTAINTY

Is conservation science advanced enough to provide definitive guidance for effective conservation policy? Yes and no. We have a large and rapidly growing body of knowledge about conservation biology. We have documented the effects imposed by edge habitats and isolation. We know which species are sensitive to fragmentation. Conservation scientists and ecologists base their work on a well-developed body of theory capable of making concrete and quantitative predictions. These predictions have been repeatedly tested and validated.

At the same time, conservation biologists are discovering new domains of ignorance—perhaps at even a faster rate than they are discovering new facts and theories. A DNA analysis of the bacteria in a teaspoonful of Norwegian soil revealed that, instead of the one or two dozen species biologists thought might be present, it contained two to ten thousand species of bacteria! The still nascent National Biological Service (NBS) is beginning to address this essential need for basic information on species occurrences, but its efforts still seem to pale before the task it faces. We need a hierarchical set of indicators with monitoring and management tiered to one another and coordinated across different spatial scales.[17]

Scientists increasingly realize how intricately ecological conditions and species interact. Invasion by some new exotic or the emergence of some new disease repeatedly takes us by surprise, often confounding our conservation efforts. Moreover, we are beginning to realize how often ecological systems display nonlinear responses to cumulative effects. Fish populations crash while experts argue over the details of their favorite models.

This situation raises a key question: how do we deal with this uncertainty? If you talk with managers you find that many are full of hubris instead of humility. If you want old growth, they will excitedly explain how to engineer old growth. Yet science often reveals further complexity and uncertainty about the future consequences of our manipulations. Scientists face uncertainty of many different kinds. We still do not know how much diversity exists, how it is distributed, or how species contribute to the persistence of other species. Are these changes in our population estimates significant trends or merely natural oscillation? When should we declare a population endangered? This uncertainty leads many scientists to urge managers to err on the side of conservation. Yet managers are trained to express confidence and to emphasize economic targets. This leads many managers to express dismay at scientists' lack of definitive answers. Small wonder, then, that scientists and managers differ so often in their position along the hubris/humility spectrum.

What consequences will this uncertainty bring for our public lands? Does it simply provide a screen for managers to hide behind? Does it preclude any confidence in designing conservation schemes? At least we should acknowledge our ignorance about ecological systems, especially during formal environmental reviews as in environmental impact statements. We should also seek to monitor the effects of our management and correct major impacts as quickly as possible. By extension, we should also lay the burden of proof on those who claim, often without evidence, that extensive and intensive forms of habitat manipulation will not adversely affect biotic systems. Ultimately, both scientists and managers must rely on the best available information and their own judgment.

FUTURE PROSPECTS

Where shall we go with diversity as a policy tool and goal? I cannot answer that. But I will tell you where conservation science is headed:

- Many scientists are becoming more involved. They are speaking out publicly and venturing into policy. The Ecological Society of America now maintains a Washington office, and it and the Society for Conservation Biology have both established policy committees.

- There is obviously a great need to scale up the amount of inventory and monitoring of our biological resources. The National Biological Service and the proposed National Institute for the Environment are both needed to provide managers with critical information with which to make decisions.

- At the same time, scientists are gaining a wider perspective. More taxa, including inconspicuous small creepy crawly things with multiple interactions, are being studied all the time. So too are water levels, habitat conditions, temporal scales, and landscape variables. The GAP Analysis Program is attempting to pinpoint which habitats and communities are most in need of protection.

- As conservation science becomes more sophisticated, as it becomes more technical, perhaps as it becomes more arcane, there will be increasing room for disagreement. Alternative points of view will emerge within the scientific community on controversial points such as conducting population viability analyses and designing reserve networks. Such controversy is likely to be exploited by those eager to minimize the role for conservation biology and its implications for resource management. Thus we can expect to see the emergence of new "experts" eager to dispute conventional points of view. We may also witness attempts to label the work of established conservation scientists as "biased" or subject to alternative interpretations. Indeed, we have already begun to hear about "bad" science.

How can we avoid this kind of conflict, expert versus expert? There is a desperate need here to integrate research and monitoring more directly with management—what is sometimes referred to as "adaptive management." We need to build learning, via replicate treatments, controls, and careful experimental design, into our management schemes. Likewise, we need to find ways to direct our research results more directly back into management. This, of course, is the great promise and hope of ecosystem management. It is also one that has yet to be fully realized.

NOTES

1. W. S. Alverson, W. Kuhlmann, and D. M. Waller, *Wild Forests: Conservation Biology and Public Policy* (Washington, D.C.: Island Press, 1994).

2. D. Simberloff, "The Spotted Owl Fracas: Mixing Academic, Applied, and Political Ecology," *Ecology* 68 (1987):766–772; S. L. Yaffee, *The Wisdom of the Spotted Owl: Policy Lessons for a New Century* (Washington, D.C.: Island Press, 1994).

3. K. A. Kohm, ed., *Balancing on the Brink of Extinction: The Endangered Species Act and Lessons for the Future* (Washington, D.C.: Island Press, 1991); D.J. Rohlf, "Six Biological Reasons Why the Endangered Species Act Doesn't Work—And What to Do About It," *Conservation Biology* 5 (1991):273–282.

4. D. S. Wilcove, M. McMillan, and K. C. Winston, "What Exactly Is an Endangered Species? An Analysis of the U.S. Endangered Species List: 1985–1991," *Conservation Biology* 7 (1993):87–93.

5. R. Tobin, *The Expendable Future* (Durham, N.C.: Duke University Press, 1990).

6. E. O. Wilson, "The Little Things That Run the World (the Importance and Conservation of Invertebrates)," *Conservation Biology* 1 (1987):344–346.

7. A. E. Magurran, *Ecology Diversity and Its Measurement* (Princeton: Princeton University Press, 1988), p. 109.

8. Alverson et al., *Wild Forests,* postscript.

9. *Sierra Club v. Marita,* Case Nos. 94-1736 and 94-1827 decided January 20, 1995.

10. See Proposed Rule for National Forest System Land and Resource Mangement Planning, 60 Fed. Reg. 18886 (April 13, 1995).

11. J. M. Diamond, "Assembly of Species Comminities," in M. L. Cody and J. M. Diamond, eds., *Ecology and Evolution of Communities* (Cambridge, Mass.: Harvard University Press, 1975).

12. B. D. Patterson and W. Atmar, "Nested Subsets and the Structure of Insular Mammalian Faunas and Archipelagos," *Biological Journal of the Linnaean Society* 28 (1986):65–82; A. Cutler, "Nested Faunas and Extinction in Fragmented Habitats," *Conservation Biology* 5 (1991):496–505.

13. R. H. MacArthur and E. O. Wilson, *The Theory of Island Biogeography* (Princeton: Princeton University Press, 1967).

14. E. O. Wilson, "Threats to Biodiversity," *Scientific American* 261(3) (1989):108–116.

15. D. Botkin, *Discordant Harmonies: A New Ecology for the Twenty-First Century* (New York: Oxford University Press, 1991).

16. W. S. Alverson and D. M. Waller, "Is It Un-Biocentric to Manage?" *Wild Earth* 2(4) (1992):9–10.

17. R. Noss, "Indicators for Monitoring Biodiversity: A Hierarchical Approach," *Conservation Biology* 4 (1990):355–364.

PART II

BIODIVERSITY'S SAFETY NET: SAVING ENDANGERED SPECIES

The sixth great extinction spasm of geological time is upon us, grace of mankind.

—E. O. WILSON

In its relatively brief history, the protection of wildlife species has focused almost exclusively on those plants and animals directly threatened with extinction. The U.S. Lacey Act of 1900, amended several times subsequently, was originally enacted to prohibit the interstate commerce of wild animals taken in violation of state law.[1] The 1934 Fish and Wildlife Coordination Act, also subsequently amended,[2] required the U.S. Fish and Wildlife Service to minimize and mitigate the adverse wildlife effects of federal projects in order to avoid species imperilment. The United States, however, did not pass an actual Endangered Species Act (ESA) until 1966, which was amended in 1969. Finally, in 1973, meaningful enforcement mechanisms were embedded in the ESA, making it, after major reauthorizations in 1978, 1979, 1982, and 1988, the powerful conservation law that it is today.

The political problems that presently beset the ESA are in many ways a reflection of the confused messages that Congress has sent to the act's implementing federal agencies, the Departments of Interior and Commerce, since the modern era of endangered species protection began in 1973. On the one hand, as National Oceanic and Atmospheric Administration (NOAA) lawyer Jason Patlis points out in Chapter 3, an explicit purpose of the ESA is to protect ecosystems upon which threatened and endangered species depend. Although biodiversity was barely a recognized concept in 1973,[3] certain sections of the act certainly echo biodiversity overtones. Nevertheless, as reflected in much of the express obligations and congressional history of the ESA, many senators and representatives believed that the act was to be a legislative tool that primarily addressed charismatic megafauna like the bald eagle and American alligator. A reasonable middle-ground supposition is that a bipartisan Congress indeed desired to protect a full panoply of fish and wildlife in 1973 but has since experienced gradual defections as its lofty goals sometimes threaten the comfort of an American society accustomed to unabridged consumption patterns.

Today, after the implementation of several other conservation laws, like the 1976 National Forest Management Act (NFMA), 1976 Federal Land Policy and Management Act (FLPMA), and the wetlands provisions of the 1972 Clean Water Act (CWA), the ESA is ideally supposed to work as a legislative safety net that catches species before they join the passenger pigeon as museum relics. But actual practice has not conformed to legal theory. The ESA has, instead, generally been a picture of crisis management. Domestic U.S. species continue to be added to the threatened and endangered list at precipitous rates. There are now over 900 U.S. and 4,000 candidate species of plants and animals on the list, compared to the 109 on the original 1973 list. While critics of the ESA point to this fact as evidence of legislation gone awry, supporters counter that the act merely reflects the dangerous disregard Americans display toward the natural world as housing tracts, road construction, and strip malls continue to proliferate around the country.

As the first administration in over a decade to attempt a good-faith implementation of the act, the Clinton ESA team finds itself in treacherous political terrain. The situation has probably only been exacerbated by the November 1994 congressional elections, which gave the Republican Party full control of both the House and Senate for the first time in fifty years. While the Clinton administration recognizes the real threats that face America's natural heritage, Secretary of the Interior Bruce Babbitt and NOAA head James Baker feel considerable political pressure to use the ESA's underestimated flexibility in order to avoid painful clashes between economic development and species protection. Since January 1993, the Interior Department and NOAA have announced numerous administrative and implementation initiatives designed to ease the burden of the ESA. Whether such moves will eventually stem the present extinction slide is unclear, but all appear to be consistent with a literal interpretation of the act.

For all the acrimony surrounding the ESA, the act actually allows economic considerations at all stages of implementation save one: the listing of a species as threatened or endangered under Section 4. At all other points—such as when critical habitat is designated and recovery plans promulgated under Section 4, when federal agencies must "consult" with the Fish and Wildlife Service (FWS) or the National Marine Fisheries Service (NMFS) on actions that may affect listed species under Section 7, and when an individual may "take" a species under Sections 9 and 10—economic factors are explicitly allowed to be considered.[4] In other words, although Congress has consistently upheld a scientifically credible accounting of the status of wildlife, it has simultaneously armed the implementing agencies with a number of cost/benefit tools when actually regulating on behalf of species.

Many believe, in fact, that this flexibility often has an adverse effect on listed species. On the one hand, as described by Patlis, recent developments in Section 7 consultation with regard to multispecies, multiagency, and program actions are welcome improvements. On the other hand, these innovations mask or exacerbate several persistent problems that hamper truly effective consultation: first, action agency biological assessments, which determine the necessity of an FWS/NMFS biological opinion, are almost always written by private parties with a financial stake in the outcome; second, FWS/NMFS biological opinions frequently allow the population of a species to go extinct because it is argued that the species as a whole will survive; third, biological opinions do not adequately consider cumulative or random effects; and fourth, reasonable and prudent measures in a biological opinion, which form the basis for FWS/NMFS incidental take permits, are usually unenforceable. Despite the seemingly esoteric nature of these problems, the mechanics of consultation are crucial because Section 7 is the only place in the ESA where federal agencies are explicitly held accountable for the effects on wildlife of their otherwise lawful actions.[5] Section 7 also possesses affirmative conservation requirements for all federal agencies, but the duty is vague and most courts have been hesitant to seriously review agency actions under it.

Driving the bulk of the controversy over the ESA are its perceived and real effects on private property rights. This is largely because no other federal statute has ever even contemplated the type of land use regulation necessary under the ESA to conserve species and their habitat. A coalition of opponents to the act, therefore, have begun to insist that the ESA, particularly Section 9's prohibition against harming listed species habitat,[6] runs counter to the Fifth Amendment of the Constitution, which states that "private property" shall not be "taken for public use without just compensation."[7] ESA supporters reply that most of these claims are greatly exaggerated by a minority of well-financed business interests striving to avoid any reasonable constraint on their profit seeking and, in any event, the ESA need not be implemented in a way that denies reasonable activities on private property. Moreover, the federal courts have *never* found that the ESA's regulatory reach constitutes a taking. Yet a growing number of conservationists, recognizing that roughly three-quarters of all listed species in the United States occupy private land at some time, are taking a closer look at species protection on private land—for the sake of property owners and wildlife alike.

Perhaps nowhere are the conflicts between natural beauty and private-led growth more pronounced than in California, which, with roughly 40,000 wildlife species and an ever expanding human population of 32 million, has been in the forefront of environmental and biodiversity protection since formal efforts began in the 1960s. As veteran attorney Lindell Marsh points out in Chapter 4, California was also the site of the first habitat conservation plan (HCP) under Section 10 of the ESA. HCPs allow nonfederal development to occur on listed species' habitat in exchange for an overall conservation plan for the species in question. Although the HCP process has been criticized by purists, Marsh argues that its more cooperative and participatory approach has increased society's support for species protection. Marsh concedes, however, that such cooperation would be less effective without some sort of regulatory stick.[8]

Most recently, the HCP process has served as a model for an even more ambitious plan to save much of natural southern California—namely its coastal sage scrub habitat and the approximately one hundred sensitive species that depend on it, including the California gnatcatcher. This effort could revolutionize ESA implementation by combining the best features of federal oversight, state regulation, and private initiative. Because there is not yet an established enforcement mechanism, it could also become a hard lesson in the difficulty and danger of leaving biodiversity enforcement to mere goodwill. With some remaining land valued at over $2 million per acre because of its prime coastal location, most of it in private hands, the effort to save the gnatcatcher and its habitat is an excellent case study for broader lessons in biodiversity conservation.

The idea behind saving coastal sage scrub is deceivingly simple: identify remaining habitat, protect the ecologically crucial habitat, and allow human development on the least sensitive habitat. In 1991, the California government took the first step by authorizing government agencies at all levels, as well as private entities, to establish protective strategies under the Natural Community Conservation Plan (NCCP) program. In 1993, when Secretary Babbitt listed the 2,600 remaining pairs of gnatcatchers as threatened under the ESA, the federal government formally entered the fray. Classifying the bird as threatened rather than endangered enabled the FWS to promulgate "special" regulations under Section 4(d) of the ESA, an example of the act's flexibility that has not often been used. Under the ESA, only endangered species are technically subject to Section 9's prohibitions against takes and federal rules, but pursuant to Section 4(d) federal rules extend to threatened species as well.[9] Although federal courts have generally frowned on allowing the take of species by regulation without a lawful permit,[10] Babbitt's gnatcatcher rule nonetheless incorporated the California state multispecies NCCP effort almost wholesale. The only real additional requirement established by the gnatcatcher rule was that no more than 5 percent of lower-grade coastal sage scrub habitat could be destroyed during the planning process, thus allowing some development to proceed.

The NCCP interim planning stage for coastal sage scrub in southern California continues to this day. And, in a controversial move, Babbitt announced in 1994 that nonlisted, NCCP-covered species that are later listed will be governed by the NCCP plan and not the formal application of the ESA. In fact, this new rule will apply to all species conservation plans developed under Section 10 of the ESA.[11] It will also place tremendous pressure on the scientific and regulatory integrity of conservation plans such as those under the NCCP, many of which are valid for fifty years.

Thus without one single action by Congress, profound innovations in ESA implementation are percolating up from nonfederal participants. While the results of these changes are still unclear, it is certain that states (and perhaps Native American tribes) will continue to play a major role in biodiversity protection. Such delegation is not without conflict. For instance, some state fish and game agencies seek to prevent federal listings with conservation plans. Whatever the efficacy of these plans, they should not obviate the clear scientific criteria established by ESA Section 4. Alternatively, the states and federal government could more fully implement Section 6 of the act, which already allows states to take over management initiatives relating to a variety of actions concerning species recovery, from assessment and monitoring to habitat protection and private incentives.[12] States could also better coordinate the protection of candidate species with the federal government, not only to prevent listing, but also to avoid duplicative efforts with the federal government.

The stickiest question for the NCCP and other state initiatives, however, is funding. In addition to the costly requirements of biological research and land planning, millions of dollars will be needed to purchase easements or fee simple title to wildlife corridors and reserves. In this age of tight government budgets, who will pay for these necessary conservation efforts? While those who seek to develop ecologically sensitive land should bear the cost of their actions, it is nonetheless unfair to saddle present users with the costs of all past development. Indeed, the search for an equitable solution to this ESA funding dilemma possesses ramifications for the broader effort of biodiversity protection on private lands.[13]

Most significantly, the challenge of private land conservation starkly reveals the massive and harmful public land subsidies that now exist in the United States. Not only does the federal government lose billions of dollars to below-market sales of timber, water, mineral rights, and grazing permits annually, but these same subsidies simultaneously increase the costs of protecting threatened and endangered species. Moreover, there exist billions of unused dollars in the Land and Water Conservation Fund (LWCF) reserve,[14] which is generated by a tax on offshore oil production and is used to purchase rights in private property every year. Other intriguing ideas include utilizing funds from the 1991 Intermodal Surface Transportation Efficiency Act,[15] assessing natural resource damages for injuries to listed species or their habitat,[16] and authorizing a federal real estate transfer tax that could be levied only by state and local governments in an approved planning area.

Assuming that a secure biodiversity funding framework can be created and maintained, Todd Olson demonstrates in Chapter 5 that creative private incentive mechanisms to support biodiversity are plentiful. His work shows that the free market and species protection are not inherently at odds but must be calibrated to reinforce each other and provide a greater sense of certainty to private parties. Olson's habitat transaction approach holds particular promise in areas like southern California, where a sufficient baseline of biological data exists and urban development pressures are strong. In more rural areas, landowners might consider establishing trust funds or insurance accounts that could finance adaptive biodiversity management actions. Similarly, the 1995 Farm Bill provides an excellent opportunity to direct payments and price supports to activities that reinforce species and ecosystem health.[17] Other noteworthy incentive-based approaches include various tax credit and deduction proposals, as well as voluntary programs that simply provide public recognition for a good deed.

For all the genuine conflict surrounding federal endangered species protection on private land, there has been at least an equal amount of hyperbole. While Americans zealously value private property rights, poll after poll confirms that they value a clean and healthy environment just as much. Despite the Fifth Amendment, the Constitution has never allowed a private property owner to do whatever he or she pleases at the expense of fellow citizens. Common law nuisance principles prevent individuals from opening a pornography store or spewing pollutants into a neighborhood at will. The difficulty with biodiversity is that its degradation has now only risen to the level of nuisance.[18] Unlike traditional examples of nuisance, the damages borne from biodiversity loss are not usually immediate and its causes are often diffuse and cumulative. But like all nuisance claims, biodiversity loss is a legitimate check on private economic activity. Defining and addressing private harm to biodiversity is the major legal question confronting Congress as it faces ESA reauthorization—and one that does not beget simple policy responses.

But if the House Republicans' recent "Contract with America" is any indication, many members of Congress will soon attempt to reconcile the age-old tension between private rights and community well-being with a quick legislative fix. In plank number eight of the contract, entitled "The Job Creation and Wage Enhancement Act," the House Republicans passed a bill on "Private Property Rights," which would enable a private landowner to demand compensation from the federal government whenever the FWS or any other federal agency enforced a law that reduced the value of his or her property by twenty percent. There are three fundamental problems with this seemingly innocuous proposal. First, it ignores two hundred years of Supreme Court jurisprudence that demands factually based inquiries on takings claims, based on the landowner's loss of any viable economic use of land and the public interest of the regulation in question.[19] Second, it would subject agency interpretation of congressional law to compensation requests and arbitration hearings from any eligible landowner at any time, thus effectively frustrating meaningful agency enforcement of law. And third, if implemented, it would drain budgetary resources to compensate private citizens for not harming a public resource, which, as its proponents well know, would lead to efforts to directly weaken the ESA.

Another provision in the Contract with America, entitled "Regulatory Impact Analyses," would ironically force each federal agency to perform a burdensome 23-step process on each final rule promulgated. By requiring unnecessary cost-benefit analysis of even regulations designed to benefit economic development, common sense protection of biodiversity would be impossible. This provision also passed the House of Representatives in March 1995 as part of H.R.9. In the Senate, however, the legislation has been stymied by the realization that almost any regulation—from worker safety and transportation oversight to food inspection and environmental protection—would be covered. Consequently, senate Majority Leader Robert Dole (R–KS) was forced to abandon the legislation in the summer of 1995. Clearly, whatever problems exist regarding private land conservation and environmental regulation, the Contract with America represents a serious threat to biodiversity protection and demands additional public scrutiny.

Indeed, the Republican ascendance in Congress comes at a time when the ESA needs strengthening, not weakening. In the spirit of President Teddy Roosevelt, the Republicans possess the opportunity to make biodiversity conservation a truly bipartisan or even nonpartisan issue. Absent a stand-alone Biodiversity or Ecosystems Protection Act, Congress could strengthen the underutilized Section 5 of the ESA, which already requires the Interior Department and Forest Service to "establish a program to conserve fish, wildlife, and plants, including those which are listed as endangered species or threatened species" (meaning that nonlisted species should also be covered by the program). Such an amendment would accomplish what every policymaker should want—namely, the prevention of species endangerment. For those species that are imperilled to the point of listings, Congress must ensure that sound science, true recovery goals, and innovative habitat management plans are embraced.

NOTES

1. Lacey Act Amendments of 1981, 16 USC §§3371–3378.
2. 16 USC §§661–667(c).

3. The late Senator Magnuson (D–WA) presciently recognized "the need for biological diversity for scientific purposes." See *Report of the Senate Committee on Commerce on S.1983, The Endangered Species Act of 1973,* Report 93-307 (July 1, 1973).

4. "The term 'take' means to harass, harm, pursue, hunt, shoot, wound, kill, trap, capture or collect, or to attempt to engage in any such conduct"; ESA, Sec. 3(18).

5. See Don Barry, David Hoskins, et al., *For Conserving Listed Species, Talk Is Cheaper Than We Think,* 2nd ed. (Washington, D.C.: World Wildlife Fund, 1994). Of the 98,237 consultations conducted by the FWS and NMFS from 1987 to 1992, only 55 projects or actions (or less than 0.6 percent) were blocked as a result of ESA Section 7.

6. "Harm in the definition of 'take' in the Act means an act which actually kills or injures wildlife. Such act may include significant habitat modification or degradation which actually kills or injures wildlife by significantly impairing essential behavioral patterns, including breeding, feeding or sheltering." See 50 CFR Sec. 17.3.

7. The U.S. Supreme Court has always used a fact-based balancing test to evaluate takings claims, including the purpose of the government's action and the economic effect on the property owner. See for example, *Penn Central Transportation Co. v. New York City,* 438 U.S. 104 (1978).

8. The U.S. Supreme Court recently upheld the federal government's authority to regulate wildlife habitat on private land. *Sweet Home v. Babbit,* No. 94-859 (June 29, 1995); see also *Palila v. Hawaii Department of Land and Natural Resources,* 639 F. 2d 495 (9th Cir. 1981); U.S. General Accounting Office, *Endangered Species Act: Information on species Protection on Nonfederal lands* (Dec. 1994); National Research Council; *Science and the Endangered Species Act* (1995).

9. 50 CFR Sec. 17.31.

10. See for example, *Sierra Club v. Clark,* 755 F.2d 608 (8th Cir. 1985).

11. See U.S. Fish and Wildlife Service and National Marine Fisheries Service, *No Surprise: Assuring Certainty for Private Landowners in Endangered Species Act Habitat Conservation Planning* (Washington, D.C., 1994). But see also Bay Area Land Watch, *Habitat Conservation Plans (HCP) on San Bruno Mountain, San Mateo, California: The Failure of the First HCPs in the United States* (Brisbane, Calif., 1993).

12. See also S.2553 (103rd Cong.). This bill, introduced by Senator Barbara Boxer (D–CA), would authorize federal financial assistance to states for the purpose of acquiring habitat necessary to carry out an ESA Section 10(a)(2) conservation plan.

13. Professor J. B. Ruhl, for example, has proposed a model based on the Coastal Zone Management Act, 16 USC Sec. 1451 et seq. Under his scheme, states would identify and nominate biological resource zones, local governments and citizens would develop plans per federal approval, and all regulation would fall under the auspices of approved plans. See J. B. Ruhl, "Biodiversity Conservation and the Ever-Expanding Web of Federal Laws Regulating Nonfederal Lands: Time for Something Completely Different?" Univ. of Colo. Law Review 66: 555(1995).

14. 16 USC Sec. 460(d), 4601–4 et seq. See also Federal Aid in Wildlife Restoration Act (Pittman-Robertson Act), 16 USC §§669–699i; Federal Aid in Fish Restoration Act (Dingell-Johnson Act), 16 USC §§777–777k; Fish and Wildlife Conservation Act (Non-Game Act), 16 USC §§2901–2911.

15. P.L. 102-240.

16. See ESA Sec. 11; see also Marine Sanctuaries Amendments of 1984, 16 USC Sec. 1443; Oil Pollution Act, 33 USC 2706(d)(1)(b).

17. See for example, the 1985 Farm Bill, Food Security Act of 1985, P.L. 99-198; 1990 Farm Bill, Food Agriculture, Conservation, and Trade Act of 1990, P.L. 101-624.

18. See Restatement (Second) of Torts §827 (changed circumstances or new knowledge may make what was previously permissible no longer so). See H.R. 925 (104th Congress), which would require compensation to private landowners if endangered species or wetlands protection lowered property values by 20% or more, and passed in the House in spring 1995. How this bill can be reconciled with speaker Newt Gingrich's view that "there are enormous interests that we have as human beings in maintaining biological diversity" remains to be seen. Interestingly, Gingrich has called for a "Biological Diversity Act." See Scott Allen, speaking in wildlife's behalf, the *Boston Globe* (May 28, 1995).

19. See for example, *Lucas v. South Carolina Coastal Council,* 112 S. Ct. 2886 (1992) (ruling that a statute prohibiting house construction on beachfront property in a historic flood zone could deny a property owner viable use of his land if no historical nuisance is found); *Dolan v. Tigard,* 114 S. Ct 2309 (1994) (ruling that a mandated transfer of private property to protect species is a taking unless a public purpose related to the transfer has been established).

REFERENCES

Ackerman, Bruce, and Richard Stewart. 1995. Reforming environmental law. *Stanford Law Review* 37:1333.

Barker, Rocky. 1993. *Saving All the Parts: Reconciling Economics and the Endangered Species Act.* Washington, D.C.: Island Press.

Bean, Michael. 1983. *The Evolution of National Wildlife Law.* New York: Praeger.

Bean, M. J., S. Fitzgerald, and M. O'Connell. 1991. *Reconciling Conflicts Under the Endangered Species Act: The Habitat Conservation Planning Experience.* Washington, D.C.: World Wildlife Fund.

Breen, Barry. 1989. Citizen suits for natural resources damages: Closing a gap in federal environmental law. *Wake Forest Law Review* 24:851.

Deane, James, ed. 1994. *Defenders Special Issue: The Race to Save Wild California.* Washington, D.C.: Defenders of Wildlife.

Defenders of Wildlife. 1995. *Saving America's Wildlife: Renewing the Endangered Species Act.* Washington, D.C.: Defenders of Wildlife.

De Gennaro, Ralph, and Gawain Kripke. 1993. *Earth Budget.* Washington, D.C.: Friends of the Earth.

Dunlap, Thomas. 1984. *The Federal Government, Wildlife and Endangered Species.* Washington, D.C.: The Conservation Foundation.

Fischer, Hank, and Wendy Hudson. 1993. *Building Economic Incentives into the Endangered Species Act.* Washington, D.C.: Defenders of Wildlife.

General Accounting Office. 1988. *Management Improvements Could Enhance Recovery Program.* Report RCED-89-5. Washington, D.C.: GAO.

Houck, Oliver. 1993. The Endangered Species Act and its implementation by the U.S. Departments of Interior and Commerce. *University of Colorado Law Review* 64:277.

Irvin, William Robert. 1993. The Endangered Species Act: Keeping Every Cog and Wheel. *Natural Resources and Environment* 8:33.

Kunich, John. 1994. The fallacy of deathbed conservation under the Endangered Species Act. *Environmental Law* 24:501.

Livingston, John A. 1981. *The Fallacy of Wildlife Conservation.* Toronto: McClelland & Stewart.

Mann, Charles, and Mark Plummer. 1995. *Noah's Choice: The Future of Endangered Species.* New York: Knopf.

McCaull, John. 1994. The natural community conservation planning program and the coastal sage scrub ecosystem of Southern California. In R. E. Grumbine, ed., *Environmental Policy and Biodiversity.* Washington, D.C.: Island Press.

Rohlf, D. R. 1989. *The Endangered Species Act: A Guide to Its Protections and Implementation.* Palo Alto, Calif.: Stanford Environmental Law Society.

Sax, Joseph. 1993. Property rights and the economy of nature: Understanding *Lucas v. South Carolina Coastal Council. Stanford Law Review* 45:1433.

Snape, William J. III and Heather Weiner. 1995. Recipe for Reauthorization of the Endangered Species Act. *Duke Environmental Law and Policy Forum* V:501.

Stevens, William. 1995. Latest endangered species: Natural habitats of America. *New York Times,* February 14.

Tobin, Richard. 1990. *The Expendable Future: U.S. Politics and the Protection of Biological Diversity.* Durham, N.C.: Duke University Press.

U.S. Department of the Interior. 1985. *Potential Funding Sources to Implement the Fish and Wildlife Conservation Act of 1980.* Washington, D.C.: Government Printing Office.

U.S. Department of the Interior, U.S. Fish and Wildlife Service. 1990. *Endangered and Threatened Species Recovery.* Washington, D.C.: Government Printing Office.

U.S. Department of the Interior, U.S. Fish and Wildlife Service. 1992. *Endangered and Threatened Species Recovery.* Washington, D.C.: Government Printing Office.

U.S. General Accounting Office. 1979. *Endangered Species: A Controversial Issue.* Washington, D.C.: General Accounting Office.

U.S. House of Representatives. 1994. Report by Majority Staff of the Committee on Natural Resources and the Environment. *Taking from the Taxpayer: Public Subsidies for Natural Resources Development.* Washington, D.C.: General Accounting Office.

U.S. National Oceanic and Atmospheric Administration. 1993. *Report of the NOAA Panel on Contingent Valuation.* Washington, D.C.: NOAA.

Chapter 3

BIODIVERSITY, ECOSYSTEMS, AND ENDANGERED SPECIES

Jason Patlis

It is almost impossible to read a law review article on the Endangered Species Act (ESA) that does not begin with some colorful characterization of the act's sweeping mandate.[1] For canine lovers, it has been dubbed "the pit bull of environmental statutes"; for high society, it has been called "the crown jewel" of environmental laws. The Supreme Court has labeled it "the most comprehensive legislation for preservation of endangered species *ever* enacted by *any* nation." Superlatives abound with reference to the ESA. What usually follows in these articles, however, is a thorough trashing of the ESA and a discussion of why it has not lived up to any of these superlatives.

With respect to ecosystem protection, there is no sweeping mandate in the ESA, nor are there any sweeping judicial decisions like *TVA v. Hill*,[2] and thus there are no failed promises. This is not to say, however, that ecosystem protection was not contemplated in the ESA. Indeed, ecosystem protection was an instrumental concept in the passage of the ESA. Although ecosystem protection has been explicitly mentioned numerous times in the legislative history of the ESA and indeed can be read into the statute itself in several instances, this legislative consciousness was never transposed into regulatory obligation or judicial interpretation. Thus the promise of the ESA, with respect to ecosystem protection, never even materialized.

Despite the lack of regulatory or judicial mandates, the implementing agencies certainly maintain authority to incorporate ecosystem protection into the implementation of the ESA. That such measures are not required by the statute does not mean they are not allowed by the statute. Such measures are being taken to some extent already, and while there are inherent limitations in the statute and existing regulations in protecting ecosystems, the ESA is the strongest tool currently available for protecting our biological diversity.

USING THE ESA FOR ECOSYSTEM PROTECTION

As this discussion focuses on using the ESA—a statute to protect individual species—for protecting ecosystems, let us begin by discussing the relationship of all three: species, ecosystem, and biodiversity. Scientists have a relatively limited understanding on all levels of biodiversity, including such issues as defining the genetic characteristics of distinct population groups, cataloging species in unexplored ecosystems such as tropical rain forests or ocean bottoms, and determining the attributes of ecosystems. Furthermore, the relationship of genes, species, and ecosystems to one another and to the larger meaning of biodiversity is not fully understood. Biological diversity can be analyzed on three levels: *genetic* diversity is a measure of the variation of genes within a species, including distinct populations within a species or genetic diversity within a population; *species* diversity is a measure of the variety of species in a region, including not only the number of different species but also the number of different taxonomic groupings; *ecosystem* diversity is a measure of the variety of groupings of species, including species abundance, age structures, and relationships among species (predatory, parasitic, symbiotic, and so forth).

Ecosystems are the least understood component of biodiversity. What we do know is that they contain a tremendous amount of organization, which puts them at the top of the organizational hierarchy of biodiversity, followed by communities, guilds, species, organisms, and genes. Ecosystems can be defined as the interactions of living organisms to the point where they have developed self-integrating and self-organizing processes. Ecosystems also include the transfers of energy and matter between these organisms and processes. Whereas a community refers to groupings of species or populations, the ecosystem comprises the physical or abiotic environment in addition to biological components. Given the need to protect biodiversity at least on the ecosystem level, the question arises whether the ESA, which currently focuses on species, can adequately serve this purpose. Would an "endangered ecosystem act" be more efficacious in protecting biodiversity than an "endangered species act"? The answer is one of policy and resource management as much as it is of science.

In terms of science, it has been established that certain "indicator species" or "keystone species" sometimes provide a measure for the health of an ecosystem; by studying these species scientists can determine trends in the ecosystems. Similarly, scientists can identify certain "umbrella species" that provide a measure for the protection of an ecosystem; by protecting these species, managers can protect the entire ecosystem. These species have been called "coarse filters" through which communities of species within an ecosystem can be protected. Given the lack of understanding regarding ecosystems, there is a strong practical incentive to use umbrella species.

Critics of this approach, however, point out that it is frequently impossible to identify an umbrella species for an ecosystem—and even if it is, protections for these "coarse filters" may not be adequate for the ecosystem itself or smaller, dependent species. An ecosystem approach considers the range of biophysical elements, such as species, communities, and landscapes, and entails an initial classification and mapping of ecosystem components, such as climate, physiography, physiochemistry, geology, soils, and vegetation. The goal is to protect the components within the ecosystem that are vital to species' survival. Although an ecosystem approach is ultimately more cost-effective, allowing managers to deal with several species simultaneously, there are a number of roadblocks to the adoption of such an approach: logistically, it involves more political entities, more parties, and additional statutory requirements; conceptually, it involves less discrete boundaries and definitions; biologically, it involves greater numbers of species, sometimes with conflicting or competing requirements; economically, it may initially require greater funding while mapping is being conducted (although costs in the long run should be greatly reduced). Others note, however, that the distinction between "single-species management" and "ecosystem management" is a false dichotomy: both are part of a continuum of necessary protections of biodiversity.

These debates aside, whether the ESA will be used as the instrument to impose these "coarse filters" is a policy decision; whether the ESA can be used as a basis for ecosystem management is likewise a policy decision. These policy issues can be addressed by the ESA without amendment. The tools are present in the ESA; they need only be applied. The questions that arise are: What tools are available, why haven't they been applied in the past, and how can they be applied in the future?

ECOSYSTEM PROTECTION AS A MANDATE OF THE ESA

The term "ecosystem" is explicitly mentioned only once in the ESA, in the preamble, which states that "the purposes of this act are to provide a means whereby ecosystems upon which endangered species or threatened species depend may be conserved."[3] Although the preamble contains the only explicit reference to ecosystems, the ESA makes clear in numerous provisions that species preservation and ecosystem protection go hand in hand. Insofar as the protection of species depends on protection of their habitats, and habitats are one of several aspects of ecosystems, all of these elements are inextricably linked with each other. This relationship is laid out in the definitions of "critical habitat" and "conservation" in Section 3 of the ESA[4] which tie habitat protection to recovery of species.

Several provisions of the ESA are applicable to habitat protection: one of the criteria for listing, reclassifying, or delisting a species under Section 4(a) of the act is present or threatened destruction, modification, or curtailment of its habitat;[5] acquisition of land to conserve listed species is authorized in Section 5;[6] and management agreements between the secretary and states can provide for administration and management of lands established for the conservation of listed species.[7] Other sections are applicable to conservation: Section 4(f) of the ESA establishes the broad charge to the secretary to develop and implement recovery plans for the conservation of the species;[8] Section 7(a)(1) provides that federal agencies have a duty to conserve listed species;[9] and nonfederal entities that seek an exemption from the prohibitions against taking listed species must develop a conservation plan pursuant to Section 10(a)(2).[10]

Even without explicit consideration of ecosystem protection, the ESA implicitly provides for the protection of ecosystems if necessary to protect individual species. The act recognizes that information about protecting endangered and threatened species is often unavailable and always changing. As a result, the ESA provides for a flexible management regime based on the "best scientific and commercial data available."[11] While the statute does not identify the precise measures necessary to protect listed species, neither does it limit the possible measures available for such protection. If a species cannot be protected without protection of its ecosystem—a fact that Congress clearly recognized—then such protection is in keeping with the scientific standard established in the ESA.

The legislative history of the ESA supports the premise that the statute was intended to preserve the biological diversity of the planet and the ecosystems that store this diversity, perhaps more than it was intended to correct the individual species that comprise these ecosystems and biodiversity. The hearings and conference reports from the original passage of the ESA are replete with discussions relating to ecosystem protection. They indicate that the broad purpose of the act, as intended at its passage, was to protect what we now call biodiversity; both species protection and ecosystem protection could thus be viewed as means to an end, rather than ends in themselves. In fact, the legislative history further indicates that species protection itself was to be done through ecosystem protection. One House Report stated:

> The essential purpose of the Act is to provide a means for protecting the ecosystems upon which we and other species depend. Another, allied purpose is to provide a specific program for the protection of endangered species.[12]

Legislative history subsequent to 1973 is bespeckled with references to both biological diversity and ecosystem protection reaffirming the original congressional intent of the ESA. Indeed, in 1978, the report of the House Committee on Merchant Marine and Fisheries stated that "the ultimate goal of the Act is the conservation of the ecosystem on which all species, *whether endangered or not,* depend for survival."[13] The report further noted that "the primary purpose of the [ESA] is to prevent animal and plant species endangerment and extinction caused by man's influence on ecosystems, and to return the species to the point where they are viable components of their ecosystems." While these passing references through the years may be a form of legislative boilerplate, the fact that they continue to be made indicates a consciousness on the part of the legislators that the ESA seeks to protect not only species but also the ecosystems essential for their survival.

Congress amended the ESA in 1982 to allow for permits to be issued to nonfederal entities for the taking of endangered species incidental to otherwise lawful activities. In the context of this amendment, the Conference report observed:

> In enacting the Endangered Species Act, Congress recognized that individual species should not be viewed in isolation, but must be viewed in terms of their relationship to the ecosystem of which they form a constituent element. Although the regulatory mechanisms of the Act focus on species that are formally listed as endangered or threatened, the purposes and policies of the Act are far broader than simply providing for the conservation of individual species or individual members of listed species.[13]

These amendments, in particular the requirement of a conservation plan, are significant in that Congress recognizes, through this operative provision of the statute rather than through the preamble, that the ESA protects more than individual species. Even as Congress prepares for a contentious reauthorization of the ESA in 1995 and beyond, most adhere to the original premise that the ESA needs to focus on ecosystems as a means to protect threatened and endangered species.

Recent Efforts to Protect Ecosystems Through the ESA

Despite the statutory language and the legislative history, it has become evident through the years that the ESA, as implemented by the National Oceanic and Atmospheric Administration (NOAA) and Fish and Wildlife Service (FWS) and interpreted by the courts, is species-oriented, even myopically at times. There are several reasons for this. To a large extent, this ecosystem-based approach was laid out in the preamble and the definitions but was never carried over to the operative provisions of the act. Furthermore, the operative provisions that most directly incorporate an ecosystem approach—protection of the species' critical habitat pursuant to Section 7(a)(2) and the duty of federal agencies to conserve listed species pursuant to Section 7(a)(1)—were interpreted by the implementing agencies and by the courts in such a way that their significance was greatly minimized.

Specifically, FWS and NMFS promulgated joint regulations in 1986 that included a definition adversely modifying critical habitat which is almost identical to the definition of jeopardizing the species. Both agencies have thus taken the position that the prohibitions against jeopardy and adverse habitat modification are largely duplicative. A number of scholars have criticized this interpretation, arguing that it undermines the broad goals of the ESA and even contravenes the act by rendering the adverse modification prohibition nugatory. Despite the mandatory language of Section 7(a)(1), which states that federal agencies shall carry out programs for the conservation of listed species, agencies maintain significant discretion in determining how and to what extent they will utilize their duties to conserve listed species. Courts have recognized a conservation duty upon federal agencies in the abstract sense, but they have refrained from delineating the scope of this duty in a practical sense.

Ecosystem considerations can be taken into account in several provisions of the ESA, however. For example: new listings of species can be determined and grouped according to the ecosystems in which they are found; recovery plans can be developed for groups of species found in a particular ecosystem and thus focus on ecosystem recovery as well as individual species recovery; conservation plans pursuant to Section 10 of the act can also address ecosystem-based considerations rather than single-species concerns. Above all, ecosystem considerations can be—and in certain instances must be—incorporated into the consultation process of Section 7(a)(2).

General Policy Initiatives

Both FWS and NMFS, as well as other federal agencies, have been moving to an ecosystem-based approach in addressing many aspects of listed species.

Indeed, FWS and NMFS recently issued a joint policy statement that formally provides an ecosystem approach to implementation of the ESA. The new policy incorporates "ecosystem considerations in Endangered Species Act actions regarding listing, interagency cooperation, recovery, and cooperative activities" and recognizes that "species will be conserved best not by a species-by-species approach but by an ecosystem conservation strategy that transcends individual species."[15] Specifically, the policy states that listing decisions will be grouped on a geographic, taxonomic, or ecosystem basis where possible and, moreover, that comprehensive status reviews across the entire range of candidate species will be conducted in conjunction with other federal, tribal, state, and private agencies. Recovery plans will be developed and implemented for communities or ecosystems where several listed and candidate species occur, in a manner that conserves the biotic diversity of the ecosystems on which listed species depend.

Moreover, twelve agencies of five departments recently signed a Memorandum of Understanding on Implementation of the Endangered Species Act, which seeks to "establish a general framework for cooperation and participation . . . in the exercise of [agencies'] responsibilities under the ESA . . . by protecting and managing their populations and the ecosystems upon which those populations depend."[16] Specifically, the agreement provides a mechanism for coordinated action and focuses on species and ecosystems equally. Most relevant to ecosystem protection through the consultation process, the agencies have agreed "to identify and resolve regional issues associated with interagency consultation undertaken pursuant to section 7(a)(2) of the ESA [such as] encouraging multi-agency, multi-project consultations [and] exploring opportunities to increase the effectiveness of programmatic consultations."[17]

Apart from these general policies and agreements, ecosystem-based efforts are being made with respect to particular species and genera. For example, NMFS has been incorporating an ecosystem-based approach into many of its activities relating to Pacific salmonid stocks. With respect to the listed species of Snake River salmon, NMFS has designated critical habitat for three species combined. This allows NMFS, as well as federal action agencies, to consider the effects on all habitat shared by all three species. Furthermore, NMFS is currently developing a single recovery plan that will address the conservation needs of these species together.

With respect to the future listings of other anadromous stocks, NMFS has initiated status reviews on a coastwide basis for all five biological species of Pacific salmon (sockeye, chinook, coho, pink, and chum) as well as steelhead and cutthroat trout. These expanded status reviews cover the range of the species in the continental United States and represent a significant step toward protecting the entire ecosystems of these species. Expanded status reviews will allow NMFS to conduct a more thorough assessment on all levels of the determination for listings—such as whether individual stocks or groups of stocks contribute to the genetic and ecological diversity of the coastwide populations, and whether individual stocks or larger populations are threatened or endangered in relation to larger groupings of the population.

In addition to NMFS's own actions regarding Pacific salmonids, federal agencies have sought to enter into agreements in an effort to prevent or postpone future listings of stocks and thereby avoid the sometimes stringent protective measures invoked upon listing. Agencies recognize that the most effective means to achieve this goal is to protect entire ecosystems of salmonid stocks. In 1994 for example, the Forest Service, National Park Service, Bureau of Land Management, FWS, and NMFS entered into a Memorandum of Understanding to conserve species "that are tending toward federal listing by protecting their habitats and ecosystems upon which they depend."[18]

Even if salmonid species have already been listed, agreements to provide broader ecosystem management are being negotiated. In 1993, for example, four federal agencies signed an agreement to coordinate federal activities regarding the San Francisco Bay/Sacramento–San Joaquin River Delta and to specifically incorporate an ecosystem-based approach into their activities.[19] This agreement, in turn, has been incorporated into a larger agreement between the same federal agencies and the state of California.[20]

Another means to address ecosystem considerations under the ESA is through Sections 4 and 10. Section 10(a) provides that the secretary may issue a permit for incidental takings by a nonfederal entity, conditioned on the development, funding, and implementation of a conservation plan that minimizes and mitigates the impacts of the incidental taking and will not appreciably reduce the likelihood of survival and recovery of the species in the wild. Conservation plans are intended to provide broad protections to both listed and nonlisted species through cooperative public and private initiatives.

FWS has recently engaged in several rulemakings, pursuant to Section 4(d) of the ESA, to incorporate state and local conservation planning into the Section 10 permit process for the threatened California gnatcatcher and the threatened northern spotted owl.[21] The rulemakings provide that certain incidental takings would be exempt from the takings prohibition and yet would not require an incidental take permit under Section 10, provided that they are in compliance with state law and specific state and local conservation planning requirements, which generally focus on ecosystem protections. There are a number of benefits to these rulemakings that help fulfill the ESA's broader goals of ecosystem protection. They focus on state-managed and regionally managed programs that address general ecosystem concerns, rather than individual landowner projects that would likely address individual species; this in turn provides for alternative, less burdensome mechanisms for compliance with the substantive mandates of the ESA. They allow the FWS to directly incorporate the state's research and planning efforts as the best available data in its decision making and allow the states to take the initiative in conservation planning.

One of the most significant operative provisions of the ESA is the no-jeopardy mandate of Section 7(a)(2). Joint regulations promulgated by FWS and NMFS provide a detailed framework for compliance with Section 7(a)(2).[22] Based on the consultation, either FWS or NMFS (depending on the species) issues a biological opinion concluding whether the proposed action is likely to jeopardize a species or not. There are two reasons why Section 7(a)(2) has become such a powerful tool: the broad definition of agency action and the scope of the effects of the action to be considered.

Both the statutory and the regulatory definitions of agency "action"—anything authorized, funded, or carried out by the agency—are tremendously broad, and this breadth has not been lost on the courts. The Supreme Court, in *TVA v. Hill*, recognized that "action" includes both proposed actions and ongoing actions, and other courts have followed this expansive interpretation. Examples of agency actions include issuance of a right-of-way permit, issuance of certain grants or loan guarantees, creation of categories of nationwide permits to allow discharges, approval of a registration program for pesticides, and announcement of a strategy regarding timber sales. The "effects of the action" that must be addressed in the consultation process are extremely broad, too, and include direct and indirect effects of the action, as well as effects of interrelated or interdependent actions. Again, the courts have broadly construed the requirement that all effects of the action be considered during the consultation process.

Section 7 Consultations

Given the scope of Section 7(a)(2),[23] the most efficacious means of incorporating ecosystem considerations into the substantive requirements to protect listed species is through the consultation process. Two types of consultation are particularly well suited for this purpose: consultations on programmatic actions of an agency and consultations on coordinated actions of several agencies.

Programmatic actions of a federal agency are programs, plans, guidelines, or frameworks established primarily for the purpose of guiding individual projects undertaken by the agency. They themselves generally do not involve any ground-disturbing physical activity. Indeed, they may not even explicitly authorize ground-disturbing activities. They do, however, establish the direction and delineate the standards, guidelines, criteria, and so forth that govern ground-disturbing activities, and in this sense they implicitly authorize ground-disturbing activities. Examples of programmatic actions include:

- Land and Resource Management Plans by the Forest Service under the National Forest Management Act, which serve as guidelines for subsequent site-specific projects within national forests

- Fishery Management Plans approved by NOAA under the Magnuson Fishery Conservation and Management Act, which provide for long-term commercial fishing practices for an entire fishery

- Nationwide permit programs established by various statutes, such as the Clean Water Act, implemented by the EPA and Army Corp of Engineers, which provide a framework under which local permits are issued by either federal or state agencies

- "State assumption programs," which are approved by a federal agency but carried out by the state, such as states' coastal zone management programs under the Coastal Zone Management Act and states' development of water quality standards under the Clean Water Act

Most programmatic actions have a common characteristic: even after they are initially adopted or approved by the federal agency, they continue to serve as guidance for subsequent site-specific projects, and in this sense they are ongoing actions. There is little argument that the initial approval of a programmatic action requires compliance with Section 7 as an agency action. For purposes of Section 7, however, the federal action is not only the agency's initial approval of the programmatic action but also its ongoing tacit approval and implementation by its continued use of the programmatic action. As long as the initial adoption or approval of the programmatic action was a federal action for purposes of Section 7 and the federal agency maintains discretion to amend or revoke the guidance incorporated in the programmatic action, Section 7 remains applicable.

When it comes to the mechanics of consulting on programmatic action, often the effects to be analyzed at the programmatic level are too remote temporally and too speculative scientifically. This problem does not negate the requirement to consider all direct and indirect effects of the programmatic action, however, nor does it allow for deferral of an analysis of the effects to the site-specific level. Rather, it requires agencies to analyze the best available data at the point at which consultation is required—at the program level—although specific data may not be available until the site-specific level analysis. There are several mechanisms available to the action agency and consulting agency for this situation. One mechanism is to use the incremental step process provided in the regulations at 50 CFR 402.14(k), which was designed expressly for program activities. Another mechanism is to develop counterpart regulations.[24] A third mechanism is to use the standard consultation procedures. The service agency can extend the consultation time frame in order to obtain more data. Even when there is still uncertainty, it can be compensated by establishing, in the programmatic opinion, a set of parameters for all subsequent projects that can be used to determine whether subsequent projects require additional scrutiny.

Another problem regarding the mechanics of consultation on programmatic actions is the nature of the biological opinion and any accompanying incidental take statement. Although programmatic actions generally do not involve ground-disturbing activities and thus may not directly result in the taking of a listed species, they may indirectly result in takings through their continuing approval and implementation at the site-specific level. In considering the full range of direct, indirect, interrelated, and interdependent effects of the programmatic action, adverse effects to listed species may be anticipated, which would trigger formal consultation. While these impacts might be addressed to a greater extent at the site-specific level, they may also be identified at the programmatic level. Indeed, some are identified only at the programmatic level.

When adverse effects may result in takings, an incidental take statement must accompany the biological opinion. Furthermore, the incidental take statement has several useful if not necessary purposes: it identifies the impacts of the action on the species; it provides reasonable and prudent measures, terms, and conditions for minimizing these impacts; and it provides an exemption from the takings prohibition for those takings identified in the incidental take statement. These purposes can be fulfilled through an incidental take statement for a programmatic action as much as for a site-specific action. Monitoring and reporting requirements are one means to help minimize takings, for example, and these are certainly appropriate terms and conditions at the programmatic level. Requiring for additional research is another means of minimizing the impact of takings. Indeed, minimizing the impacts on listed species may be more effective at the programmatic level than at the site-specific level.

Even though programmatic consultations may be species-oriented, they necessarily involve a broader-based, longer-term, more comprehensive approach for protection of listed species, which provides significant protection to the ecosystems as well. For these reasons, the resource management objectives expressed earlier can be more readily attained through programmatic consultations than through site-specific actions. For example, programmatic actions involve decisions that are not expressed in site-specific

actions—such as establishment of multiple-use goals and objectives; establishment of standards and guidelines; establishment of management areas
and wilderness allocations as well as standards for those areas; designation of
habitat suitability for certain activities; and establishment of monitoring
requirements. All these decisions can address landscape-level effects for particular species—as well as effects to the ecosystem itself that will adversely
affect individual species—which can be analyzed only at the program level.
Whether one subscribes to the approach of protecting umbrella species or to
an ecosystem approach, these decisions are a prerequisite for adequately
addressing either.

Given that such analyses are essential for addressing the role of individual
species in the ecosystem, one might consider whether they can be done at the
site-specific level rather than the program level, especially in light of the
expansive definition of the "effects of the action." It is difficult to develop a
meaningful analysis of the watershed or landscape-level impacts on a site-
specific level. These analyses might not even be appropriate or feasible at the
site-specific level. It is even more difficult to conclude that any single site-
specific project would jeopardize listed species. To analogize: it is nearly
impossible to say that a single pack of cigarettes will cause cancer; yet if you
look at a program to smoke a pack a day for fifteen years, you can readily
conclude that cancer is a risk.

In addition to programmatic actions, FWS and NMFS consult on coordinated actions, which include joint actions by two or more agencies as well as
different actions by several agencies on a related issue. Both programmatic
and coordinated actions derive their benefit through analytical and administrative economies of scale; the difference is that programmatic actions have a
vertical relationship with subsequent site-specific actions, while coordinated
consultations have a horizontal relationship with other interconnected activities.

One issue is whether consultations can be conducted with both federal
agencies and nonfederal agencies, even where the nonfederal entity may not
be an "applicant," as defined in the regulations. As long as there is a sufficient
federal nexus to the action, courts will generally find that Section 7 is applicable. Another issue concerns coordination between the consulting service
agencies. Substantively, there should be consistency in data, analyses, and
conclusions by the service agencies—both in determining the best available
scientific and commercial data and in using those data to evaluate the effects
of different actions on the same species or similar actions on different species.
Procedurally, there should be consistency in the mechanics of consultation as
well.

Agencies may coordinate activities for ESA purposes for one of two reasons: in an optimistic vein, agencies are realizing that their activities do not

occur in isolation and that efficient ecosystem management requires an analysis of agencies' collective effects; in a pessimistic vein, certain ecosystems are in such dire straits that multiple species are being listed as endangered or threatened in these areas, thus forcing agencies to consider their combined impact on a variety of species. Whether the government is being proactive or reactive, however, the result is the same: these coordinated efforts result in a more holistic, ecosystem-based approach to resource management.

The importance of such coordinated actions is illustrated by PACFISH,[25] a joint aquatic habitat and riparian management strategy developed by FS and BLM. NMFS is currently conducting status reviews for all five species of salmon, as well as steelhead and cutthroat trout, throughout their range in the continental United States. One study has identified 214 salmonid stocks at risk, of which 134 are on FS lands and another 109 are on BLM lands. The PACFISH strategy will be used across five states and will affect the 243 stocks on federal lands. On the most local level, PACFISH establishes riparian conservation zones that will protect streams; on a larger level, entire watersheds will be identified for special management; on a larger level still, the selection of watersheds to be managed will be based on an overall ecosystem-based approach. PACFISH addresses many effects of most federal habitat-related actions on salmonids and thus represents a holistic approach with respect to these habitat-related impacts. However, PACFISH addresses only standards and guidelines used for site-specific actions, which is only one of several factors in land-use planning.

Another illustration of coordinated actions involves those of NMFS, FWS, EPA, and BOR regarding the San Francisco Bay and Delta, an ecosystem in critical condition as evidenced by several recent listings under the ESA.[26] Moreover, Congress passed the Central Valley Project Improvement Act (CVPIA) to protect the Central Valley and Trinity River basin ecosystems and their fisheries resources.[27] Specifically, the CVPIA mandates a host of actions to protect and restore wildlife populations, including the dedication of 800,000 acre-feet of the Central Valley Project's annual yield for fish and wildlife and habitat restoration. Coordination among the federal agencies and between the federal agencies and the state has been formalized through several agreements that will facilitate interagency planning and provide additional impetus to move toward an ecosystem-based approach. Even before the agreements, NMFS had consulted with both BOR and the state on the Central Valley Project and the State Water Project, which are closely tied to one another, as laid out in a coordinated operations agreement.[26] Moreover, both FWS and NMFS are jointly consulting with EPA on EPA's promulgation of water quality standards in the bay and delta, which address water quality criteria for salinity, temperature, and dissolved oxygen, among other measures.

The ecosystem protections afforded by coordinated consultations are somewhat different than those afforded by programmatic actions. In terms of resource management, coordinated consultations provide a forum that overcomes many of the hurdles cited earlier. For example, coordinated consultations will bring together several agencies and thereby overcome political boundaries, improve dialogue, and increase cost-effectiveness from the outset in protecting a newly listed species. In terms of the science, coordinated consultations provide an opportunity to do the mapping and other analyses that are necessary to determine the protections needed for ecosystems. Moreover, they provide an opportunity to better protect individual species across their natural ranges and thereby protect the entire ecosystems of those species.

WHERE DO WE GO FROM HERE?

The biological diversity of the planet is disappearing at a staggering rate, and unlike the great extinction episodes of the past, this loss is the consequence of the poor stewardship of one of the species comprising that diversity—humankind. While our scientific understanding has been propelled by new research, there is an overwhelming lack of knowledge regarding the basic elements of biological diversity. The fundamental facts that pertain today—a lack of knowledge, a rapid loss of biodiversity, and an ability to influence this loss—are the same fundamental facts that existed in 1973 and formed the basis for the Endangered Species Act. Indeed only now, as we begin to comprehend the severity of the threat to our planet's biodiversity, can we begin to appreciate the prescience of Congress in 1973.

The ESA, in one sense, is a simplistic statute that provides a simplistic mandate: protect the species living on this planet because we may never know what we are losing until it is lost, at which point it is too late. Congress recognized in 1973 that the protection of species is only a means to an end; the essence of the Endangered Species Act is the preservation of biological diversity. In another sense, however, the ESA is an extremely complex statute that provides complex means of implementation: it reaches both public and private entities; it requires analyses of the biological needs of threatened and endangered species; it requires projections of effects of human activities; it requires identification of thresholds of effects to those species; and it requires all of these in light of much scientific uncertainty on each element.

Although the ESA's implementation focuses on species protection, the act's purpose focuses on ecosystem protection and biological diversity. Perhaps Congress originally believed that species protection was the best means to preserve biodiversity. But whenever ecosystem protection is the best means to achieve the same goal, then the ESA provides the authority to do so. Indeed, one can argue that ESA may even require it. The question then becomes: what aspect of the ESA's implementation is best suited for protecting ecosystems? The complex implementation, to some extent, contains the flexibility to achieve the mandate.

This discussion has considered several tools currently being applied—general policies with respect to listings, recovery plans, and conservation programs; use of habitat conservation plans; and consultations on programmatic and coordinated actions—each with its own benefits in protecting ecosystems. While these initiatives can be taken without amendment to the ESA, they would acquire greater strength if the ESA were amended to explicitly provide for them.

These actions, however, do not provide either complete solutions to the threat to biodiversity or complete means to ecosystem protection. Rather, they are practical steps in preventing the continuing demise of thousands of species—and reversing this trend in many other species—while more thorough solutions can be developed. These measures can serve as a form of intensive care for endangered species and ecosystems, but the solutions we need to develop are those that form sweeping scientific, legal, and ethical tenets that will protect the biological diversity across boundaries and generations.

NOTES

1. 16 USC 1531 et seq.

2. *Tennessee Valley Authority v. Hill*, 437 U.S. 153 (1978).

3. 16 USC §1531(b).

4. 16 USC §1532.

5. 16 USC §1533.

6. 16 USC §1534.

7. 16 USC §1535.

8. 16 USC §1533(f).

9. 16 USC §1536(a)(1).

10. 16 USC §1539(a)(2)(A).

11. 16 USC §1533(b)(1)(A); 16 USC §1536(a)(2).

12. H.R. Report 93-412, 93rd Cong., 1st Sess. (1973), reprinted in Congressional Research Service, *A Legislative History of the Endangered Species Act of 1973, as amended 1976, 1977, 1978, 1979, 1980* (1982).

13. H.R. 887, 94th Cong., 2nd Sess. (1976).

14. H.R. Conf. Report 835, 97th Cong., 2nd Sess. (1982).

15. See Notice of Interagency Cooperative Policy for the Ecosystem Approach to the Endangered Species Act, 59 *Fed. Reg.* 34273 (July 1, 1994).

16. Memorandum of Understanding Between U.S. Dept. of Agriculture (Forest Service, Soil Conservation Service), U.S. Dept. of the Army (Corps of Engineers), U.S. Dept. of Commerce (NMFS), U.S. Dept. of Interior (BLM, BOR, FWS, Minerals Management Service, National Park Service), U.S. Dept. of Transportation (Coast Guard, Federal Aviation Administration, Federal Highway Administration), signed Sept. 28, 1994.

17. Ibid.

18. Memorandum of Understanding Between U.S. Dept. of Interior (FWS, BLM, NPS) and U.S. Dept. of Commerce (NMFS), Jan. 25, 1994.

19. Agreement for Coordination on California Bay/Delta Issues, signed by FWS, NMFS, Bureau of Reclamation, and EPA, Sept. 10, 1993.

20. Framework Agreement Between the Governor's Water Policy Council of the State of California and the Federal Ecosystem Directorate, signed by Bureau of Reclamation, FWS, NMFS, EPA, and California EPA and California Water Policy Council, May 1994.

21. Notice of Intent to Prepare an EIS on Proposed Rule for the Conservation of the Northern Spotted Owl, 58 *Fed. Reg.* 69132 (1993).

22. See 50 CFR Part 402.

23. 16 USC 1536(a)(2).

24, See 60 *Fed. Reg.* 39921 (August 4, 1995).

25. U.S. Dept. of Agriculture (Forest Service) and U.S. Dept. of Interior (BLM), Environmental Assessment for Managing Anadromous Fish-Producing Watersheds in Eastern Oregon and Washington, Idaho, and Portions of California (March 1994).

26. NMFS listed the Sacramento winter-run chinook in 1989 and in December 1993 uplisted it to endangered status given declining run sizes. See 59 *Fed. Reg.* 440 (Jan. 4, 1994). The FWS has currently listed delta smelt as threatened and has proposed listing the Sacramento splittail as threated, as well as proposing critical habitat for the delta smelt.

27. P.L. 102-575, 106 Stat. 4600 (1992).

28. See NMFS, Biological Opinion for the Operation of the Federal Central Valley Project and the California State Water Project, 1993.

Chapter 4

CONSERVATION PLANNING
UNDER THE ESA: A NEW PARADIGM

Lindell L. Marsh

In March 1993, the U.S. Fish and Wildlife Service listed the California gnatcatcher as threatened under the federal Endangered Species Act. The gnatcatcher occupies coastal sage scrub habitat covering more than 400,000 acres, ranging from Los Angeles to the Mexican border, and perhaps another 2 million acres in Mexico. The ESA prohibits the "taking" of the species, defined to include killing, harming, or harassing individuals of the species. Large-scale conservation plans are now being prepared to conserve not only the habitat of the gnatcatcher but coastal sage scrub habitat and, more generally, the biodiversity of southern California. This planning is being done under the state's Natural Community Conservation Planning Program (NCCP) framework,[1] as well as other local multiagency initiatives.

The ESA originally envisioned protection for individual species—the grizzly bear, gray wolf, sea otter, snail darter, desert pupfish, and others. In 1983, however, a major paradigm shift occurred in the ESA with the formulation of the San Bruno Mountain Habitat Conservation Plan (HCP) and the addition of Section 10(a) to the act, permitting the incidental take of endangered species under a conservation plan that did not "appreciably reduce the likelihood of the continued existence and recovery of the species in the wild."[2] The San Bruno Mountain HCP in San Mateo County, California, was a multiple-species plan addressing the conservation of fifty-one species, both listed and unlisted, as a biological community. In retrospect, the plan and the process leading up to it were part of a far larger paradigm shift in the governance institutions of this nation.

Specifically, the San Bruno Mountain planning process and Section 10(a) contemplated a focus on the biological community, including both listed and unlisted species. The Conference Report regarding the 1982 amendments to the ESA provided that "in enacting the Endangered Species Act, Congress recognized that individual species should not be viewed in isolation, but must be viewed in terms of their relationship to the ecosystem." Further, the report noted that "although the regulatory mechanisms of the Act focus on species that are formally listed . . . the purposes and policies of the Act are far broader . . . and allow unlisted species to be addressed in the plan." The report stated that "to the maximum extent possible, the Secretary should utilize this authority to encourage creative partnerships between the public and private sectors and among governmental agencies in the interest of species and habitat conservation," crediting the San Bruno HCP as the model for these provisions.[3] Section 10(a) also proposed proactive planning for conservation with consideration of possible economic development. As in a painting, the idea was to focus first on the negative space, in order to determine the outlines of what had been considered the positive space—space for urban development. Assurances that the plan would be honored were also envisioned.

THE DEEP MEANING OF THE HCP PROCESS

But the addition of Section 10(a) and the HCP process reflected deeper changes in our governance structure. Preceding the San Bruno Mountain process, there were four key historical concepts of relevance.

First is the prevailing anthropomorphic view of the world, flowing from Genesis, that humankind stands apart from the environment and should dominate and control the animal community for its own benefit. In contrast, for example, is the view of many native Americans that humans are part of that community.

Second is the Western world's use of "fragmentation" as a way to think about things and control the environment. Examples of fragmentation abound in systems of taxonomy, physics, medicine, business, and industry, where we find the organization of assembly lines: each worker has his or her own job, sphere of concern, and authority. I am reminded of Thomas Jefferson's conceptualizations: his garden—small square plots with a separate species in each; the decimal monetary system; the range and township system of mapping—dividing the landscape into a grid.[4] The product, of course, is the grid system of towns and agricultural areas that you see when driving or flying across the country.

The third concept is representative democracy: the empowerment of the individual as the source of authority, with specific and limited authority then being provided to specific agencies and organizations.[5] For example, author-ity is being given to corporations to act as individuals in wielding extensive power for the economic benefit of their shareholders. Similarly, authorization is given to agencies such as the U.S. Fish and Wildlife Service to regulate for the protection of endangered species. In stark contrast is the culture of the Quakers and their reliance on consensus, or the lack of corporate authority among Native Americans, such as California's Yurok Indians. In many cases within the Native American culture, there is no "tribe" that can speak for and bind the individual member.[6]

The last concept is the judicial model of conflict resolution inherited from England, resulting in adversarial, quasi-judicial decision-making pro-cesses—effective in determining the facts in retrospect and assigning guilt but very ineffective in providing a framework for prospective group plan-ning.

The governance system that embodied these four concepts was quite effec-tive in providing for the economic development of this nation. The strength of the system was its many points of action and control. However, its weak-ness was its difficulty in addressing the complex issues that transcend the many fragments making up the system. Throughout the system, points of authority were established utilizing "command and control" mechanisms, often controlling vast systems of subordinate components. The picture that comes to mind is the image of Harold Geneen, past president of ITT, sur-rounded by filing trunks, each containing the vital records of a separate ITT subsidiary under his personal control. His was the creative vision that con-trolled the entire system. Agencies, such as the U.S. Fish and Wildlife Service, were similarly given the authority to protect endangered species using com-mand and control mechanisms. Concerns lying outside the authority of these fragmented centers of authority were not well addressed—such as intergen-erational equity and protection of noneconomic environmental value—and in fact individuals within an "organization" were discouraged from consider-ing such extraneous concerns. Further, the language of the power structure reflected this authoritarian bent in that "goals," rather than "concerns," were articulated.[7]

Following the Depression and the enormous successes of World War II, not only winning the war but also creating the world's most devastating weapon, and then the economic growth period that followed including inter-national efforts such as the Berlin Airlift and the Marshall Plan, some have suggested that we viewed ourselves as superhuman and only slowly began to rethink our own limitations.[8] With the 1960s, however, we began to worry that our institutions were not meeting the demands of change and the prob-lems that transcended our fragmented governance structure. This concern took a number of different forms and became the subject of broad explo-ration in the following years.

Most obvious were the writings of a number of authors concerned with the environment—Rachel Carson, Marjory Stoneman Douglas, Aldo Leopold, Garrett Hardin, Paul and Ann Ehrlich—and the convening of meetings such as Earth Day.[9] Second were the many attempts to use the command and control mechanisms to address specific problems: the need for environmental studies and reports, air and water quality, floodplains, historic and cultural resources, open space, scenic rivers, endangered species, and more. Some of these efforts began to address the issue of fragmentation. For example, the National Environmental Policy Act (NEPA) required the consideration of alternatives that transcended the authority of the lead agency. We began to explore the innovative use of "plans" that transcended jurisdictional boundaries,[10] and other innovative approaches were suggested to refocus the legal system on underlying concerns rather than the rights and interests of people.[11] "Scoping" under NEPA was instituted to provide for greater collaboration.[12] More subtly, there was a new wave of spiritual and psychological ideas: Martin Buber's concepts of "I/Thou," communes, psychotherapy, group therapy, T-groups, the concept of "dialogue," and so forth.[13]

We also looked to other cultures, such as Japan, and a plethora of books were written on the Japanese management systems and Japanese processes such as the tea ceremony.[14] Some were even thinking about how change itself is addressed. In 1960, for example, Thomas Kuhn presented the idea of paradigm shifts.[15] The drawbacks of "fragmentation" were explored by writers focusing on developments in physics stressing connectedness and chaos—for example, the idea that the movement of butterfly wings over China affects weather in the United States—and underscoring the limits of "control" by arguing for humility in our ability to comprehend and control our environment.[16] The gurus of business culture started exploring such concepts as "team building," "management by values," the "virtual organization," and "partnering," ideas that move away from the authoritarian command and control management pyramid toward a flatter management structure. This new structure transcends the legalistic boundaries of our fragmented public and private-sector organizations.[17] And ethical issues were increasingly raised regarding intergenerational equity, sustainable development, and the allocation of the world's resources.[18]

A Product of Its Time

Although we did not fully appreciate it at the time, the San Bruno Mountain planning process was a product of its time and reflected these broader explorations, as have the conservation planning processes that followed. They reflect a profound transformation that is occurring in the United States' system of governance. The San Bruno Mountain HCP addressed the ecosystem, naming fifty-one species of concern both listed and unlisted. While the species-oriented provisions of the ESA provided a bottom line for the protection required, the focus was on the ecosystem. From a conceptual perspective, the view was that once the underlying concerns were satisfied, specific issues, such as the adequacy of protection for the individual species or the very definition of terms such as "species," could be more easily addressed. Assurances that the HCP would be honored were provided by an implementing agreement entered into by the U.S. Fish and Wildlife Service, the California Fish and Game Department and Parks and Recreation Department, the county, three cities, and a number of landowners. This may well have been the first such agreement to bridge the federal, state, local, and public/private chasm and provide for assurances and limitations on further regulation. It should be noted that in 1979, California had authorized "development agreements" that, generally, could freeze local land regulations.[19]

"Focused planning" became a helpful concept: the idea that the effort would focus on a specific species, issue, or concern—but with the understanding that in order to address the focused point, a broader set of issues and concerns would also be considered. Thus the line between planning for a species, for wildlife, for other concerns, was transcended.

Collaboration of the entire "constituency of interests" was critical to the plan's consummation. The collaboration involved more than cooperation; it was more in keeping with the spirit of Buber's "I/Thou" relationship. It was respectful; the concerns of all sides were honored. The intent was to come to a consensus among the affected agencies and interests. It was in keeping with recent concepts of business culture—"principled," "partnering." It did not dwell on whether certain standards had been satisfied, but whether the underlying concerns of the interests had been addressed. It built relationships of trust and consideration. I can recall that, at the outset, the attorney for the local environmental group and I had agreed that we would try to reconcile our concerns, not compromise them.

Other process elements, too, have been helpful in achieving success in these efforts:

- Facilitation: we developed this element in a conservation planning process regarding North Key Largo, employing a "facilitator" to assist the constituency in developing an acceptable plan. This approach has since been used in various southern California efforts as well.

- Common technical support: we used a common team of experts and technicians working under the facilitator.

- Involvement of the "constituency of interests": this constituency was to be convened and orchestrated by a lead agency.

- Application of the underlying NEPA logic: we wanted a process involving the affected constituency that focuses on the particular concern or action; considers alternatives (brainstorming) that transcend artificial governance boundaries; scopes the issues and evolves thorough technical analysis to identify relevant impacts; and narrows the alternatives and lists a preferred set of actions.

- Box and ratchet: we established a "box" to assure that the constituency would stay together to complete the plan and a "ratchet" to move the process to completion.

- Compliance: the "command and control" regulations of the involved agencies provide the bottom-line requirements to be met by the plan.

A MAGNIFICENT EXPERIMENT

The benefits of the approach are clear. It provides a greater opportunity for creativity and produces better and wiser decisions with greater breadth, decisions that are farsighted and comprehensive. Better relationships are developed, as well, relationships of trust and willingness to cooperate in addressing the next concern, relationships that will better serve all of us over the long term. The visionary intent of this paradigm shift is to add to the brilliance of representative democracy—the many points of action and the ability to collaborate in a focused, respectful, and principled manner.

The southern California multispecies/NCCP processes are a magnificent experiment that promises to develop this paradigm by focusing on the conservation of species while offering the opportunity to address broader issues of biodiversity, landscapes,[20] and quality of life—and ultimately the issue of sustainable development. While the discussion in San Diego began by focusing on wildlife habitat, for example, it is shifting to a discussion of the relationship of wildlife habitat conservation to planning for transportation, urban density, air quality, and energy conservation. Addressing habitat conservation may fit with broader efforts to redesign our urban systems to be more efficient, less wasteful, and more livable. Indeed, the process may promote increasing respect among the participants and may be extended to issues focusing on urban ills or international problems of resource use, consumption, and waste.

NOTES

1. California Fish and Game Code §2800 et seq.

2. 16 USC §1539(a)(2)(B)(iv).

3. 97th Cong. 2nd Sess., H.R. Report 97-835, Sept. 1, 1982.

4. Public Land Law Review Commission, *History of Public Land Law Development* (Washington, D.C., 1968), p. 61.

5. See Gorton Wood, *The Radicalism of the American Revolution* (New York: Random House, 1991).

6. See A. L. Kroeber, *Handbook of the Indians of California* (New York: Dover, 1976), an unabridged republication of the work originally published by the Government Printing Office in 1925 as Bulletin 78 of the Bureau of American Ethnology of the Smithsonian Institute.

7. See Michel Foucault, *The Order of Things* (London: Tavistock, 1970), discussing the role of words and language in power structures.

8. Daniel Yankelovich, *New Rules: Searching for Self-Fulfillment in a World Turned Upside Down* (New York: Random House, 1981).

9. See Rachel Carson, *Silent Spring* (Boston: Houghton Mifflin, 1963); Marjory Stoneman Douglas, *The Everglades: River of Grass* (New York: Rinehart, 1947); Aldo Leopold, *Sand County Almanac* (New York: Oxford University Press, 1949); Garrett James Hardin, *Managing the Commons* (San Francisco: Freeman, 1977); Paul Ehrlich, *The Population Bomb* (New York: Ballantine Books, 1968); and Paul and Ann Ehrlich, *Extinction: The Causes and Consequences of the Disappearance of Species* (New York: Random House, 1981).

10. Ira M. Heyman, "Innovative Land Regulation and Comprehensive Planning," *Santa Clara Law* 13 (1972):183; Herome Muys, "Interstate Compacts and Regional Water Resources Planning and Management," *Natural Resources Lawyer* 4 (1973):153; "Regional Government for Lake Tahoe," *Hastings Law Journal* 22 (1971):705.

11. Christopher Stone, *Should Trees Have Standing?* (Los Altos, Calif.: W. Kaufmann, 1974); Joseph Sax, "The Public Trust Doctrine in Natural Resource Law: Effective Judicial Intervention," *Michigan Law Review* 68 (1971):473.

12. Nicholas Yost, *The Governance of the Environmental Affairs—Towards Consensus* (Aspen: Aspen Institute for Humanistic Studies, 1982).

13. Martin Buber, *I and Thou* (New York: Scribner's, 1958); see also Lawrence Halprin, *The RSVP Cycles: Creative Processes in the Human Environment* (New York: Braziller, 1969).

14. Soshitsu Sen XV, *Tea Life, Tea Mind* (New York and Tokyo: Weatherhill, 1979).

15. Thomas S. Kuhn, *The Structure of Scientific Revolutions* (Chicago: University of Chicago Press, 1970).

16. See, for example, James Gleick, *Chaos* (New York: Penguin, 1987); Fritjov Capra, *Tao of Physics*, 3rd ed. (Boston: Shambhala, 1991); and *The Turning Point* (New York: Simon & Schuster, 1982).

17. See, for example, John A. Byrne, "The Horizontal Corporation," *Business Week,* Dec. 20, 1993, p. 76.

18. For intergenerational equity see Edith Weiss, "In Fairness to Future Generations," *Environment,* April 1990, p. 7. For sustainable development see *Our Common Future,* Report of the World Trade Commission, Environment and Development, Commissioned by the United Nations (Oxford: Oxford University Press, 1987), and, more recently, Paul Hawken, *The Ecology of Commerce: A Declaration of Sustainability* (New York: HarperCollins, 1993). For the allocation of global resources see *Declaration of Principles Governing the Sea Bed and Sea Floor, and Subsoil Thereof, Beyond the*

Limits of National Jurisdiction, UN General Assembly, Dec. 17, 1970, G.A. Res 2749, 25 G.A.O.R. Supp. (No. 28), UN Doc. A/8028 (1970).

19. California Gov. Code §§65864 et seq.

20. See Tony Hiss, *The Experience of Place* (New York: Knopf, 1990).

Chapter 5

BIODIVERSITY AND PRIVATE PROPERTY: CONFLICT OR OPPORTUNITY?

Todd G. Olson

This chapter challenges the notion that the preservation of biodiversity is inherently at odds with private property ownership and property rights. It not only explores how private property can be enlisted to become a force for conservation, but also describes the "habitat transaction method" as a tool that aligns the interests of private property owners with specific conservation objectives.

IS PRIVATE PROPERTY THE ENEMY?

To hear some conservationists, one would gather that private property is the bane of their existence. Except for the rare philanthropist, they say, people seem to own property for their own private gain, which ultimately requires some kind of development of the land. If property owners had their way, they say, all of the private property in the country would eventually be developed. If only the federal government had had the foresight not to give away millions of acres of land to homesteaders! That was, without a doubt, the single greatest government-caused environmental debacle in American history. Right?

As the reasoning goes, we cannot take back what was given away—so we must at least control the use of privately owned land to avert environmental hemorrhaging. We must insist that traditional notions of property rights are outmoded and unable to deal with modern problems. Accordingly, we must construct theories that limit the rights of landowners to use the land in any old way they choose. Landowners must be held responsible to society as a whole. Landownership cannot be absolute. The public has a vital interest in natural land. Thus it is reasonable to regulate the use of private land to require private landowners to bear their public responsibility in the use of their land. The Supreme Court must belong to the stone age not to recognize this logic and interpret the takings clause of the Fifth Amendment accordingly. Right?

This line of reasoning sounds perfectly reasonable to many conservationists. Yet it has a socialist ring to many property owners. The result has been a backlash that appears to question not only the validity of regulating land use for the greater public good but also whether conservation is even a legitimate public goal. Endangered species? No such thing! Well, maybe the bald eagle, but a snail darter? A snail? A fairy shrimp? A kangaroo rat? And what about this wetlands stuff? If I water my lawn too much, the government is going to regulate my puddles! It's all a big land grab by communist environmental wackos!

Such rhetoric casts the conflict as anti-property-rights conservationists versus anti-conservation property-rights advocates. Conservation versus property rights. Nature-lovers versus profit-makers. Government versus business. The environment versus the economy. A battle for the ages. A battle which, if anyone wins, everybody loses. This nihilistic zero-sum game will arbitrarily, unpredictably, and cyclically harm and help the natural environment and harm and help the economy. The only way out is for both sides to redefine the enemy. In fact, the true enemy is common to both sides. And if the common enemy is recognized by both sides, the result can be staggeringly beneficial for both the environment and the economy.

THE REAL ENEMY OF CONSERVATION

When an endangered species is discovered on a desired land, the owner may be told that he or she may not put the land to any economic use. The land is highly valued by society, but can be rendered valueless to the landowner. Whatever the landowner's moral motivations may be, the economic incentive is to hide, diminish, or destroy the resource that society considers of great value. The economic interests of landowners are pitted against biodiversity, creating a burden on both landowners and biodiversity alike. This situation is the norm for modern regulation of sensitive biological resources on private lands.

The perverse incentive problem described above has tremendous implications for how we ought to think about protecting biodiversity on private lands. Even if the Supreme Court permitted maximum regulation against the diminution of biodiversity on private lands, to implement such regulation might be as likely to bring harm to the environment as to protect it, as landowners act, both legally and illegally, to protect their economic interests. Penalties and enforcement could indeed be stepped up, but at great risk of rapidly eroding public support for conservation efforts.

The problem of perverse incentives is illustrated by at least two experiences in California. The California gnatcatcher was recently listed as threatened. The listing process, however, went on for months, and landowners were well aware of the impending listing. It should not be surprising to learn that during the listing process an unusually large amount of gnatcatcher habitat was destroyed—legally—to avoid the economic loss that would occur after the species was listed. Another example can be found up and down the Central Valley, where farmers disk their fallow lands continually in order to avoid occupation by endangered species. Such disking is an additional cost to farmers, but the practice has become an insurance policy against having the value of farmland taken away or diminished by the federal Endangered Species Act.

Even if laws protecting biodiversity could be strictly enforced, a policy that sets the environment and private property fundamentally at odds cannot long endure. Such a practice could not survive politically or economically, even if it could survive under the Constitution. In the long run, then, our energy is misplaced by focusing on Fifth Amendment jurisprudence regarding regulatory takings because greater regulation is not likely to result in sufficient protection of biodiversity.

The common enemy of conservationists and landowners is an economic system that fails to take into account the social value of biodiversity—and even creates incentives to destroy biodiversity. Our economy produces food, clothes, houses, entertainment, medical services, and so on because people are rewarded for producing these goods and services. The same economy, with its current regulatory overlay, systematically penalizes those who protect biodiversity. Conservation is not the enemy of private property if owners of private property are appropriately rewarded for conservation just as they are for other land uses. Private property is not the enemy of conservation if the profit motive behind property ownership is enlisted to protect biodiversity rather than to destroy it.

The answer, then, is a new kind of economy—one that recognizes the value of biodiversity just as it recognizes the value of tennis shoes; one that fully recognizes the value of maintaining land in a natural state just as it recognizes the value of developing it. In such an economy, private landowners can become vigilant and faithful stewards of natural lands. Indeed, an army of private landowners who are rewarded for sound conservation management might actually be better stewards of natural lands than is the federal government, as the government is tugged at by a variety of political and fiscal concerns that may not be in the best interests of conservation. Creating such an economy may be a tall order, but it may also be the only sustainable way to protect biodiversity over the coming decades and centuries. For this project, conservationists and property rights advocates must join as allies against an economic system that damages both the environment and the economy.

Toward a New Land Economy

Ambitious as it may sound, the focus for a long-term strategy for protecting biodiversity should be on developing a new land economy that takes into account the value of biodiversity in much the same manner as it takes into account the value of houses and shopping malls. Various means might be used to develop such economies on local, regional, national, and international scales. One such strategy is described later in the chapter. Two ingredients, however, are essential to any such approach: creating a standard method for measuring biodiversity and creating a method for translating the biodiversity measurement into economic value.

Measuring Biodiversity

For a good to become part of the economy, its value must be determinable. Most goods are valued according to consumer preference—the most preferred pair of tennis shoes will fetch the best price. In the case of biodiversity, consumers will not be setting prices, so some other way of determining the conservation value of land must be found. Some soul searching is required. Is maximizing the number of surviving species the most important consideration? Are some species more ecologically critical than others? Should species that are exotic to a region be given lower value or even a negative value? Should aesthetic value to humans play a role? What about known medicinal and other scientific research values?

At present, the ESA articulates the clearest public policy goal driving the definition of biodiversity—that of preventing the extinction of species. Better formulations may be possible, but the ESA is the law. As a practical matter, definitions of the conservation value of land are likely to be derived from the nonextinction goal of the ESA until some other mandate gains similar prominence.

Biologists may be reluctant to articulate standard measures of conservation value, particularly if the measurement is to be used in forming public policy.

Without some form of measurement, however, policy determinations regarding conservation value will be ad hoc decisions leading to public skepticism regarding the very concept of conservation value. Moreover, an ad hoc approach will not lead to the creation of a market that takes conservation value into account. The difficulty of formulating measures of conservation value can be moderated by at least the following factors:

- Limiting the use of a measurement standard to a particular geographical region

- Demanding a measurement standard at a level of precision necessary only to achieve specified conservation objectives

- Designing systems to permit revision of measurement standards as scientific understanding is refined

Once a measurement standard is established, it becomes possible to compare the conservation value of various actions, such as permanent land set-asides, restrictions on the type or level of future development, habitat restoration or enhancement, habitat management, and so forth. What remains is to create a means to translate the conservation value of such actions into economic value.

Translating Conservation Value into Economic Value

There are various ways of converting conservation values into economic values. One strategy is to establish a conservation trust fund and use the money to "buy" units of conservation value. These funds could come from private donations, development impact fees, local bond issues, state or federal conservation grants, utility fees, or other broad-based fees that reflect land usage. The trustees of the fund would then "buy" conservation actions by direct negotiation, by offers to compensate certain conservation actions at a specified price, or even by general offers to pay a specified price per unit of conservation value, based upon a clearly defined measure of conservation value. Such trusts could range from the small, narrowly focused, and privately funded to the national or international, broad in scope, and publicly funded.

The Defenders of Wildlife Wolf Compensation Fund is an example of a successful private fund for purchasing conservation value. Money is paid to ranchers for allowing the wolves to come and go on their property. The compensation is based on head of livestock lost to wolves. Permitting the wolves to thrive on one's property is a form of conservation action for which Defenders pays compensation out of a special fund.

In the current economy and federal budgetary climate, funding for large-scale conservation planning is scarce at best. Another general strategy is to facilitate new development that is compatible with the conservation goals and use a portion of the economic value generated by the new development to pay for conservation actions in other places, typically in the same general area. One such technique is a system of tradable conservation credits called the "habitat transaction method."

THE HABITAT TRANSACTION METHOD

The habitat transaction method is one technique for modifying a regional economy to incorporate the inherent value of biodiversity.[1] With this method, conservation objectives are expressed in terms of a total amount of conservation value that will be preserved. If a permit is sought under the ESA, the conservation value to be preserved must be sufficient to satisfy the criteria of Section 10(a) of the ESA. A process is then established for measuring the initial conservation value of all the land in the planning area, expressed in terms of standardized "conservation units." Any landowner who agrees to conserve or restore habitat within the planning area receives credits based on the conservation value he or she adds to the reserve system. Any landowner proposing a project that would cause a loss of conservation value must offer a number of credits based on the loss of conservation value that would result from the development. Landowners who receive credits for conservation actions may use the credits to mitigate projects elsewhere within the planning area or may sell the credits to any other landowner who needs credits to mitigate project impacts.

Thus demand for development creates a corresponding demand for conservation; the conservation activities that result will create a reserve system that should meet the conservation objectives. In addition, an adaptive management scheme, based on research and monitoring programs, is put in place to ensure appropriate habitat management, necessary midcourse corrections in the plan, and a safety net against unforeseen circumstances. The following sections describe the habitat transaction method in more detail.

Measuring Conservation Value

The central biological premise of the habitat transaction method is that objective measures of conservation value can be defined in terms of conservation units—indicators of long-term conservation value for specified conservation objectives. Conservation units are used to quantify the conservation that must occur to assure achievement of those objectives and to determine acceptable incremental trade-offs between conservation and other land uses. Conservation units are defined in two basic steps—first the definition of habitat quality and then the adjustment of habitat quality assessments based on landscape-level factors to arrive at conservation value.

For individual species planning, habitat quality reflects the extent to which the physical, biological, and other environmental characteristics of an area correspond to the habitat characteristics of the target species. For multiple-species planning, habitat qualities for target species are considered in concert; the definition of quality then reflects overall multiple-species planning goals. For whole ecosystem planning (that is, planning for ecological communities), quality can be measured in either of two ways (preferably by both): by physical properties that reflect ecosystem diversity, function, or health, such as topographic diversity, watershed integrity, or proximity to other protected lands; or by biological properties, such as the distribution and abundance of selected indicator species, vegetational community composition, or proportion of invasive alien species.

Sound conservation planning must, however, look beyond habitat quality assessments to the roles of myriad factors that determine conservation value—that is, the ability of an area to support species of concern over the long term. Such factors include habitat size and configuration, landscape linkages or corridors, edge effects, species interactions, and consideration of such phenomena as threats from invasive species and the roles of unoccupied habitats, special landscape features, and habitat refugia in population persistence. All these factors are considered in defining conservation units, the currency used to facilitate market exchange, and in selecting a "conservation ratio," the number of conservation units that must be conserved for each unit lost in order to realize long-term conservation objectives.

A simple, yet robust, definition of conservation value for a particular habitat type can be developed using the following scheme. First, habitat quality points are assigned to habitat areas with a range of values between 0.0 and 1.0 points per acre, based on the extent to which the land is characteristic of the subject habitat type. Points are assigned according to soil types, slope and aspect, elevation, quality of characteristic vegetation, presence or absence of indicator species, and the like. The point system can then be used to make a rough habitat quality map of the planning area.

Second, the habitat quality points are adjusted according to the size and contiguity of the patches of habitat in the planning area. The contiguity adjustment is based on how extensively the patches of habitat are connected in contiguous areas. To make the adjustment for contiguity, the habitat quality value of each parcel is multiplied by a factor based on the size of the contiguous patch of habitat of which it is a part. These factors are determined by using a curve like the one shown in Figure 5.1.

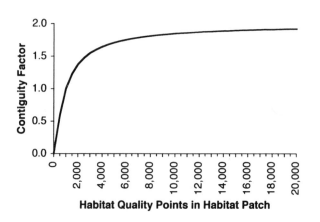

FIGURE 5.1
Contiguity factor.

Applying the contiguity factor devalues fragmented habitat and assigns higher value to connected habitat. This effect can be illustrated by applying the factor to three configurations in which each square has 200 habitat quality points (Figure 5.2).

Finally, habitat values are further adjusted according to the overall configuration or shape of the habitat patches. The "rounder" the configuration, the closer the shape factor will be to 1; the more linear or irregular the configuration, the closer the shape factor will be to zero. The formula

$$Shape\ Factor = 2\pi\left(\frac{\sqrt{A/\pi}}{P}\right)$$

is used to determine this factor, based on the combined land area (A) and combined perimeter (P) of all the habitat patches in a given configuration. The effect of the shape formula can be illustrated by applying it to three configurations that have the same contiguity-adjusted value but varying shape factors (Figure 5.3). The final shape-adjusted values represent the conservation value of each of these configurations in terms of conservation units.

The foregoing definition of conservation value takes into account inherent habitat quality, patch sizes, connectivity and fragmentation of habitat, length and width of habitat corridors, exposure of habitat to unprotected edges, and

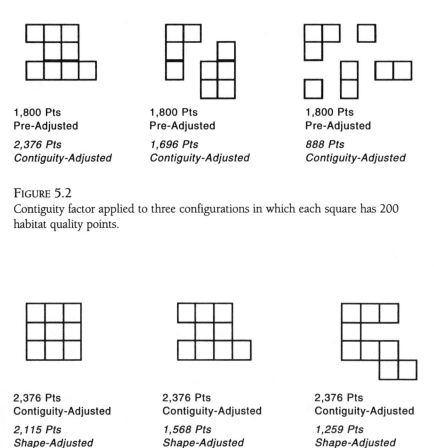

1,800 Pts
Pre-Adjusted

2,376 Pts
Contiguity-Adjusted

1,800 Pts
Pre-Adjusted

1,696 Pts
Contiguity-Adjusted

1,800 Pts
Pre-Adjusted

888 Pts
Contiguity-Adjusted

FIGURE 5.2
Contiguity factor applied to three configurations in which each square has 200 habitat quality points.

2,376 Pts
Contiguity-Adjusted

2,115 Pts
Shape-Adjusted

2,376 Pts
Contiguity-Adjusted

1,568 Pts
Shape-Adjusted

2,376 Pts
Contiguity-Adjusted

1,259 Pts
Shape-Adjusted

FIGURE 5.3
The effect of the shape formula applied to three configurations that have the same contiguity-adjusted value but varying shape factors.

the general roundness of the habitat configuration. This basic approach can be easily adjusted to take into account other important considerations as well.

Since the habitat transaction method provides that landowners will receive credits or will be required to pay credits based on the definition of conservation value, they will have a strong incentive to cooperate with adjacent landowners to protect land in configurations with long-term conservation value and, conversely, to avoid actions that would significantly diminish long-term conservation value. Reducing the definition of conservation value to an objective formula facilitates efficient transactions and allows landowners to calculate readily the costs and benefits of various development and conservation scenarios.

Using the techniques for measuring conservation value outlined here, the habitat transaction method assures that habitat areas comprising a predetermined conservation value—taking into account both habitat quality and reserve design requirements—will be protected. The method then uses market forces to determine an economically efficient means of protecting that conservation value. The adaptive management scheme, including reserve management, research, and monitoring components, is established to respond to the inevitable shortfalls in scientific data that result in uncertainties associated with the definition of conservation values and other elements of plan design.

Economic Considerations

The cost of habitat acquisition using the habitat transaction method is inherently covered by the credit-trading mechanism itself—new development pays the price by purchasing credits to compensate for its impacts on habitat. In addition to such costs, however, the up-front costs of planning and biological studies, the ongoing costs of administration, and the ongoing costs of reserve management must also be covered. Since endangered or threatened species crises are the result of accumulated impacts of existing development (which typically has made no contribution toward habitat conservation), costs should be allocated as broadly as possible to all of the public who benefit from the realization of conservation goals.

While the efficiency of the habitat transaction method should significantly reduce costs to present owners of undeveloped land of mitigating endangered species impacts (and would distribute costs more equitably among such landowners), mitigation costs for landowners in at least some geographical areas would remain daunting. Although this is not the place to resolve this issue, every effort should be employed to reduce the burdens presently borne by owners of undeveloped land and spread the cost of endangered species protection broadly and fairly. Various methods can be used in conjunction with the habitat transaction method to reduce costs to landowners: capital gains tax breaks on the sale of credits, density bonuses for landowners who must offer credits, open space credit for landowners who must offer credits, public acquisition of land for the reserve system, and the contribution of appropriate public lands to the reserve system. Other implementation costs (besides land acquisition) also should be spread using such means as state and federal grants, state and local bond measures, surcharges on broad-based commodities such as water and energy, and special real estate taxes on users of land generally.

The Habitat Transaction Method vs. Traditional Regulation

The traditional approach to land regulation is to require avoidance of certain project-specific impacts where possible and to require mitigation for impacts that cannot be avoided. Section 10(a) of the ESA, as commonly applied, has taken this approach. Here we compare traditional project-by-project regulation with the habitat transaction method in various respects.

Biological basis. Under traditional regulation, biology is applied on a project-by-project basis. Yet it is difficult to know how project impacts and project mitigation fit into the larger regional picture, particularly when the project is small. The habitat transaction method explicitly acknowledges the biological requirements of the species or other resources to be protected and expresses them as quantifiable objectives. The program then creates a reserve system through "habitat transactions" that is designed to meet these biology-based objectives.

Cohesiveness of reserve areas. It is difficult to use traditional regulation to build a regional reserve system, because mitigation is offered on an ad hoc, project-by-project basis. The habitat transaction method assures a cohesive reserve system by defining conservation units to take into account such considerations as reserve shape and connectivity. Parcels of land that can contribute in a meaningful way to the reserve system are given higher credit value. Conversely, disincentives are included for actions that could fragment or unlink important habitat areas.

Monitoring. Conservation goals are rarely articulated clearly under traditional regulation, so traditional regulation is rarely monitored for success or failure. The habitat transaction method, however, clearly defines conservation objectives and then monitors achievement of the objectives and requires that the plan be adjusted if necessary to meet the objectives.

Administration. Traditional regulation often involves little initial planning, but parcel-by-parcel review is intensive and expensive. Although the habitat transaction method requires significant up-front planning, it then avoids parcel-by-parcel disputes over the adequacy of project mitigation measures, making the program efficient for both the public and the private sectors.

Boundary lines. When planning is done using traditional regulation, it is common to draw lines on maps to indicate what areas must be preserved, what areas may be developed, and so forth. Drawing such lines draws immediate opposition from landowners placed in the more restrictive categories, and possibly even inverse condemnation claims. Under the habitat transaction method, however, no arbitrary boundaries are used to divide landowners into one class that benefits from the plan and another class that does not.

Efficiency. Because of its ad hoc nature, traditional regulation is tedious, time-consuming, and expensive. Under the habitat transaction method, landowners desiring to pursue development projects have an efficient means of doing so—either by setting aside land of sufficient conservation value or by purchasing credits from others who have set aside habitat of sufficient conservation value. Project-by-project review of mitigation measures is not necessary.

Incentives. Traditional regulation, as noted earlier, often creates perverse incentives to hide or destroy valuable habitat. Under the habitat transaction method, landowners with valuable habitat can realize the fair market value of that land as habitat; the higher the habitat value of land, the more credits a landowner will receive for conserving it. The landowner's incentives are much more closely aligned with the conservation objectives.

Property rights. Traditional regulation is under increasing scrutiny by the Supreme Court. Even when regulation is on solid constitutional ground, it generates great animosity among landowners, particularly the smaller landowners. Under the habitat transaction method, however, landowners are not forced to conserve land, nor are they prohibited from developing land. They can make their own economic choices to maximize their profits in the context of the conservation credit system. This approach is likely to withstand scrutiny under the Fifth Amendment and is much less likely to provoke the ire of property owners.

FINDING NEW WAYS TO SAVE BIODIVERSITY

Environmental lawyers and conservationists are often engaged in debates over how much regulation can be done without resulting in a "taking," in accordance with the most recent Supreme Court decisions. Traditional regulation, however, creates conflicts with private property interests that are difficult to enforce and leave large segments of the public bitter concerning conservation efforts. As natural land resources near urbanizing areas diminish, the conflict between private use of property and conservation interests will only intensify under the present regulatory scheme. This chapter suggests that conservation strategies can be developed that utilize the profit motive to the advantage of conservation. The habitat transaction method is one such strategy that is designed to be employed on a regional scale.

As we move into the next century, our society faces a choice of the means by which it will attempt to conserve biodiversity. We may continue down the traditional regulatory path and further institutionalize the custom of engaging in battle after battle pitting conservation against private property. Alternatively, we may find ways to incorporate the value of biodiversity into our local, regional, national, and even international economies in order to make private property an ally in the preservation and conservation of biodiversity.

NOTE

1. Much of this description of the habitat transaction method is derived from Todd G. Olson, Dennis D. Murphy, and Robert D. Thornton, "The Habitat Transaction Method: A Proposal for Creating Tradable Credits in Endangered Species and Habitats," in Hank Fischer and Wendy E. Hudson, eds., *Building Economic Incentives into the Endangered Species Act* (Washington, D.C.: Defenders of Wildlife, 1993), pp. 27–36.

PART III

INTERNATIONAL PROTECTION: BEYOND HUMAN BOUNDARIES

Humanity, from the standpoint of other species, is a plague.
—MICHAEL SOULÉ

I'm now fighting for my own species.
—JACQUES COUSTEAU

International biodiversity law presents two significant obstacles. Not only must it deal with the interdisciplinary challenges of biodiversity itself, but it is also stuck with the inherently diffuse and sometimes chaotic character of international law generally. Because there is no real central authority in global affairs, the preeminent issue under international law is enforcement. The lack of enforcement mechanisms often renders international obligations meaningless, but their presence immediately raises sovereignty concerns. Finding a balance is the study of international law.

Nowhere are the challenges and opportunities of international environmental protection more apparent than in the 1992 Convention on Biological Diversity (CBD).[1] Finalized at the United Nations "Earth Summit," signed by almost every country in the world, and now ratified by well over a hundred nation-states, the CBD is our planet's seminal biodiversity blueprint. It possesses two fundamental pillars: to recognize biodiversity conservation as a legitimate and important international goal and to facilitate the equitable and sustainable use of global biological resources.[2] In the United States, despite the facts that the Clinton Administration signed the convention in 1993 and that the Senate Foreign Relations Committee approved the convention 16–3, Sen. Jesse Helms (R–NC) and Majority Leader Robert Dole (R–KS) have blocked the ratification in the 104th Congress.

Although the CBD's forty-two articles, two annexes, and preamble are all interwoven to a certain extent, the treaty possesses several basic conservation obligations, which will continue to be fleshed out by future Conferences of the Parties (COP). Article 3 states the well-accepted principle of international environmental law that countries have the sovereign right to treat biological resources in any way they wish,[3] so long as their activities do not harm the environment beyond their borders.[4] Article 6 asks countries to develop national strategies for the conservation and sustainable use of biodiversity and to integrate such strategies across all economic and policy sectors. The heart of the CBD is Article 8, which requires, "as far as possible and appropriate," a number of on-site conservation measures from endangered species protection to ecosystem restoration. Finally, under Article 26, the CBD asks countries to report to the COP its measures to implement the convention.

Despite the temptation to impose advanced biodiversity protection regimes on countries around the world, even practices and policies in highly developed countries demonstrate the decentralized nature of biodiversity protection. Universal standards are important, but they must be implemented by people at the local level. This is particularly true in developing countries, which house a significant portion of the world's biodiversity and are starving for economic investment. The rudimentary question of international biodiversity law, therefore, is defining what type of economic development is sustainable to meet the human needs of today and tomorrow.[5] Not surprisingly, then, all four chapters in this section address the crucial question of sustainability and its relationship to the double-edged sword of international enforcement.

In Chapter 6, for instance, Leesteffy Jenkins, describes the legal difficulties of using international trade restrictions as an enforcement tool. Short of war, trade leverage is often the only effective means to achieve international environmental enforcement. Environmental trade measures, however, are under increasing attack from the rules of the General Agreement on Tariffs and Trade (GATT).[6] This trend is expected to continue under the recently concluded Uruguay Round of GATT,[7] which not only created a new powerful World Trade Organization (WTO) with binding but secretive dispute settlement provisions, but also saddled environmental trade measures with highly burdensome tests that could easily imperil a host of nondiscriminatory laws. As one prominent example, trade law continues to disallow trade measures that seek to regulate imports based on how a product is made. Such import restrictions, called "production and process method" (PPM) measures in trade vernacular, include initiatives like local recycled paper content require-ments and federal dolphin-safe tuna regulations. Indeed, PPMs cut to the very heart of all environmental protection, including the use of ecolabels, which allow consumers to make informed retail decisions. Although the WTO will not possess the power to directly overturn U.S. laws, it will allow challenging countries to levy retaliatory trade sanctions against the United States, thus placing enormous pressure on Congress and state governments to capitulate.

Trade is also at issue in Peter Jenkins' Chapter 7, which discusses the per-nicious effects of nonnative or "exotic" species. These intruding species, which are wreaking havoc on ecosystems and their natural functions, are increasingly the result of human trade and transport (as well as the inten-tional stocking of species such as game fish). Estimated economic damage by these species runs well into the billions of dollars annually. As just one of many examples, the introduced Asian clam in several California bays is dis-placing native mollusks and reducing levels of phytoplankton bloom as it reaches densities of 30,000 clams per square meter. Although Article 8(h) of the CBD directly seeks the prevention and control of exotics, the issue is not on any current agenda of the WTO Committee on Trade and Environment (CTE). Moreover, domestic efforts to control such species may be at risk by the Uruguay Round disciplines.

The problematic relationship between environmental law and interna-tional trade rules is particularly acute in the area of marine biodiversity. Because many threats to marine ecosystems are PPMs (such as overfishing), efforts to enforce biodiversity-related standards with trade measures are problematic. In Chapter 8, Suzanne Iudicello points out that trade leverage has historically been quite successful in negotiating and implementing inter-national fisheries agreements. She stresses, however, that the myriad threats to marine biodiversity demand an ever broader approach. While the scien-tific and technical hurdles of managing the world's vast marine ecosystems are daunting, she notes that it is imperative to move beyond traditional sin-gle-threat, single-species approaches.

The biodiversity agendas of other international institutions are the topic of Chapter 9 by Scott Hajost and Curtis Fish. First and foremost are the UN Commission on Sustainable Development and the Global Environmental Facility, both specifically charged with biodiversity protection. Also signifi-cant are the lending practices of multilateral development banks like the World Bank, whose projects can have a tremendous impact on biodiversity for better or worse, as well as "debt for nature" swaps engineered by the International Monetary Fund. While ad hoc domestic and regional efforts to protect biodiversity will continue to be very important, the eventual success of global biodiversity efforts may very well hinge on the formal and informal international cooperation discussed in Chapter 9.

Still, the central instrument of international cooperation will be the CBD itself. By design, however, the CBD is not meant to be the only accord protecting biodiversity. Article 23.4(h) expressly instructs the CBD Secretariat to cooperate with the executive bodies of other applicable international agreements. This interface can occur by placing the issue of cooperation on the CBD Secretariat work program or by asking the CBD's Subsidiary Body on Scientific, Technical, and Technological Advice (SBSTTA) to draft a report on the topic.[8] To be successful the CBD will need to rely on multiple instruments and policies aimed at biodiversity protection. In this regard, the CBD is not only the culmination of over a century of international conservation efforts, but also the nerve center of all present biodiversity initiatives.[9]

Although living natural resource measures have existed for several thousand years, the first international wildlife treaty was not consummated until 1886, when Germany, Luxembourg, the Netherlands, and Switzerland agreed to regulate salmon fishing in the Rhine River. For the next half century, wildlife treaties focused almost solely on specific species suffering from overexploitation. Examples include the 1900 Convention for the Preservation of Wild Animals, Birds, and Fish in Africa,[10] the 1911 Treaty for the Preservation and Protection of Fur Seals,[11] and the 1916 and 1936 Conventions for the Protection of Migratory Birds.[12]

One of the most prescient international wildlife treaties, the Convention on Nature Protection and Wildlife Preservation in the Western Hemisphere (WHC),[13] came into force in 1942. A regional precursor to the CBD, the WHC seeks to protect species of special concern and authorizes habitat protection, trade restrictions, and scientific collaboration between parties. Although the WHC suffers from the lack of its own institutional structure to this day, its substantive provisions have served as a model for a number of regional conservation agreements, including the 1968 African Convention on the Conservation of Nature and Natural Resources,[14] the 1982 Convention on the Conservation of Antarctic Marine Living Resources,[15] the 1982 Convention on the Conservation of European Wildlife and Natural Habitats,[16] and the 1983 Convention on the Conservation of Migratory Species of Wild Animals.[17] Even the 1976 Agreement on the Conservation of Polar Bears,[18] which is primarily concerned with overharvesting, reflects the WHC's original concern for ecosystem and habitat protection.

More recent international accords, such as the UN Convention on the Law of the Sea (UNCLOS) discussed in Chapter 8 by Suzanne Iudicello, have begun to focus on habitat types beyond regional boundaries like the high seas. Two other international agreements, the 1975 Convention on Wetlands of International Importance (Ramsar)[19] and the 1975 Convention Concerning the Protection of the World Cultural and Natural Heritage (World Heritage Convention),[20] establish site-specific lists to protect applicable habitat or sites wherever they occur. The Ramsar Convention, for example, recognizes the ecological functions of wetlands and the flora and fauna they support. While neither Ramsar nor the World Heritage Convention actually commits parties to binding obligations they do not unilaterally agree to, both conventions have focused international attention on limiting certain human development. They also established workable funding mechanisms that were utilized by the CBD in Articles 21 and 39.

Forest habitat, which contains more than 60 percent of the world's terrestrial biodiversity, still does not possess a binding conservation treaty. While there are commodity accords like the International Tropical Timber Agreement,[21] they have been unable to establish meaningful restraints on global timber production. Many conservationists hope that both the CBD and the Commission on Sustainable Development will be able to build upon the nonbinding forestry principles established at the Rio Earth Summit and eventually create a protocol pursuant to Article 28 of the CBD. Some timber-producing countries, however, such as Canada, Brazil, and Malaysia, would like to negotiate a forest agreement outside the CBD in order to avoid or weaken scientifically accepted biological and ecological forestry principles. Perhaps the recent Desertification Agreement, also on the agenda at the Commission on Sustainable Development, can produce conservation gains for forests and other ecosystems.

By far the most successful international agreement to date relating to biodiversity is the 1975 Convention on the International Trade in Endangered Species of Wild Fauna and Flora (CITES),[22] which several contributors mention in this section. CITES has established comprehensive limits on the multibillion-dollar wildlife trade industry and subsequently has become a powerful international conservation tool. Most important, it has focused squarely on the issue of enforcement by requiring each party to take measures to penalize wildlife trade in contravention of CITES. The U.S. government, for example, has implemented this mandate under the Endangered Species Act and the Pelly Amendment to the 1967 Fisherman's Protective Act. If the CBD is ever to approach CITES' effectiveness, it will eventually need to adopt similar enforcement mechanisms.

CITES also has considerable flexibility. Depending on their degree of endangerment, species are listed in one of three appendixes. Appendix I lists those species threatened with extinction; commercial trade is generally prohibited and requires both an export and import permit. Appendix II specimens are those that may become threatened with extinction unless trade in such species is subject to strict regulation; commercial trade in these species requires an export permit verifying that trade will not be detrimental to the survival of the species. For Appendix III species, countries can unilaterally ask fellow signatories to check their export permits on specimens to help enforce domestic legislation in those countries.

In recent years, CITES has become embroiled in several acrimonious disputes over the acceptable limits to certain wildlife trade. When items like elephant ivory are traded, at issue is the very definition of sustainability embedded in the CBD. Many conservationists believe that with species numbers so low due to overexploitation, the precautionary principle dictates against further trade unless it is certain not to harm the species overall. Others argue that low populations are the direct result of regulation, which should be replaced with managed ownership of wildlife to provide the incentive for species survival. The latter argument, however, is rather extreme: it would reduce all life to human monetary value and eviscerate traditional notions of government wildlife management.

Separating these two disparate views on elephant conservation and wildlife trade is, again, the issue of international enforcement. For example, sustainable trade in elephant hides and meat would probably not be objectionable to the CITES parties if they were convinced that such trade would not lead to widespread ivory smuggling. Even controlled trade in ivory might pass muster with an effective enforcement regime, though the human *need* for ivory (as opposed to meat and hides) should raise powerful ethical objections against elephant kills for solely luxurious purposes. At present, because many illicit wildlife traffickers are linked to the powerful drug and weapon cartels, a move to free trade in elephant parts would probably lead to the elephant's extinction.

International free trade rules were created after World War II to combat domestic protectionism, which many economic historians believe greatly contributed to the Great Depression. Conservationists are now deeply concerned, however, that free trade is being used by some as a club to beat down democratically passed social laws, including those related to biodiversity. Several recent GATT decisions have ruled against countries' trade restrictions without any discernible proof of economic protectionism, effectively allowing some multinational corporations (MNCs) to avoid enforceable environmental standards. Ironically, as trade bureaucrats tout the efficiency of "uniform" environmental laws that would lower environmental standards in many developed countries, many business enterprises support trade restrictions that level the playing field against less environment-friendly competitors.

Like the general political debate over ecology and economics, the tension between trade and the environment must eventually focus on internalizing broad social costs not captured by private exchanges—dirty air, polluted water, degraded habitat—into the price of consumed products. Although trade has the very real potential to unshackle the chains of poverty and catalyze sustainable biodiversity conservation for the developing world, in its present form it is creating disincentives for effective biodiversity protection. In simple terms, nothing but goodwill is now stopping MNCs from investing and developing around the world in ways that would harm biodiversity. And this investment and development inevitably lead to international trade. Because almost 75 percent of the world's $5 trillion worth of annual trade is conducted between MNCs, 40 percent of which is *intra*corporate, it is no wonder that MNCs have been GATT's most vigilant lobbyists.

In fact, holding multinational actors accountable to international and domestic biodiversity standards may be the greatest challenge presently facing the global legal system. The swift intercontinental flow of goods, services, and capital now affects development patterns and biodiversity in unprecedented ways. MNCs have been a chief beneficiary of modern technology, which has had the effect of enabling multinational actors to conduct business with decreasing government and citizen oversight. If the WTO is truly interested in sustainable development, its newly created Committee on Trade and Environment (CTE) must develop rules of investment for the capital that drives both development and trade. Reasonable international biodiversity investment and development standards would almost certainly yield discernible results.

Although the United Nations has drafted a Code on Conduct of Transnational Corporations,[23] it is an empty shell ignored by most national governments and international businesses. The international community's inability to deal rationally with this problem highlights two tenets of international law in the late twentieth century: binding and meaningful international agreements are difficult to attain; and in the absence of such agreements, the United States has the power to take unilateral action that fills the power void.

While other governments do not always respond favorably to unilateral displays of power, not all unilateral actions are the same. U.S. trade sanctions under the Pelly Amendment are not the same as the United States holding itself to its own environmental laws when acting in other countries. The latter was the case, for instance, when the Clinton administration's Bureau of Reclamation and Export-Import Bank declined to participate in construction of the Three Gorges Dam project in China because to do so would have been illegal under the U.S. Endangered Species Act and National Environmental Policy Act.[24]

Similarly, the U.S. government could require its own citizens and corporations to abide by U.S. environmental laws when operating abroad, thereby preventing private American investment from harming global biodiversity.[25]

This policy initiative would surely evoke a different response than U.S. trade restrictions, and its effect on biodiversity protection might well be more positive. Although Congress is generally hesitant to regulate U.S. businesses in a way that might disadvantage them in the global marketplace,[26] compelling reasons exist for a Foreign Environmental Practices Act (FEPA). First, numerous economic studies have correlated strong economies with strong biodiversity and environmental laws. Second, there is growing evidence that certain industries, particularly those relating to natural resources and biodiversity, migrate to countries with less stringent environmental standards for profit maximization. Third, an increasing number of MNCs are already establishing high uniform environmental standards and succeeding competitively. Fourth, FEPA would benefit relatively small and predominantly domestic businesses, who already must play by U.S. environmental rules and, moreover, represent the backbone of American society.

Perhaps the ultimate challenge posed by international environmental law is redefining national sovereignty for the twenty-first century. At what point does an action by a sovereign irreversibly harm the global interest in biodiversity? No longer does individual behavior occur in isolation. No longer can national governments control every event within their borders. And no longer are international institutions powerless bodies devoid of any enforcement capabilities. But international rules are all greatly in flux. An immensely complicated power struggle between government accountability and economic efficiency is now under way. The Biodiversity Treaty, for one, reflects this struggle but does not resolve it. Indeed, the debate over sovereignty cuts to the core of international law because it raises not only the thorny issue of enforcement, but also the question of when cooperation becomes coercion. The chapters that follow offer their own perspective to this unfolding drama.

NOTES

1. 31 I.L.M. 818.

2. While most commentators identify three objectives of the CBD—conservation, equity, and sustainable use—I believe that sustainable use is a necessary component of both biodiversity conservation and equitable sharing and, as such, need not be listed as a separate objective.

3. See Principle 21 of the Stockholm Declaration, adopted by the United Nations Conference on the Human Environment (1972).

4. See *U.S. v. Canada ("Trail Smelter" Arbitration)*, 3 R.I.A.A. 1905 (1941).

5. See World Commission on Environment and Development; *Our Common Future* ("The Brundtland Report"), 1987.

6. 61 Stat. A3, 55 U.N.T.S. 188, opened for signature Oct. 30, 1947.

7. GATT Doc. MTN/FA, 33 I.L.M. 9 (Dec. 15, 1993).

8. See CBD, Art. 25.

9. Indeed, one could argue that the CBD is a binding version of the 1982 UN World Charter for Nature, which states that "ecosystems and organisms, as well as the land, marine, and atmospheric resources that are utilized by man, shall be managed to achieve and maintain optimum sustainable productivity but not in a way as to endanger the integrity of those other ecosystems with which they co-exist." See U.N.G.A. Res. 37/7.

10. 94 B.F.S.P. 715 (signed by the European colonial powers in Africa).

11. 37 Stat. 154 (signed by Japan, Russia, the United Kingdom on behalf of Canada, and the United States).

12. 39 Stat. 1702 and 178 L.T.S. 309, respectively. The 1916 treaty was signed between the U.S. and the U.K. (on behalf of Canada) and the 1936 treaty was signed by the U.S. and Mexico and included protection of game mammals.

13. 161 U.N.T.S. 193; 56 Stat. 1374.

14. 1001 U.N.T.S. 3.

15. 19 I.L.M. 841.

16. Europ. T.S. no. 104 ("Berne" Convention).

17. 19 I.L.M. 15 ("Bonn" Convention).

18. 13 I.L.M. 13.

19. 996 U.N.T.S. 245.

20. U.N.T.S. no. 15511, vol. 1037, p. 151.

21. See for example, UN Doc. TD/TIMBER.2/L.9 (1994).

22. 12 I.L.M. 1085.

23. UN Doc. E/1988/39/Add.1 (1988).

24. See for example, *Defenders of Wildlife v. Lujan,* 911 F.2d 117 (8th Cir. 1990), *rev'd on other grounds, Lujan v. Defenders of Wildlife,* 112 S. Ct. 2130 (1992).

25. See, for example, *U.S. v. Mitchell,* 553 F.2d 996 (1977); see also 59 *Fed. Reg.* 51552 (Oct. 12, 1994) (rulemaking by National Atmospheric and Oceanic Administration that clarifies illegality under the Marine Mammal Protection Act of any individual or vessel, subject to U.S. jurisdiction, setting purse-sein nets on dolphins to catch tuna, regardless of the flag of the fishing vessel).

26. But see H.R. 910 (104th Cong.), which has over twenty cosponsors and would require the U.S. State Department to draw up a code of conduct for U.S. businesses operating overseas.

References

Angier, Natalie. 1994. Redefining diversity: Biologists urge look beyond rain forests. *New York Times,* November 29, p. C1.

Daly, Herman, and John Cobb. 1994. *For the Common Good.* Boston: Beacon Press.

de Klemm, Cyrille, and Clare Shine. 1993. *Biological Diversity Conservation and the Law: Legal Mechanisms for Conserving Species and Ecosystems.* Gland, Switzerland: IUCN/World Conservation Union.

Drucker, Peter. 1994. Trade lessons from the world economy. *Foreign Affairs* 73:99.

Dunoff, Jeffrey. 1994. Institutional misfits: The GATT, the ICJ and trade–environment disputes. *Michigan Journal of International Law* 15:1043.

Edwards, Stephen. 1995. *Conserving Biodiversity: Resources for Our Future.* Washington D.C.: Competitive Enterprise Institute.

Ehrlich, Paul, and Anne Ehrlich. 1990. *The Population Explosion.* New York: Simon & Schuster.

El-Ashry, Mohamed. 1994. Preserving species is everybody's business. *Earth Times,* December 15, p. 28.

Esty, Daniel. 1994. *Greening the GATT.* Washington, D.C.: Institute for International Economics.

Favre, David. 1993. Debate within the CITES community: What direction for the future? *Natural Resources Journal* 33:875.

Fitzgerald, John. 1992. The Biological Diversity Treaty of UNCED. *Endangered Species Update* 9. Ann Arbor: University of Michigan School of Natural Resources.

French, Hilary. 1995. *Partnership for the Planet: An Environmental Agenda for the United Nations.* Washington, D.C.: Worldwatch Institute.

French, Hilary. 1994. Making environmental treaties work. *Scientific American,* December, p. 94.

Gore, Albert. 1992. *Earth in the Balance.* Boston: Houghton Mifflin.

Griesgraber, JoMarie, ed. 1994. *Rethinking Bretton Woods: Toward Equitable, Sustainable and Participatory Development.* Washington, D.C.: Center for Concern.

Krattiger, Anatole, Jeffrey McNeely, William Lesser, Kenton Miller, Yvonne St. Hill, and Ranil Senanayake, eds. 1994. *Widening Perspectives on Biodiversity.* Gland, Switzerland: IUCN/International Academy of the Environment.

Krugman, Paul. 1994. *Peddling Prosperity.* New York: Norton.

Lyster, Simon. 1985. *International Wildlife Law.* Cambridge: Grotius.

Martin, Philip. 1993. *Trade and Migration: NAFTA and Agriculture.* Washington, D.C.: Institute for International Economics.

Murakami, Masahiro. 1995. *Managing Water for Peace in the Middle East: Alternative Strategies.* Tokyo: United Nations University Press.

Neff, Alan. 1990. Not in their backyards either: A proposal for a foreign environmental practices act. *Ecology Law Quarterly* 17:477.

Nothdurft, William. 1992. *Going Global.* Washington, D.C.: German Marshall Fund.

Owens, Delia, and Mark Owens. 1992. *The Eye of the Elephant.* Boston: Houghton Mifflin.

Pain, Stephanie. 1994. Cracking wildlife crimes. *New Scientist,* August, p. 21.

Ponting, Clive. 1991. *A Green History of the World.* New York: St. Martin's.

Porter, Gareth. 1992. *The United States and the Biodiversity Convention: The Case for Participation.* Washington, D.C.: Environmental and Energy Study Institute.

Porter, Michael. 1991. Green competitiveness. *Scientific American,* April, p. 168.

Qing, Dai. 1994. *Yangtze! Yangtze!* Toronto: Earthscan.

Reich, Robert. 1992. *The Work of Nations.* New York: Vintage.

Rich, Bruce. 1994. *Mortgaging the Earth.* Boston: Beacon Press.

Robison, Bruce. July 1995. Light in the ocean's midwaters. *Scientific American* 60.

Sands, Phillipe, ed. 1994. *Greening International Law.* New York: The Free Press.

Snape, William J. III. 1993. What Will Happen to the Critters: NAFTA's Impact on Wildlife Protection. *Natural Resources Journal* 33: 1077.

Snape, William J. III and Naomi Lefkovitz. 1994. Searching for GATT's Environmental Miranda: Are Process Standards Getting Due Process? *Cornell International Law Journal.* 27:777.

Sweden, Government of. 1994. *Biological Diversity in Sweden.* Solna: Swedish Environmental Protection Agency.

Texas Center for Policy Studies. 1993. *Biodiversity Protection in the Texas/Mexico Border Region.* Austin: TCPS.

United Kingdom, Government of. 1994. *Biodiversity Action Plan.* London: HMSO.

United Nations. 1993. *Agenda 21, Rio Declaration, Statement of Forest Principles.* New York: UN Department of Public Information.

United Nations Comission on Sustainable Development. 1995. *Conservation of Biological Diversity: Report of the Secretary General.* E/CN .17/1995/7. New York: United Nations.

United Nations Environment Programme. 1994. *The UNEP Biodiversity Programme and Implementation Strategy.* Geneva: United Nations.

U.S. Trade Representative. 1994. *The GATT Uruguay Round Agreements: Report on Environmental Issues.* Washington, D.C: Government Printing Office.

Vienna Convention on the Law of Treaties. 1980. UN Doc. A/CONF.39/27; 8 *I.L.M.* 679.

Wold, Chris. 1995. *The Biodiversity Convention and Existing International Agreements: Opportunities for Synergy.* Washington, D.C.: The Humane Society of the United States/International.

World Bank. 1992. *Development and the Environment.* Washington, D.C.: World Bank.

World Bank. 1994. *Implementing the Convention on Biological Diversity: Toward a Strategy for World Bank Assistance.* Washington, D.C.: World Bank.

Chapter 6

USING TRADE MEASURES
TO PROTECT BIODIVERSITY

Leesteffy Jenkins

The use of trade measures to achieve biodiversity, animal welfare, and other environmental objectives has become a subject of serious debate within the international community. While there is little doubt that most of these trade measures conflict with current interpretations of the rules governing international trade in the General Agreement on Tariffs and Trade (GATT), little attention has been paid to the environmental, conservation, or animal welfare perspective. Have such measures in fact helped achieve legitimate environmental, conservation, or animal welfare goals? Or could those same objectives have been attained as effectively using other mechanisms? And lastly, has the use of these trade measures undermined the free trade system?

The answers to these questions are not easy and cannot be answered fully here. My purpose, rather, is to present the wildlife conservation and animal welfare point of view in order to further constructive dialogue. Moreover, I offer suggestions for GATT reforms to make trade rules compatible with the goals of wildlife conservation and animal welfare regulation.

SANCTIONS, STANDARDS, AND THE ENVIRONMENT

There are two types of trade measures: sanctions and standards. Sanctions are punitive trade measures. Typically the product being embargoed is unrelated to the goal being sought. An example of such a measure is the U.S. Pelly Amendment to the Fisherman's Protective Act.[1] Under this act, the U.S. president may embargo products from any country found to have "diminished the effectiveness" of an international program for endangered or threatened species. The product to be embargoed does not have to be connected to the species protected.

Standards, by contrast, regulate the terms under which products are imported. Unlike sanctions, standards are not typically punitive and are usually nondiscriminatory. *Product* standards relate to the physical characteristics of a good, such as quality, size, or performance; *process* standards, or more accurately process and production methods (PPMs), relate to how a good is produced. Most wildlife conservation and animal welfare laws that utilize trade measures use PPMs. Some PPMs relate directly to the good being traded. For instance, there is a U.S. law restricting market access for wild-caught birds to producers from countries that demonstrate they have a regime ensuring the birds are harvested sustainably and humanely. In this case, the resource being protected (birds) is identical to the product being imported (birds). Other PPMs may not be directly related to the good being traded. Take, for example, the Marine Mammal Protection Act's tuna–dolphin provisions. Under the act, the protected resource, Eastern Pacific dolphins, is different from the product being imported, yellowfin tuna. Dolphins are associated with yellowfin tuna because many dolphins die in purse-seine tuna nets. Another example of this type of regulation is the U.S. High Seas Driftnet Act, wherein the protected species are marine mammals and other pelagic species, including fish, while the regulated import is solely fish.

The trade and environment debate has become mired in labels. Developed countries are sometimes accused of being "eco-imperialists" by developing countries. Legitimate environmental laws are sometimes characterized as "protectionist." The United States has been accused of being the only country to act "unilaterally" regarding environmental concerns. It has been argued, too, that the use of environmental trade measures will lead down a "slippery slope" of economic protectionism. These characterizations do nothing to encourage serious dialogue or resolve this important issue.

Few would deny that a country has the sovereign right to develop and enforce its own values. Yet trade measures used for wildlife conservation or animal welfare purposes are no more than a mechanism to ensure that democratically chosen values are enforced at home. Countries that use such measures are in essence making a value judgment: that the citizens of the country do not want to trade in fish caught in driftnets, or fur caught with leghold traps, or cosmetics tested on animals. Instead of outward-looking, many of these laws are more properly characterized as inward-looking: a reflection of who we are. A constructive approach to this topic would be to determine whether individual trade measures can in fact achieve environmental, conservation, or animal welfare goals—and if so, how trade rules can be made more compatible with these goals.

While trade measures are often criticized for not being the "best" or "least-trade restrictive" solution to environmental or animal protection goals, in most cases they represent the most *practical* political solution. Most environmental laws are passed by means of a democratic decision-making process in which compromise is a key element. Diverse constituents are involved in the process: environmentalists, producers, retailers, consumer groups. When democratically elected officials take into account the concerns of all these constituents, the end result is usually a law that gives everyone something, but gives no one everything. For example, while many conservationists and animal welfare constituents may prefer a complete moratorium on bird imports or the intentional setting on dolphins while fishing for tuna, such a solution may not be politically feasible.

Nevertheless, from an environmental perspective, incremental movement is better than no movement at all. So while economic considerations may play a role in shaping environmental solutions, in most cases it is the environmental goal, not a desire to protect domestic industries from foreign competition, that creates an impetus for a law in the first place.

The United States is one of many countries that enact environmental regulations without reference to an international agreement or restrict trade in products for environmental, conservation, or animal welfare purposes. Later we will look at European Union and Canadian laws that also could be characterized as "unilateral." Perhaps we should be asking not whether "unilateral" measures may be implemented but, rather, under what circumstances should trade measures be used?

Some people argue that if we permit the use of process standards for environmental and animal protection goals, we will be unable to prevent their abuse for economic protectionist purposes. This claim is appealing, but it is inaccurate: there are many ways in which rules can be fashioned to ensure they are not used to protect commercial industries. For example, a rule can be established that ensures promulgation and enforcement of a process standard must be accompanied by provisions for technology sharing and technological assistance to developing countries that compete in the market in question. Such rules should discourage industry from using process standards improperly.

TRADE MEASURES IN ACTION

There are a number of instances where trade measures have been successfully employed for environmental purposes. The fight over leghold traps is an instructive example. These traps are so barbaric that they have been banned in more than sixty-five countries. The tremendous force with which the trap slams down on its victim's paw or limb is akin to slamming a car door on one's hand. In such a state of suffering, animals often chew off their own limb in attempting to escape. "Nontarget species" such as endangered species and domestic pets are victims of these traps, as well, thus harming biodiversity.

In 1988, the European Parliament adopted the first of several resolutions attacking the cruelty of leghold traps. The resolution called for labeling of imported furs to indicate whether the animals were caught in leghold traps. In 1991, the European Community addressed the issue of leghold traps more directly by banning the use of the steel-jaw leghold trap in European Union countries, as well as prohibiting the importation of fur pelts from animals trapped with this method. This regulation is to go into effect January 1, 1996.[2] At that time a country wishing to continue selling fur in the European Union must do one of two things: either prohibit all use of the steel-jaw leghold trap or use internationally accepted humane trapping standards for specified species.[3] The European Union has interpreted "humane trapping standards" to exclude any leghold trap, irrespective of whether such traps are considered to be humane by any international body.

In approving the regulation, the European Council determined that only through specific legislation pertaining to leghold traps could they eliminate this animal cruelty. Although the regulation is not yet operative, it is providing a strong incentive for developing more humane trapping methods. Some European Union countries continue to use leghold traps on a limited basis, as well as the countries of Canada, the United States, and Russia, which export fur pelts caught in these traps into the European Union. But already over half of the European Union nations prevent the use of steel-jaw leghold traps. Other countries could adapt to the EU regulation by developing and using less barbaric trapping devices.

The use of trade measures for the protection of marine mammals has also been successful. In 1972, the United States passed the Marine Mammal Protection Act (MMPA).[4] The dolphin provisions at issue directed the U.S. treasury secretary to ban the importation of commercial fish or products from fish caught with commercial fishing technology that results in the incidental kill or incidental serious injury of dolphins and other marine mammals in excess of U.S. standards. In 1984, the MMPA was amended to require that each nation wishing to export yellowfin tuna to the United States document that it had adopted a dolphin conservation program "comparable" to that of the U.S. fleet. In 1988 the MMPA was further amended to provide that the number of dolphin mortalities of a foreign fleet could not exceed 1.25 times that of the U.S. fleet. In 1990, Mexican yellowfin tuna were embargoed by the treasury secretary under the comparability provisions of the MMPA. Secondary embargoes—targetting countries that import tuna from primary contries—were instituted in 1992. When Mexico subsequently filed a GATT complaint, a GATT panel ruled in 1991 that the U.S. law violated the GATT. Although Mexico agreed to suspend the case before final resolution, the

European Community (as a secondary country) subsequently filed a related case in which a similar result was reached.

The purpose of the MMPA provisions is to reduce to zero mortality the number of marine mammals killed as a result of commercial fisheries. In the Eastern Tropical Pacific (ETP), an estimated 7 million dolphins have been killed in thirty years by U.S. and foreign fishermen using purse-seine nets to harvest yellowfin tuna. The U.S. law has been effective in achieving its goals. The number of dolphin mortalities in the ETP was reduced from a high of 423,678 in 1972 to 27,292 in 1991. In 1992, the mortality rate in the ETP was reduced further to below 5,000. Since 1981, the U.S. tuna fleet has operated under MMPA regulations that permit up to 20,500 dolphins to be killed annually. Improvements in dolphin release methods, however, combined with the fact that the U.S. fleet in the ETP had dwindled from more than forty vessels to about seven vessels in 1992, resulted in an actual U.S. dolphin mortality in 1993 of just 115 animals. During the same period, foreign fleets, primarily those of Mexico and Venezuela, grew proportionately.

Originally the MMPA required foreign governments to certify that they had a dolphin conservation program comparable to the U.S. program. Once the certification was made, the requirements of the law were met. Positive certifications were received on a routine basis from all countries that imported yellowfin tuna into the United States, including Mexico and Venezuela. Suspecting that these certifications were incorrect, U.S. environmental organizations began to investigate. An environmentalist posing as a crew member was able to document on film that foreign fleets were killing thousands of dolphins and that in fact no efforts were being made to reduce dolphin mortality. As a result of this information, Congress again amended the MMPA to provide that the foreign fleet mortality rate could not exceed 1.25 times that of the U.S. fleet. As the U.S. fleet reduced its kill quota, foreign fleets would be required to do so as well if they wished to gain access to U.S. markets. The ultimate goal: an effective mortality rate of zero.

From an environmental perspective this goal was particularly important, as surveys indicate that some populations of dolphin are being severely depleted. In fact, in 1993 the U.S. National Marine Fisheries Service (NMFS) reported that the population of offshore spotted dolphin (*Stenella attenuaia*) is severely depleted and estimated to be only 23 percent of its original size.[5] The offshore spotted dolphin is one of the primary stocks affected by the ETP tuna fishery. To date the MMPA provisions have not resulted in an overall competitive advantage for the U.S. tuna industry in the ETP.[6] If anything, the law has been a disincentive within the U.S. industry to continue fishing in the ETP.

Trade measures have also been used to protect sea turtles. In 1989, the U.S. Congress passed a law that protects sea turtles.[7] The act prohibits the importation of shrimp and shrimp products from any producing country that does not have an adequate sea turtle conservation program as defined by the act and does not require its shrimp vessels to use turtle excluder devices (TEDs). The act, as originally passed, required all shrimp imported into the United States after 1991 to be harvested with the use of comparable sea turtle protection technology. (Producers were given two years to phase in TEDs, and the United States continued to seek treaty partners for an international agreement on sea turtles.) The U.S. secretary of state later promulgated regulations giving nations an additional three years to come into full compliance with the law.

The purpose of the act is to promote global protection of six species of endangered sea turtles seriously imperiled by fishing practices of the shrimp industry. Five of the six species regularly inhabit U.S. waters. Incidental capture and drowning by shrimp trawling vessels is one of the major causes of human-induced mortality: estimates of up to 50,000 drownings a year have been reported for the United States and the toll from the worldwide shrimp fleet may exceed 150,000 annually. As the largest consumer nation of shrimp (75 percent are imported), the United States has the responsibility to ensure that shrimp produced for its market do not destroy endangered sea turtles.

In 1978, the United States began a research program to reduce incidental mortality from shrimp trawling. By 1981 a turtle excluder device had been designed that was at least 97 percent effective at releasing turtles unharmed. Today there are seven approved models that are more than 97 percent effective. In 1983, NMFS had a program in place that encouraged voluntary use, but the program was ineffective and there was still little use of TEDs. In 1987, NMFS issued regulations requiring the use of TEDs by vessels of the U.S. shrimp fleet where sea turtles and shrimp fishers had a high likelihood of contact. With additional data, it became evident that TEDs were needed on virtually the entire southeastern shrimp fleet. By 1991, nearly the entire U.S. commercial fleet was required to use TEDs. Where TEDs are used, stranding of drowning turtles has been significantly reduced.

But sea turtles are migratory species that move through the waters of many nations and into international waters during their annual migrations. Clearly, protecting a species in one part of its range, only to drown it as it moves between nesting and feeding grounds, would not save the species from extinction. Although TED requirements have now been extended to foreign fleets, the law permitted ample time for shrimp producers to comply. Moreover, the United States has provided other countries training and technical assistance on the use of TEDs. These devices are inexpensive, simple, and easy to use. Modifications of TEDs now under way will allow these devices to reduce other unwanted by-catch—thus protecting other fisheries and the biological diversity of marine ecosystems.

Another example of success is the use of trade measures to enforce laws protecting birds. Many of the world's exotic bird species have become severely depleted. As the world's largest importer of wild-caught birds, the United States attacked this problem in 1992 by passing legislation regulating (and in some cases banning) the importation of exotic birds. The Wild Bird Conservation Act bans the importation of ten species of exotic birds named in a recent CITES report as being threatened by continued trade.[8] The act also directs the Secretary of the Interior to ban or set quotas on the importation of all (both CITES and non-CITES) species of exotic birds from any country that has not implemented a management program which provides for conservation of the species and its habitat, for humane methods of capture, transport, and maintenance of the species, and for effective enforcement of illegal trade, as well as a variety of other conservation goals. To date no countries have been embargoed or allocated quotas.

As originally drafted, the act applied only to species listed in Appendixes I and II of CITES. This was unsatisfactory to the conservation community, however, because past trading history demonstrated that traffickers would simply shift the market to non-CITES species, thus putting increased pressure on species that had not previously been imported in large numbers. The United States passed this law because several populations of wild birds were being depleted and foreign governments seemed unable to prevent the illegal trafficking in exotic bird species. This is not a protectionist law because the United States is not a major producer of exotic birds.

The campaign to limit the use of driftnets on the high seas has been strengthened by U.S. laws that utilize trade measures. The High Seas Driftnet Fisheries Enforcement Act was enacted in 1992.[9] The act directs the secretary of commerce to prohibit the importation of all fish, fish products, and sportfishing equipment of any nation or nationals that continue to conduct large-scale driftnet fishing beyond the exclusive economic zone (EEZ) of any nation after December 31, 1992. Specifically, the Driftnet Act directs the secretary of commerce to determine whether a violation has occurred. Following such a determination, the president must consult with any nation so named for the purpose of obtaining an agreement to terminate large-scale driftnet fishing. If no agreement is reached within ninety days, the president must direct the Secretary of Treasury to prohibit the importation of fish, fish products, and sportfishing equipment from the offending nation.

The purpose of the Driftnet Act is to complement UN Resolution 46/215, which calls for a worldwide moratorium on driftnet fishing by December 31, 1992. The UN Resolution, though a multilateral agreement, has no enforcement provisions. The United States thus seeks to carry out enforcement by means of its domestic law. The UN Resolution was in response to evidence that large-scale driftnet operations are highly destructive to living marine resources and ocean ecosystems and pose an especially significant threat to slow-reproducing species like marine mammals, birds, and sharks, which take many years to recover.

In 1991, the United States, in Section 307(1)(M) of the Magnuson Fishery Conservation and Management Act, prohibited the practice of large-scale driftnet fishing by U.S. nationals and vessels—not only within the exclusive economic zone of the United States but beyond the EEZ of any nation as well. Moreover, the United States helped facilitate cooperative agreements with Russia, Japan, and other concerned fishing nations regarding the use of large-scale driftnets outside a country's EEZ. Despite these efforts, fisheries resources continued to decline, especially in the Bering Sea. As a result, after the UN Resolution passed, the United States enacted the Driftnet Act to ensure that the UN global moratorium takes effect and that unregulated fishing practices in the central Bering Sea are reduced or eliminated. While no countries have been embargoed under this act, there is evidence that several countries continue to use driftnets in violation of the UN Resolution.

If trade is to be made compatible with environmental, biodiversity, and animal protection goals, GATT and regional agreements such as NAFTA will need to integrate environmental concerns into trade. The most evident ways such an integration might occur are through the development of strong enforcement mechanisms—including the use of trade sanctions in international environmental agreements—and through the legalization of process standards under GATT.

Few international environmental or wildlife conservation agreements (IEAs) contain adequate enforcement mechanisms. As a result, decisions of IEAs are routinely ignored by member countries that do not agree with them. Consequently, IEA organizations such as the International Whaling Commission (IWC), the Inter-American Tropical Tuna Commission (IATTC), and CITES have a greatly diminished capacity for protecting the resources for which they have responsibility.

In recent years, the United States has used the threat of trade sanctions as a means of encouraging countries to comply with their international obligations under both CITES and the IWC. The primary law that permits the United States to impose trade sanctions under such circumstances is the Pelly Amendment to the Fisherman's Protective Act of 1967. Under the Pelly Amendment, as noted earlier, the president may impose trade sanctions on any country that "diminishes the effectiveness of any international program for endangered or threatened species."[10]

Although it has been criticized for engaging in unilateral action to protect wildlife, the United States had never actually imposed trade sanctions on any country for violating an IEA until 1994.[11] Furthermore, the Pelly Amendment—the only U.S. law under which trade *sanctions* have been threatened—can be invoked only when countries have failed to comply with their obligations under IEAs or are in some way diminishing the effectiveness of an international conservation program. To date, the mere threat of trade sanctions has been sufficient to encourage the vast majority of intransigent countries to comply with their international obligations.[12] Not surprisingly, some opponents of the Pelly Amendment claim that it violates GATT—rather than denouncing it as an ineffective means of protecting the global environment and wildlife resources.

The development of multilateral enforcement provisions, including trade sanctions, by IEA organizations would reduce the necessity for unilateral action in most circumstances in which the United States has threatened trade sanctions—and would greatly diminish, though not necessarily eliminate, the necessity for unilateral action to protect environmental and wildlife resources. Ideally, an IEA would have the power to authorize its members to impose trade sanctions against intransigent parties, as well as against non-member countries that reduce the effectiveness of the IEA. Sovereign rights would not be infringed upon if member countries were not *required* to impose trade sanctions but, rather, were urged to do so at their discretion. Such a scheme would have the added advantage of permitting member countries to vote in favor of trade sanctions even if, for political or other reasons, actual imposition of trade sanctions was not feasible for the voting country. Until IEA organizations develop the capacity to enforce international wildlife agreements, however, individual countries will continue to play an important role in ensuring that international objectives are met.

SUGGESTIONS FOR REFORM

A reform of GATT rules will be necessary if trade measures are to be used truly effectively. As currently interpreted, GATT does not recognize trade measures as a legitimate means of enforcing environmental objectives. If trade sanctions are to develop as a legal enforcement mechanism in the context of IEAs, reforms will need to be made to the technical legal rules in GATT. Moreover, the contracting parties must recognize that process standards are a legitimate means of enforcing environmental, conservation, and animal welfare objectives.

Currently, GATT does not permit member nations to use PPMs as the basis to regulate trade in goods. But if the environment is to be effectively protected, trade rules must explicitly recognize that many environmental and conservation objectives cannot be achieved unless countries are able to regulate unsustainable PPMs.[13] Concerns such as the threatened loss of habitat or species, or an increased level of pollutants in local and global environments, should be a legitimate basis for imposing restrictions on the importation and exportation of goods and the utilization of natural resources. If we are to protect our environment, however, countries must be able to discriminate between products that are physically "alike" but were produced in drastically different manners—and be able to adopt trade regulations that take these differences into account.[14]

International organizations have no means of accomplishing their goals other than through state action. Nation-states, in effect, implement the objectives of IEAs. Any GATT reforms must therefore recognize that state action taken alone (if it meets specified criteria), or in accordance with an IEA, presumptively accords with the exception provisions contained in GATT Article XX.[15] Although the GATT panel in the first tuna-dolphin case suggested that trade restrictions authorized by an international agreement may be permissible, a test case has not yet been made.

If GATT is to coexist harmoniously with global environmental objectives, there must be recognition that environmental, habitat, and species degradation knows no boundaries and, moreover, that protection of global resources must be comprehensive if environmental protection is to be achieved. This means that countries must be able to act both individually and collectively to protect global and domestic natural resources.

Although parties to an IEA may agree to waive their GATT obligations pursuant to the GATT waiver provisions,[16] such provisions could not be construed to apply to countries that are not members of the IEA. Thus, for instance, if the IWC tried to authorize trade sanctions against Iceland for violating the IWC ban on commercial whaling, Iceland (a nonmember country) could challenge any trade action taken in accordance with the IWC decision at GATT. The irony is that GATT could be used in this situation as a haven for countries that show the least respect for international institutions. Until there are GATT reforms, countries have an incentive not to join IEAs that adopt trade sanctions as an enforcement mechanism or to withdraw from such agreements whenever they wish to ignore decisions of an IEA. Unless international trade rules are modified, IEAs will not be able to effectively prohibit nonmember countries from engaging in behavior contrary to the goals of IEAs.

There is growing awareness that the international trading system has an effect on biodiversity, animal protection, and the environment. Trade measures in some cases have evolved as the most effective means toward these ends. Indeed, the international dialogue is no longer denying the role of environment in trade; today it is attempting to determine how much environmental protection should be considered. When comprehensive animal and environmental protection provisions have been integrated into trade laws, consumers will become more willing to open their doors to foreign producers and international businesses will gain the stable new markets that the GATT signatories envisioned.

NOTES

1. 22 USC Sec. 1978 (1988, Supp. V).

2. The regulation went into effect for domestic producers on January 1, 1995, and will apply to foreign producers on January 1, 1996.

3. The listed species are muskrat, sable, fisher, badger, ermine, beaver, wolf, bobcat, marten, racoon, otter, lynx, and coyote. See Annex 1 of Council Regulation 3254/91 referred to in Art. 3(1).

4. 16 USC Sec. 1361 et seq. (1988) (as amended U.S.C.A. Sec. 1361 (Supp. 1993).

5. 58 *Fed. Reg.* 58285 (Nov. 1, 1993).

6. In 1990, U.S. tuna companies ceased any purchase, processing, or sale of tuna caught by encircling dolphin.

7. P.L. 101-162, Sec. 609, Nov. 21, 1989, 103 Stat. 1037.

8. The Wild Bird Conservation Act of 1992, 16 U.S.C.A. Sec. 4901 et seq. (Supp. 1993). Eight of the listed species are Appendix II birds for which commercial trade is not currently banned under the Convention on International Trade in Endangered Species of Flora and Fauna (CITES). Two species have since been moved to CITES Appendix I. See 57 *Fed. Reg.* 57510.

9. P.L. 101-582, Sec. 101, codified at 16 USC 1826a.

10. 22 USC Sec. 1978(a)(2).

11. The United States recently imposed trade sanctions against Taiwan for its continued trade in rhinoceros horn and tiger parts.

12. Since 1972, Pelly certifications have occurred on fifteen occasions. On at least eight of those occasions, the certified country brought its behavior into compliance with the IEA.

13. Because IEAs would depend on domestic enforcement of trade sanctions, domestic laws would have to be adopted authorizing such action. In the United States, for instance, the Endangered Species Act of 1973, 16 USC 1531 et seq. (1988, Supp. IV 1991) (as amended U.S.C.A. Supp. 1993), domestically implements U.S. obligations under CITES. These domestic laws may violate current GATT rules.

14. Changes of this type would reflect the "precautionary principle" that environmental degradation should be prevented, rather than controlled. The international community is beginning to realize that destructive processes can cause environmental harm. For instance, Art. 4, para. 4, of the Montreal Protocol provides that "the Parties shall determine the feasibility of banning or restricting, from States not a party to this Protocol, the import of products *produced with,* but not containing, controlled substances" (emphasis added).

15. Current GATT jurisprudence, however, may not recognize a state's unlimited right to act to protect resources outside its territorial jurisdiction. See GATT, United States Restrictions on Imports of Tuna (unpublished decision), GATT Report DS21/R (Sept. 3, 1991), pp. 48, 50. But see also GATT, United States Restrictions on Imports of Tuna (II), GATT Report DS29/R (May 20, 1994).

16. GATT, Art. XXV.

Chapter 7

HARMFUL EXOTICS IN THE UNITED STATES

Peter Jenkins

In the early 1900s, a tree fungus was introduced to the United States by way of diseased nursery plants imported from Europe or Asia. It quickly spread through the once magnificent eastern stands of American chestnut, killing millions of these ecologically and economically valuable trees. Virtually all that remains of wild chestnuts now are scattered old stumps that send up sprouts which quickly die. The fungus that causes chestnut blight is one of thousands of exotic species—species spread beyond their natural ranges by humans—established in the United States.

Both intentional and unintentional releases of exotic species have caused serious ecological and economic problems. Apart from the extensive damage caused by exotic pests and weeds to forestry, agriculture, and other economic interests, exotic species have been a significant factor in native species endangerment and extinction. They are a particular threat in vulnerable island ecosystems—like Guam, for example, where, since World War II, nine of the island's eleven native forest-dwelling bird species have been extirpated by one introduction, the brown tree snake. Extraordinary measures are necessary to keep the brown tree snake out of Hawaii, where its impact could be equally devastating.

Table 7.1, prepared by Michael Bean of the Environmental Defense Fund for the Office of Technology Assessment (OTA), illustrates the role

TABLE 7.1
Contribution of Nonindigenous Species (NIS) to Threatened and Endangered
Species Listings by the U.S. Fish and Wildlife Service Category of impact on
threatened and endangered species

		Category of impact on threatened and endangered species		
Group	Total number of threatened and endangered species	Species where NIS contributed to listing	Species where NIS are a major cause of listing	Species where NIS are *the* major cause of listing
Plants	250	39 (16%)	—	14 (6%)
Terrestrial vertebrates	182	47 (26%)	3 (2%)	19 (10%)
Insects*a*	25	7 (28%)	—	2 (8%)
Fish	86	44 (51%)	8 (9%)	5 (6%)
Invertebrates*b*	70	23 (33%)	1 (1%)	1 (1%)
Total	613	160	12	41

Note: Includes species listed through June 1991.
*a*Includes arachnids.
*b*Includes mollusks and crustaceans.

Source: M. Bean, "The Role of the U.S. Department of the Interior in Non-Indigenous Species Issues," contractor report prepared for the Office of Technology Assessment, November 1991.

exotic species play in threatened and endangered species listings.[1] In more than half of the weakened endangered fish, for example, exotics have contributed to the listing. The right-hand column indicates that in 5 to 10 percent of all vertebrate groups, the major cause of the threatened or endangered listing is the introduction of exotics. These figures are based on 1990 data and likely understate the problems. Exotics frequently act in combination with habitat loss and other factors in an "extinction vortex" that eliminates native species locally, regionally, or altogether.[2]

Exotics can harm native species in many ways: competition (zebra mussels crowd out and kill native mussels in the Great Lakes and beyond); predation (free-ranging house cats kill millions of songbirds annually); infection (Dutch elm disease has devastated our native elms); and hybridization (introduced rainbow trout have genetically swamped rare southwestern trouts like the Apache trout and Gila trout). Indeed, exotics are the most overlooked threat to native biodiversity. Aside from causing or contributing to the extinction of native species, invasions of exotics result in biological homogeneity as pests and weeds achieve global ranges—the opposite of biological diversity. Human developments, and their associated habitat destruction or disturbance, create opportunities for invasions by "weedy," human-adapted generalists like starlings and rats.

Exotics can change basic ecosystem processes, as well, such as the frequency and intensity of wildfires. Melaleuca, an Australian tree that has invaded one-half million acres of the Everglades, burns extremely hot because of its high oil content. Although melaleuca fires kill nearby native plants and their seeds, the melaleuca seeds survive the hot temperatures and thrive after fires, leading to dense monospecific stands. Melaleuca also transpires great volumes of water and creates high ground, both of which contribute to the drying of marshlands. Unless these trees are controlled, the Everglades will be changed permanently. A massive control effort using herbicides and handpulling of seedlings is under way, but it is not keeping pace with the invasion.

Ecological damage from exotic species is in many cases slow and undramatic, taking decades. Because of the insidious, unsexy nature of this problem, policymakers have responded weakly. Current laws range from international treaties to federal and state statutes and regulations to local ordinances. Recently OTA undertook the first ever comprehensive review of these laws as well as the policy issues posed by exotics. OTA's report, *Harmful Non-Indigenous Species in the United States*,[3] concluded that there are numerous gaps which Congress should address. In fact, OTA found that more than 4,500 exotic species, predominately insects and weeds, have become established in the United States and hundreds have caused economic and ecological harm.

Controlling or eradicating harmful exotic species, called the "nasty necessity" by conservation biologists, is sometimes frustrated by powerful opposition. It usually requires pesticides, herbicides, shooting, snaring, and other lethal methods, which environmentalists, animal rights activists, and others have often opposed. Snaring of feral pigs and goats to protect remote, vulnerable, natural areas of Hawaii, for example, is opposed not only by hunter groups but by People for the Ethical Treatment of Animals (PETA) and other humane groups.[4]

Does this exotics issue seem like it's getting too complicated and controversial for the U.S. Congress to address? It has been so in the past, and the 104th Congress is even less likely to take a pro-environment stance on this issue. Many well-entrenched economic interests, such as the pet, aquarium, and nursery industries, as well as segments of the agriculture, livestock, and timber industries, oppose tighter restrictions that would reduce imports of exotic species, even though they themselves have a lot at risk. The timber industry, and our native forests, could be devastated by another disease like the chestnut blight, yet some sawmill operators support the import of potentially infested raw logs from Siberia. It takes a compelling horror story—like the ecologically and economically disastrous zebra mussel invasion in the Great Lakes—to get Congress to intervene. Congress acted too late to stop the zebra mussel, and Congress will likely continue to react only after disasters occur. Now let us turn to the international, federal, and state laws on exotic species and explore some areas where new approaches are needed.

INTERNATIONAL LAW

The most important pathway of harmful exotics into U.S. ecosystems is not via intentional releases. Nor is it contraband smuggled by tourists in their suitcases. Rather, it is unintentional importation through international trade. That is, exotics frequently "stow away" on ships, on plants, and in shipping containers and packing material. The trading partners now of biggest concern to the United States are those with similar ecosystems that have potentially harmful species preadapted to surviving in U.S. ecosystems. These include Chile, New Zealand, South Africa, and Russia. Liberalization of trade with these and other countries is leading to increases in U.S. imports that may carry new harmful exotics. The North American Free Trade Agreement (NAFTA) and the Uruguay Round of General Agreement on Tariffs and Trade (GATT) will accelerate this process. The U.S. government's response appears inadequate to prevent this increased trade from resulting in a wave of harmful introductions. More inspectors and better technologies have not been funded to keep pace with the increases. And international law regulating exotic species threats to biodiversity is weak.

There are two key international conventions—the IPPC (International Plant Pest Covention) and the CBD (Convention on Biological Diversity)—though many other minor and little-enforced provisions on exotic species can be found scattered throughout various other international instruments. Some of these provisions directly address exotics; others address them indirectly—for example, provisions that call for preventing habitat degradation.[5] (See Appendix Table 1.) The IPPC presently deals with agricultural pests only. The IPPC is used as a coordinating mechanism to protect agriculture from pests and could be expanded to protect biodiversity rather than just agriculture. The CBD is weak as far as exotic species are concerned. This is unfortunate, because the initial draft by the International Union for Conservation of Nature and Natural Resources (IUCN) included a relatively strong exotics provision. It would have established a complete list of scientific authority styled after the Convention on International Trade in Endangered Species (CITES), as well as a listing process focusing more attention on exotic species. The final draft, however, containes weak, fuzzy language that basically says countries should attempt to eradicate exotic species and prevent their introduction. It lacks specificity and is unenforceable, primarily because of its vagueness.

FEDERAL LAW

One of the most important U.S. laws that can protect native biodiversity from exotic species invasions is the Lacey Act,[6] which is supposed to prevent injurious introductions into the United States. This act, however, lists only twenty-two prohibited species or genera. It is poorly enforced, as well, largely because the U.S. Fish and Wildlife enforcement division is underfunded. Moreover, the Lacey Act leaves most decision-making power regarding intentional releases to the states.

The Federal Noxious Weed Act represents a good instrument to protect biodiversity,[7] but it has not been used to its full potential. It has been narrowly interpreted by the U.S. Department of Agriculture. Only recently has it been used to address major ecological threats such as melaleuca.

The National Environmental Policy Act[8] (NEPA) clearly needs to be applied to major trade initiatives such as NAFTA. The Bush administration's so-called environmental impact report on NAFTA did not even address risks from agricultural pests or other exotic species associated with increased trade with Mexico, and no other study has done so either. NEPA and state environmental policy acts need implementing regulations more specifically addressing potential exotic species threats. Increased trade with Mexico following NAFTA, and a lack of equivalent increases in inspection and prevention measures, create a gateway for exotic species importation. The exotics would not necessarily originate in Mexico; species could come from other countries into Mexico and then be shipped across the U.S. border. The U.S. Department of Agriculture's Animal and Plant Health Inspection Service (APHIS) has never required an environmental impact statement (EIS) for any proposed new species importation. EISs on other issues such as dams and highways must begin to address potential exotic species threats.

Opportunities exist under the Endangered Species Act[9] for environmental litigators to bring more cases like *Palila v. Hawaii Department of Natural Resources*,[10] where the state of Hawaii was challenged for supporting exotic game animals that were destroying the habitat of endangered birds. The court ordered the state to remove the exotic goats. Similar examples that could be challenged include federal Bureau of Reclamation and other agencies' management of water projects in the Southwest that allow exotic fish, such as rainbow trout, to outcompete and hybridize with our endangered native southwestern trouts.

STATE LAW

The OTA report, cited earlier, contains a detailed analysis of each state's regulation of intentional fish and wildlife introductions. (See Appendix Table 2.) States retain most of the authority under the Lacey Act to decide on new introductions. Comparing written state laws on this subject requires caution, though, because each of the fifty states has a unique ecological, agricultural, and institutional setting. (See Tables 7.2 and 7.3.) Florida, Georgia, Hawaii, Montana, and Utah are five states with fairly comprehensive systems in place, and they serve as reasonable models. Mississippi, South Dakota, Texas, and West Virginia have major gaps in their laws.

While there are several exemplary state laws, state approaches lack comprehensiveness on the whole and fall short in enforcement. The problem is that many states lack adequate resources to determine whether new introductions will harm their native species, and they lack tough and enforceable legal standards to prevent harmful introductions. They only prohibit a few species already known to be harmful. This approach, known as the "dirty list," parallels the Lacey Act approach just mentioned. Yet few potential new exotics have been studied enough to know whether they should be on the prohibited list.

The most restrictive approach is to prohibit all new exotics except those individually evaluated and listed as allowed—that is, a "clean list." Only Hawaii, under tough new legislation adopted in 1991, takes the "clean list" approach for virtually all introductions. Drastic measures were necessary because both intentional and unintentional introductions have devastated Hawaii's flora and fauna. About 90 percent of Hawaii's native species are endemic. No other state receives so many new introductions annually (averaging almost twenty-five per year), and no other state has so

TABLE 7.2
Gaps in Legal Authority

Vertebrate group	Legal authority over *importation* omits (or only partially covers) the group		Legal authority over *release* omits (or only partially covers) the group	
	Number	States	Number	States
Mammals	9	CT, IA, LA, ND, OR, SC, TX, WI, WV	10	CT, MI, MS, ND, OH, RI, SC, TX, VT, WV
Birds	8	IA, LA, ND, OR, SC, TX, WI, WV	8	MI, ND, OH, RI, SC, TX, VT, WV
Fish	4	IA, ND, NJ, WI	1	MS
Reptiles	10	IA, LA, MI, ND, OR, PA, SC, TX, WI, WV	9	MI, MS, ND, OH, RI, SC, TX, VT, WV
Amphibians	10	AK, IA, LA, MI, ND, OR, PA, SC, TX, WI	9	AK, MI, MS, ND, OH, RI, SC, TX, VT

Sources: Office of Technology Assessment, (1993) and Center for Wildlife Law, University of New Mexico Law School, "Selected Research and Analysis of State Laws on Vertebrate Animal Importation and Introduction," contractor report prepared for the Office of Technology Assessment, April 1992.

high a proportion of exotic species established in the wild (now about 33 percent of the state's flora and fauna). As a result, Hawaii leads the nation in biological imperilment. In fact, about one-third of the plants and birds listed, or proposed for listing, under the Endangered Species Act are Hawaiian.

More states should follow Hawaii's lead in imposing tough, enforceable laws to avoid repeating that state's history of biological imperilment. A clear legal standard—"prohibit all new introductions unless they have been proven to be safe"—provides a leverage point for citizens, neighboring states, or other affected parties to compel agencies to slow the flow of harmful invasions. In other words, if the agencies do not analyze a proposed introduction as required in the law, they could be sued and possibly enjoined from undertaking the introduction. This suggestion would

TABLE 7.3
Decision-Making Standards Used by States

Decision-making standard[a]	For importation permission		For release permission	
	Number	States	Number	States
Agency has no discretion; action prohibited	1pt[b]	VTpt	6pt	AKpt, FLpt, GApt, KYpt, MDpt, WApt[c]
Mandated study of potential ecological impacts	1pt	FLpt	3pt	FLpt, **HI**pt, **MT**pt
Determination of potential impacts defined broadly enough to include all ecological impacts	18+5pt	AL, **CA**pt, CO, **CT, DE, FL**,pt **GA, HI,** ILpt, **IN,** KY, **MD,** ME, **MN,** NC, NE, **NH NY,** SCpt, TN, **UT,** VTpt, **WA**	15+12pt	AL, AZpt, CO, **CT,** GApt, DE, HIpt, ILpt, **IN,** IA, KYpt, **MD**pt, ME, MN, MSpt, **MT**pt, NC, NE, NH, **NY,** SCpt, TN, TXpt, **UT,** VApt, WApt, **WI**
Determination of potential impacts *not* defined broadly enough to include all ecological impacts	8+4pt	AZ, AKpt, **CA**pt, ID, ILpt, **MT, NJ,** NM, NV, PA, RIpt, **VA**	4+6pt	AZpt, ID, ILpt, **NJ,** NV, OKpt, ORpt, PA VApt, WApt
No specific decision-making standards	17+3pt	AKpt, IA, KS, LA, **MA, MI,** MO, MS, ND, OH, OK, OR, RIpt, SCpt, **SD, TX, WI,** WV, WY	15+6pt	AKpt, AR, **CA,** KS, LA, **MA, MI,** MSpt, MO, ND, NM, OH, OKpt, ORpt, RI, SCpt, **SD, TX**pt, VT, WV, WY

[a]"Decision-making standard" refers to the requirements legally imposed on, or adopted by, the permitting agencies when they exercise discretion.

[b]Some states treat different groups of vertebrates differently. This is designated, where applicable, by using the abbreviation "pt" after the state initial to indicate the entry covers only "part" of the vertebrates regulated. They are totaled separately.

[c]The 18 states indicated in boldface have general environmental policy statutes, regulations, or executive orders that may overlay nonindigenous species permitting and require higher decision-making standards with regard to environmental impacts than the standard indicated. They are: CA, CT, HI, IN, MD, MA, MI, MN, MT, NJ, NY, NC, SD, TX, UT, VA, WA, WI.

Sources: Office of Technology Assessment (1993) and Center for Wildlife Law, University of New Mexico Law School, "Selected Research and Analysis of State Laws on Vertebrate Animal Importation and Introduction," contractor report prepared for the Office of Technology Assessment, April 1992.

not meet much resistance from state agencies. When OTA surveyed the heads of the main fish and wildlife agencies regarding the implementation of their own laws, more than one-third rated their own list of prohibited species as "too short." Many wanted additional legal authority from their legislatures, and they typically commented that their present authority left potentially harmful activities—such as increasingly popular exotic game farming—uncovered. Like the laws themselves, there is great variability in state enforcement.

Except for Hawaii and California, states generally do not effectively monitor imports originating within the United States. A popular or wide-ranging species introduced into one unrestrictive state can soon be taken, or spread on its own, to the others. Most of the state agencies surveyed rated their own implementation and enforcement resources as "less than adequate." About one-fifth rated their resources as "much less than ade-quate." For the sixteen agencies that cited additional resources needed to match their responsibilities, the desired increases averaged 50 percent. Clearly, states need to take exotic species more seriously.

TWO RECOMMENDATIONS

In closing, I offer two recommendations. First: one ready solution exists for the lack of adequate laws covering intentional introductions—that is, legally mandating adherence to decision-making protocols. These proto-cols are step-by-step criteria developed by experts to determine whether an introduction should proceed. (See Appendix Table 3.) Many such expert protocols exist. For example, the American Fisheries Society has a protocol for deciding whether to approve an exotic fish introduction. But no jurisdiction has an enforceable legal requirement that fisheries man-agers must follow. Would it be unreasonable to hold managers to stan-dards that their own professional societies have endorsed?

Second: The more difficult task of reducing unintentional introductions through international trade will require much more preemptive risk analy-sis by biologists, aided by the legal leverage that environmental lawyers can provide. Serious ecological risks should be grounds to prevent the opening of a new trade item or even the opening of a new international trade route until the risk is reduced to an acceptable level. Otherwise, as more and more damaging invasions of exotics occur in the next few decades, U.S. biological diversity will be sacrificed on the altar of free trade.

Appendix

Appendix Table 1
Main International Treaties with Provisions Related to Exotic Species

---

Multilateral Treaties Directly Addressing Exotic Species:

- International Plant Protection Convention; signed by the United States in 1972
- Convention on Biological Diversity; signed by the United States in 1993
- Convention on the Law of the Sea; signed by the United States in 1994

Bilateral Treaties Directly Addressing Exotic Species:

- Convention on Prevention of Diseases in Livestock (U.S.–Mexico); signed in 1928
- Boundary Waters Treaty of 1909 (U.S.–Canada); in particular the Great Lakes Water Quality Agreement of 1978 as amended in 1987
- Convention on Great Lakes Fisheries (U.S.–Canada); signed in 1954
- Convention Concerning the Conservation of Migratory Birds and Their Environment (U.S.–USSR); signed in 1976

Multilateral and Bilateral Treaties Indirectly Addressing Exotic Species:[a]

- Convention Concerning the Protection of the World Cultural and Natural Heritage; signed in 1973
- Convention on International Trade in Endangered Species of Wild Fauna and Flora (CITES); signed in 1975
- Convention on Wetlands of International Importance Especially as Waterfowl Habitat; signed in 1985
- Convention on Nature Protection and Wildlife Preservation in the Western Hemisphere; signed in 1942
- Convention for Protection and Development of Marine Resources of the Wider Caribbean Region; signed in 1983
- Convention for the Protection of Migratory Birds (U.S.–Canada); signed 1916
- Convention for the Protection of Migratory Birds and Game Mammals (U.S.–Mexico); signed in 1936

The bilateral migratory bird treaties focus on harvest restrictions and include general provisions to preserve important habitats. The United States would be obligated to protect such habitats if they were threatened by exotic species. However, these older treaties tend to be less comprehensive and lack adequate legal mechanisms to enforce obligations.

Note: Dates given are for U.S. signature. Agreements were established and opened for signature either in the same year or up to several years earlier. The Convention on Biological Diversity has not yet been ratified by the U.S. Senate.

[a]These generally protect habitats or groups of indigenous species deemed to have major conservation significance.

Sources: S. Lyster, International Wildlife Law (Cambridge: Grotius, 1985); U.S. Congress, Office of Technology Assessment, Technologies to Maintain Biological Diversity, OTA-F-330 (Washington, D.C.: Government Printing Office, 1987).

Key State Statutes and Regulations on Importation and Release of Fish and Wildlife

State	Statutory authority	Authority in regulations
Alabama	9-2-13	220-2, -.26, -.93
Alaska	16.05.251, -.255(8), -.920, -.940(10), 20(17)	5 AAC 41.005, -.030, -.070, -92.029
Arizona	3-2901; 17-306	R12-4-401, -405, -406, -410, -412, -413
Arkansas	15-46-101	Game and Fish Comm. Code Book §§04.07; 18.12; 32.12- .16; 42.05, -.09
California	Fish and Game Code	Fish and Game Comm. regs. §§171-171.5; 236; 670.7; 671.1-671.5
Colorado	33-6-112, -114, -114.5	Art. VII.007; -.008, -.009
Connecticut	26-40a, -55, -56	26-55-1, -2
Delaware	3 §7201, 7 §741, -772	Dept. of Nat. Res. and Envir. Control, Div. of Fish and Wildlife regs. 10, 14
Florida	370.081; 372.26, -.265, -.922, -.98, -.981	Vol. 14, 39-4.005; 39-6; 39-12.004, -.011; 39-23.006-.008; 39-23.088
Georgia	27-5-1, -2, -4, -5, -7	391-4-2-.06; 391-4-3-.12
Hawaii	142-94, 150A-6, -7, -8; 197-3	Title 4, ch. 18, 71; Title 13, ch. 124
Idaho	36-104(6), -701	13K 1, 5.4, 7; 13L3
Illinois	8 §240; 56 §10-100, -105; 61 §2.2, 2.3	17 IAC 3,1-6.7, -10-1, -10-11
Indiana	14-2-7-20, -21	310 IAC 3.1-6.7, -10-1, -10-11
Iowa	109.20, -.47, -.83	none
Kansas	32-965, -1004	23-16-1; 115-20-3
Kentucky	150.180	301 KAR1:115; -:120; -:122; 1:171; 2:040; 2:080
Louisiana	56:20; 56:319, -:319.1	Title 76, §107
Maine	7 §1809, 12 §6071, -7202, -7204, -7237, -7237a, -7239, -7240, -7613	Tab 402, Pt. IV, §7.60; Dept. Marine Res. regs. ch. 24

(Continues)

Key State Statutes and Regulations on Importation and Release of Fish and Wildlife

State	Statutory authority	Authority in regulations
Maryland	Agric. Code 5-601; Health-Gen. 18-219, 24-109; Nat. Res. 4-11A-02, 10-903	08.02.14.05, -.07; 08.03.09.0; 08.02.11.05K
Massachusetts	131 §19, -19A, -23	321 CMR 2.12, -9.00-9.02
Michigan	300.253 §3.(1), -(8), 300.257; 300.258(m) 304.2 §2(a); 305.9; 308.115a; 317.81	Wildlife Conservation Act Comm. Order update 92, 9/17/91: §§4.2, 5.2, 5.5
Minnesota	17.45, -.497; 84.967, -.968, -.9691; 97C.515, -.521	Dept. of Nat. Res. Comm. Order No. 2450, published in June 22, 1992, State Register, ch. 6216, 6250
Mississippi	75-40-113; 79-22-9, -11	Dept. of Wildlife Conservation Public Notice Nos. 1405, 2768
Missouri	252.190; 578.023	3 CSR 10-4.110, -.134
Montana	75-1-201; 87-3-105, -210, -221; 87-4-424	12.7.602, -.701; 12.6.1506, -.1507, -.1512, -.1514, -.1515
Nebraska	37-713, -719	Title 163m ch. 2, §§0002, 004.03, 008.08
Nevada	503.597; 504.295	503.110, -.140
New Hampshire	207:14; 211.62(e) I and II (previous provisions are reenacted in HB 1183, ch. 171 of 1992 Laws), 211:64; 212:25 and 467:3	FIS ch. 800
New Jersey	23:4-50; 23:4-63.1, -63.2, -63.3, -63.4; 23:5-30, -33.1	7:25-4.1 et seq., -5.1 et seq., -10.1 et seq.
New Mexico	17-3-32; 77-18-1	Reg. 667, ch. 5, art. 3 §A
New York	Ag. and Market Laws §74-9; Env't'l Cons. Law §11-0507, -0511, -0917, -1703, -1709, -1728	Title 6, pt. 174; pt. 180, §180.1
North Carolina	113-158, -160, -274, -291, -291.3, -292	TO:52B.0212; T15A:03B.0108; T15A:10B.0100; T15A:10C.0211
North Dakota	20.1-01-02; 20.1-02-05.14; 20.1-04-03	29-04-04-01, -03; 30-04-04

(*Continues*)

Key State Statutes and Regulations on Importation and Release of Fish and Wildlife

State	Statutory authority	Authority in regulations
Ohio	1533.31	1501.31-19-01
Oklahoma	29 §§5-1003, 6-504, 7-801	800.25-25
Oregon	498.052, -222.b, -242; 609.309	635-07-515, -522, -523, -527, -585, -600, -615, -620
Pennsylvania	30 §2102; 34 §102, -2163, -2961, -2962	58 §§71.1-71.6, 73.1-73.2, 77.7, 137.1
Rhode Island	4-11-2; 4-18-3, -5; 20-1-12; 20-10-12; 20-17-9	Dept. of Envir. Mgmt. Div. of Fish and Wildlife, Rules and Regs., nos. 61-63; Dept. of Health, Rules and Regs., R4-18-IWA, §§2.0, 3.0, 4.0
South Carolina	50-11-1760; 50-13-1630; 50-16-20, -40, -60	none
South Dakota	41-2-18, -3.13, -13.1, -13.3	41:07:01:11; 41:09:01:02; 41:09:02:02; 41:09:02:06.01; 41:09:08; 41:14:01
Tennessee	70-2-212; 70-4-401,	Rules of Tenn. Wildlife Resources Agency, -403, -412 ch. 1660-1-18-.01(5), -.02(2), -.02(5), -.03(1), -.03(4), -.03(5)
Texas	Ag. Code §134.020; Parks and Wildlife Code §12.015, 66.007	31 TAC 52.202-.401, 55.201 et seq., 57.111 et seq., 57.251 et seq.
Utah	23-13-5, -14	R657-3-1 et seq., -16-1 et seq.
Vermont	10 §4605, -4709	Fish and Wildlife Regs. Governing Importation of Wild Birds and Animals
Virginia	28.1-183.2; 29.1-521, -531, -542, -545	325-01-1. sec. 5, 325-01-2. secs. 1-4; 325-02-27 §§12, 13; 325-03-1 §§5, 6
Washington	75.08.295; 77.12.020, -.030, -.040; 77.16.150	220-20-039, -040; 232-12-017, -271
West Virginia	20-1-2; 20-2-13	none
Wisconsin	29.47(6), -.51, -.535	NR 19.05; 105.03
Wyoming	23-1-302; 23-3-301; 23-4-101	Game and Fish Comm. regs., ch. X

APPENDIX TABLE 3
Prominent Decision-Making Protocols

Codes of Practice and Manual of Procedures for Consideration of Introductions and Transfers of Marine and Freshwater Organisms, European Inland Fisheries Advisory Commission, Food and Agriculture Organization, United Nations, Rome, Italy, and International Council for the Exploration of the Sea, Copenhagen; revision published in 1988.

Guidelines for Introducing Foreign Organisms into the United States for the Biological Control of Weeds, Working Group on Biological Control of Weeds, joint Weed Committees of the U.S. Departments of Agriculture and Interior; revised in 1980. (The U.S. Department of Agriculture has developed several other guidelines for the importation, interstate movement, and field release of various types of organisms for biological control.)

Guidelines for Re-Introductions—Draft, Re-Introduction Specialist Group, Species Survival Commission, International Union for Conservation of Nature and Natural Resources, Gland, Switzerland; proposed in 1992.

IUCN Position Statement on Translocation of Living Organisms, International Union for Conservation of Nature and Natural Resources, Gland, Switzerland; approved in 1987.

Position Statement on Exotic Aquatic Organisms' Introductions, American Fisheries Society, United States; revision adopted in 1986.

Protocol for Translocation of Organisms to Islands, New Zealand; proposed in 1990.

Research Protocol for Handling Nonindigenous Aquatic Species, U.S. Fish and Wildlife Service, National Fisheries Research Center, Gainesville, Florida, adopted by the Federal Interagency Aquatic Nuisance Species Task Force in 1992.

The Planned Introduction of Genetically Engineered Organisms: Ecological Considerations and Recommendations, Ecological Society of America; proposed in 1989.

Sources: J. T. Carlton, "Man's Role in Changing the Face of the Ocean," *Conservation Biology,* 3(3) (Sept. 1989): 270–272; D. L. Klingman and J. R. Couison, "Guidelines for Introducing Foreign Organisms into the United States for the Biological Control of Weeds," *Bulletin of the Entomological Society of America* 19(3) (1983):55–61; J. M. Tiedje et al., "The Planned Introduction of Genetically Engineered Organisms: Ecological Considerations and Recommendation," *Ecology,* 70(2) (1989):298–315; D. R. Towns et al., "Protocols for Translocation of Organism to Islands," *Ecological Restoration of New Zealand Islands* (Wellington: Department of Conservation, 1990).

NOTES

1. U.S. Congress, Office of Technology Assessment, *Harmful Non-Indigenous Species in the United States,* OTA-F-565 (Washington, D.C.: Government Printing Office, 1993).

2. M. E. Gilpin and M. E. Soulé, "Minimum Viable Populations: Processes of Species Extinction," in *Conservation Biology: The Science of Scarcity and Diveristy* (Sunderland, Mass.: Sinauer, 1986), pp. 19–34.

3. OTA-F-565.

4. P. T. Jenkins, G. Nugent, and L. Maquire, "Ungulate Control in Hawaii: Recommendations for Research," Consultant's Report to Hawaii Animal Control Research Consortium (Honolulu, 1994), p. 39.

5. OTA-F-565.

6. 16 U.S.C.A. 667 et seq., 18 U.S.C.A. 42 et seq.

7. 2 U.S.C.A. 2801 et seq.

8. 42 U.S.C.A. 4321 et seq.

9. 7 U.S.C.A. 136; 16 U.S.C.A. 4601-9 et seq.

10. 471 F. Supp. 985 (D. Hawaii 1979), aff'd 639 F.2d 495 (9th Cir. 1981).

Chapter 8

PROTECTING GLOBAL MARINE BIODIVERSITY

Suzanne Iudicello

In discussing biological diversity, it is essential to remember the marine environment. Everyone talks about the rain forest and all the insects being lost there, but indeed the ocean covers almost three-fourths of the planet and, at least in the view of some scientists, may account for more than 95 percent of the part of the biosphere that supports life. Certainly there are more types of life in the ocean than on the land.

Marine biodiversity is of vital importance to humankind. Nearly 71 percent of the earth's surface is covered by oceans, which hold 97 percent of the water on earth.[1] The oceans perform vital functions such as regulating the global climate, moderating local temperatures, removing carbon dioxide (the primary greenhouse gas) from the atmosphere, and providing a major source of protein for human consumption. In some countries, more than half of the animal protein that people eat comes from the sea.[2] In Asia, more than a billion people rely on fish as their primary source of protein, as do many other people in island nations and along the coast of Africa.[3] Marine photosynthesis produces one-third to one-half of the global oxygen supply.[4]

Moreover, the biological diversity of the oceans is an invaluable and scientific resource. The sea is far richer in major groupings (phyla) of animals than the land; nearly one-half of all animal phyla occur only in the sea.[5] Scientific researchers are now more frequently turning to the sea to search for medical cures and unique compounds. Sea sponges have provided antileukemia drugs, bone graft material has come from coral, red algae has produced diagnostic chemicals, and anti-infection compounds have come from sharkskin.[6]

Losses of marine biodiversity pose a serious threat to these vital functions and values.

THE TROUBLE WITH *MARE LIBERUM*

For most of human history, people have seen the ocean as a limitless and unchangeable resource. But the oceans are not beyond human influence, and we must act now to preserve them. For, just as on land, diversity in the sea is in jeopardy. The problem emanates from five sources of human activity: pollution, alteration of habitats of marine organisms, introduction of alien species such as the zebra mussel in the Great Lakes, climatic and atmospheric changes, and overexploitation. What are the international regimes that could be used to protect biological diversity in the ocean? The short answer is none. There are no international treaties or regimes that focus specifically on conserving diversity in the seas—partly because marine environmental conservation, the legal and institutional framework for governing human activities at sea, lags two decades behind its terrestrial counterpart.

There are, however, instruments that could contribute to the conservation of diversity: for example, the international treaties and agreements and institutions that control the way we conduct fishing. When we talk about conserving diversity, we are talking about conserving diversity at the genetic level, the species level, and the system level. Diversity does not mean merely conserving whales, or dolphins, or bluefin tuna, or tube worms; it is the whole array at every level in the system. Thus I want to offer three cautionary notes.

Caveat 1: Single-species treaties and quota setting and allocation measures are not necessarily protective of diversity in the oceans.

Caveat 2: The consensual nature of international law makes it very difficult to use broad approaches anywhere but inside a state's exclusive economic zone (EEZ); that is, its tough to get a consensus to zone an area of the ocean.

Caveat 3: International ocean law is especially protective of the traditional notion of freedom of the seas. This notion is antithetical to the assertion of a coastal state's jurisdiction over distant water fleets, over other nations, sometimes even within that country's own waters.

Overexploitation of fish is one component of a threat to biodiversity. Newspaper headlines and television news broadcasts are featuring families and entire communities in the Canadian Maritimes picketing on the docks with signs, and New England fishermen parking their cars in the streets and demonstrating. The reason is that they are angry about impending regulations. Why is there regulation impending now after all these years? It is not because of a so-called collapse of the groundfish populations off the Grand

Banks. It is because of decades of overexploitation. Today flounder and had-dock, two of the most valued groundfish species, are thought to be commer-cially extinct and may even be approaching biological extinction—something marine scientists did not think was possible of an organism that reproduces with the frequency fish do.

The Peruvian anchovy catch, another indicator and once the largest catch in the world, was growing until the 1950s and 1960s. Then it collapsed from 80 million tons to fewer than 2 million tons. The catch began to recover but is on a downturn again. In the Bering Sea, Alaskan pollock, according to peo-ple in this business, is a healthy fishery. It is now one of the world's largest single-species fisheries. In fact, it is the largest-volume fishery in the United States. But accompanying the same historic rise and growth of that fleet is a decline in seabirds, marine mammals, and other fish that depend on the juve-nile pollock as their prey.

Overfishing is even thought by some to be causing genetic changes in cer-tain fish species. Swordfish in the Atlantic, for example, have been reduced to less than 40 percent of their spawning population of two decades ago. The average size of a mature female swordfish today is less than 70 pounds; twenty years ago, such a fish would have weighed between 115 and 200 pounds. The taking of the mature large fish, because of their high value, has been so intense that as a reproduction mechanism, the species are reaching sexual maturity at a younger and younger age and spawning earlier and ear-lier: babies having babies.

These are but a few examples of the result of a centuries-old tradition of *mare liberum,* freedom of the seas. This is the guiding principle of most ocean governance and is certainly behind fishery management—or lack of it, depending on your perspective. Documented catches of fish rose from a mere 5 million tons in 1900, to a peak of 86 million tons in 1986, before being forced downward.[7] For many years fishers kept the catch numbers climbing by abandoning overexploited stocks and concentrating on new species. The unsustainability of this trend is reflected in the decline in catches that has occurred since 1986.[8] When examining diversity, we have to remember that freedom of the seas and freedom of fishing are very old concepts indeed. They have been around a long time, so we have a lot to overcome in terms of our advocacy.

When examining international treaties that set quotas and allocations of those quotas, we cannot be concerned only with the directed catch—for example, how many swordfish are officially taken. The other concern is that indirect catch, also called by-catch, or incidental take, may be an even greater threat to diversity than targeted fishing. Researchers estimate that in the Dutch region of the North Sea, large trawlers rake every square meter of the seabed annually, plowing over the inhabitants: plants, worms, crustaceans, and other organisms.[9] The shrimp fisheries of the world throw away 10 pounds of marine organisms for every pound of shrimp landing at the port. Longlines, driftnets, purse seines, and virtually every type of fishing gear can be operated and applied indiscriminately. In the process, fishermen haul up and throw overboard dead turtles, seabirds, marine mammals, and billions of pounds of fish a year.

ATTACKING THE PROBLEM

What should we do about this—and why is it happening? Demand for food for the world's increasing population has accelerated fishing efforts. The United Nations Food and Agriculture Organization (FAO) estimates that virtually every commercially exploited species has been depleted, overexploited, or fully exploited and that something must be done quickly. The FAO once estimated 100 million pounds a year of potential production from the world's fisheries, but this may be an unachievable dream. For the first time in the history of fishing, the annual catch has declined in the world for three consecutive years after centuries of continuous growth. Twice as much money, vessels, technology, and effort is being invested and yet we cannot seem to pull out the fish. Worldwide expenditures on fishing amount to an estimated $124 billion . . . in order to catch only $70 billion in fish.[10] Obviously government subsidies are keeping more people fishing than the environment can support.[11] Less clear, but no less disturbing, are the implications of churning the seabed, raking the eelgrass, discarding tons of unwanted carcasses, or grinding them up to be applied on land as fertilizer.

A limited number of regimes and frameworks have been created to regulate ocean and distant-water fisheries. Few have conservation of fish as their primary strategy. For many, the objective is to maximize the catch of fish of a commercial species on behalf of the industry working with the fishery. The idea of maximum sustainable yield—the driving idea behind fisheries management—is that you make sure you take out of the ocean as much fish as you can, leaving just exactly enough so that there is something the next time around. Of course, the precautionary principle has been lost in the rush to catch the fish. If conservation of marine biodiversity—including marine species that are not the target of a market—is the goal, then advocates must look to other sources of international law.

What are some of the possibilities for getting a handle on this problem? One of the obvious handles is the United Nations Convention on the Law of the Sea (UNCLOS). After unsuccessful attempts to widen coastal state jurisdiction, the 1982 conference extended jurisdiction to 200 miles, placing limitations on freedom of fishing on the high seas and qualifying rights of distant-water fishing nations. The United States signed UNCLOS III on July 29,

1994,[12] after resolving long-standing concerns regarding its deep-seabed mining provisions,[13] but has not yet ratified the treaty. The precise status of the United States in regard to UNCLOS III may be irrelevant, however, because many important fishing countries, the United States among them, have incorporated into their domestic laws the principles reflected in the convention.[14] Many experts have agreed that "UNCLOS is not only a treaty but a codification and articulation of the present state of the rules applicable to the oceans" and, as such, is binding on both signatories and nonsignatories as customary international law,[15] especially those provisions related to international navigation and the rights and duties of coastal states.[16]

Article 56 of the convention gives coastal states sovereign rights out to 200 miles, including authority to conserve and manage living resources (Article 61). The coastal nation must ensure, using conservation and management measures, that the living resources of the EEZ are not threatened by overexploitation. The 1982 conference did, however establish a few limitations— namely, access to a nation's fishery zone by a foreign vessel was solely within the jurisdiction of the coastal state, within its discretion and subject to its laws and regulations.

Moreover, the conference imposed new obligations on high-seas fishing nations to facilitate conservation and to devise cooperative regimes to manage the high-seas fisheries. For the straddling stocks—those that occur both within the EEZ and in an area beyond and adjacent to the EEZ—they were urged to seek such regional mechanisms. For highly migratory species (defined in UNCLOS as tuna, tunalike species, and certain cetaceans that move considerable distances over vast expanses of ocean), the convention requires parties to cooperate directly or through appropriate international organizations for conservation. Despite this direction, certain species, particularly highly migratory ones, continued to decline. Some of these declines gave rise to the Mexico Conference on Responsible Fishing in 1992, followed by the UN Conference on Highly Migratory and Straddling Stocks in 1993, the latter an outgrowth of sessions at the Rio Earth Summit.[17]

This, then, is the international regime. Problems and ambiguities in the UNCLOS regime remain: lack of enforcement mechanisms, dispute resolution, compatibility between domestic and international management, consistency in measures throughout the range of fish, monitoring for compliance, information collection, and reduction of effort and other concerns. Essentially it is lacking what most other international regimes have, namely enforcement, and everything depends on the consent of the parties. But a regime does exist and it does have some guiding principles.

Regional fishery organizations and agreements, while somewhat more efficient at fishery management, also have their shortcomings. These organizations include the International Convention on the Conservation of Atlantic Tunas (ICCAT), fondly known to some as the "international convention to catch all the tuna." Also included are the International North Pacific Fisheries Commission (INPFC), the Inter-American Tropical Tuna Commission (IATTC), the Northwest Atlantic Fisheries Convention (NAFO), and the International Pacific Halibut Commission (IPHC). Several regional organizations are aimed at very specific single-species regimes: salmon in the North Pacific, halibut as it occurs between the United States and Canada, and Atlantic salmon disputes between the United States and Canada. They are singularly oriented to one type of fish and focus on such issues as "how much do you get?" and "how much do I get?" and "how fast do we catch them?" While their stated objectives may be to conserve the stocks they target, in reality they are aimed at maximizing the catch of a particular species, not conserving diversity. Recently a few of these bodies have explored other management measures, such as efforts to reduce by-catch through improved gear technology, fishing operations, and practices.[18]

Conservationists, however, have been able to use these regional agreements to reach beyond issues of the target catch. For example, it was the U.S. implementation of the allocation of salmon to Japan under the INPFC that entrained the series of events leading to the *Kokechik* case.[19] In that case the court, in construing the Marine Mammal Protection Act of 1972,[20] held that the secretary of commerce could not grant permission to a group of Japanese fishermen to "take" a quota of Dall's porpoise when the secretary knew that other protected species, such as fur seals, would also be ensnared. The court found that the agency could not issue a permit for only one of the protected species when it knew others would be taken as well, despite the fishery's inability to meet the conditions allowing such takes. This court decision was responsible for the shutdown of driftnetting in the North Pacific for one summer.

Conservationists should examine treaties and conventions for ways to expand directives beyond their principal aims. The INPFC was basically an agreement among the United States, Japan, and Canada determining how many salmon, squid, and so forth the Japanese were going to be allowed to catch in U.S. waters. But it was also the framework of the convention that enabled environmentalists to push for observers to grapple with the driftnet issue. Similarly, the ICCAT treaty governing Atlantic tuna continues to be used by the convention to moderately scale down the catches. The Convention on International Trade in Endangered Species (CITES) is a multilateral treaty regarding the export, import, and transit of certain species of wild animals and plants—trade that poses a threat to their continued survival. The goal of the convention is to prevent overexploitation of listed species whose survival is jeopardized. And while it is somewhat effective as a conservation tool, it kicks in only after a severe depletion of listed species and does not act to protect species before they are threatened with extinction. Environmentalists in 1992 and 1994 threatened attempts to list a marine fish—the Western Atlantic bluefin tuna, along with some other highly valuable commercial species—in various appendixes of CITES, an action that would have required monitoring the trade in those fish, and then pushed for more stringent measures in the actual setting of quotas.

THE BIG STICK: TRADE SANCTIONS

The United States has used domestic legislation successfully to pursue goals of marine species preservation on an international scale. Such measures could be used by other nations to pursue conservation of marine biodiversity. Certainly one nation can influence the behavior of other nations toward marine species through trade and economic measures—for example, by imposing trade sanctions and measures against nations engaging in environmentally destructive behavior. Other methods are more direct and aim at halting the destructive behavior itself—such as imposing bans on fishing threatened stocks or bans on certain fishing methods.

For more than twenty years, the threat of trade sanctions has been a fundamental instrument of U.S. international fisheries and marine conservation policy.[21] Domestic statutes such as the Marine Mammal Protection Act, the Endangered Species Act of 1973, the Lacey Act Amendments of 1981, and the 1989 Sea Turtle Conservation Amendments to the Endangered Species Act all contain provisions restricting the importation of fisheries products from nations refusing to comply with U.S. environmental standards for protecting marine living resources. One key measure is the Pelly Amendment to the Fisherman's Protective Act,[22] which a variety of other acts have invoked in their embargo provisions. Under the Pelly Amendment, the secretaries of commerce and interior are authorized to determine whether foreign nations are acting in a way that threatens the effectiveness of an international fishery conservation agreement or international program for endangered or threatened species—and if so, to make an official certification.[23] Once a certification has been made regarding a foreign nation, the president may prohibit imports from that country.[24]

The use of unilateral trade sanctions has increased since 1990, and these methods of achieving compliance with environmental standards have the advantages of allowing timely action and being less expensive than international negotiations. These sanctions are perceived by a broad spectrum of political constituent groups as the most effective method, and possibly the only feasible method in some cases, for changing foreign nations' behavior.[25] Those groups include environmental organizations, commercial and recreational fishermen, labor unions, and consumer protection advocates, among others. The use of unilateral trade sanctions has also received broad support in Congress.[26]

This approach may be constrained, however, under the General Agreement on Tariffs and Trades (GATT) and, potentially, under UNCLOS III. Recent actions taken under GATT have been distinctly hostile to the use of trade sanctions to achieve environmental goals.[27] An additional problem could arise if the United States becomes a state party to UNCLOS III, and the convention enters into force. The international community has long expressed hostility toward the use of unilateral trade sanctions by the United States and can be expected to use all available methods to challenge such practices, since these trade sanctions potentially violate many substantive rights provided in UNCLOS III.[28] If the United States became a state party, then other state parties could rely on the convention's compulsory dispute settlement provisions to prevent U.S. imposition of unilateral sanctions.[29] While international law does not explicitly prohibit such unilateral measures for political purposes, there is a consensus among legal scholars that such measures are impermissible where a state is a party to an agreement that contains a dispute settlement mechanism.[30] Resolving these issues could have a significant impact on the ability of individual nations to impose unilateral trade sanctions to further goals of conserving marine biodiversity on an international scale.

BEYOND TRADE SANCTIONS

Other ways to address international behavior threatening marine biodiversity are more direct than trade sanctions—measures such as direct bans on fishing certain types of stocks, for example, and the use of specific types of fishing gear or methods. An example of this type of method is the campaign against the use of large-scale driftnets on the high seas. Driftnets kill staggering numbers of nontarget species, including whales, dolphins, turtles, and birds.[31] Indeed, environmental activism created a swell in public opinion against driftnet fishing that led to U.S. domestic legislation such as the Driftnet Impact Monitoring, Assessment, and Control Act of 1987.[32] The concern demonstrated over the impact of driftnets, not only from the United States but internationally, prompted the UN General Assembly to declare a moratorium on large-scale pelagic driftnet fisheries that began December 31, 1992.[33] Marine biodiversity can be positively affected by such campaigns.

But threats other than overexploitation must also be addressed, such as the physical alteration of ecosystems, pollution, the introduction of alien species, and atmospheric changes, namely global warming and climate change. Ecosystems can be totally destroyed—or fragmented to such an extent that they can no longer function—by activities such as logging, construction of marinas, dredging, and mining. Coastal wetlands, coral reefs, and other ecosystems are being converted or degraded at rates that are disturbingly high by historical standards,[34] and many marine species are threatened with extinction, owing mostly to habitat loss. Minimal efforts, if any, have been made internationally to deal with this crisis and its effects on marine biodiversity—with one exception, a recent initiative by the International Union for the Conservation of Nature (IUCN), which has undertaken efforts to conserve coral reefs.[35]

Certainly there are possibilities for addressing environmental harm from atmospheric changes. The Vienna Convention for the Protection of the Ozone Layer, for example, was adopted on March 22, 1985, and entered into force on September 22, 1988.[36] This convention, which provides for general aims of research and monitoring ozone depletion, also specifically provides for the adoption of protocols and annexes. The Montreal Protocol on Substances That Deplete the Ozone Layer, adopted in September 1987, addresses how atmospheric change may affect diversity and is considered one of the most significant international achievements for protecting the environment from adverse effects caused by humans. Several marine environment conventions are concerned with dumping and accidental spills of oil and hazardous materials. Land-based activity, rather than vessel or marine activity, has been recognized as the major source of marine pollution.[37] Pollution can come from sewage (nutrients), chemicals, toxins, and sediments. Domestic clean water legislation, while not directed specifically at ocean degradation, has been a help. Broader coordination for pollution efforts has come from such sources as the UN Environmental Program's adoption in 1985 of the Montreal Guidelines for the Protection of the Marine Environment Against Pollution from Land-Based Sources, which encourages states and international organizations to use the guidelines in developing bilateral, regional, and global agreements to control pollution.

In sum, then, there are tools among international and regional authorities to conserve marine biodiversity against the threats of overexploitation, ecosystem degradation, pollution, and atmospheric change. The problem is that these tools were not designed specifically for this purpose. Just as the scientific and marine resource management communities wrestle with new concepts like biodiversity, the legal community must begin integrating cross-disciplinary, multifaceted concepts into both international and regional legal regimes. For now, at least, advocates are faced with the challenge of sharpening the tools for the job of marine biodiversity conservation.[38]

NOTES

1. Peter Weber, *Abandoned Seas: Reversing the Decline of the Oceans,* Worldwatch Paper 116 (Washington, D.C.: Worldwatch Institute, 1993), p. 5.

2. Elliot Norse, *Global Marine Biological Diversity* (Washington, D.C.: Center for Marine Conservation, 1993), p. xviii.

3. Weber, *Abandoned Seas,* p 9.

4. Ibid., p. 8.

5. Norse, *Global Marine,* p. xxviii.

6. Weber, *Abandoned Seas,* pp. 10–11.

7. Ibid., p. 32.

8. Ibid., pp. 32–33.

9. Ibid., p. 36. See also Norse, *Global Marine,* pp. 110–111.

10. Weber, *Abandoned Seas,* p. 47.

11. Ibid., pp. 45–46.

12. *Congressional Record,* vol. 140, no. 101, S. 9975–76, and S. 10046–48, July 28, 1994.

13. John P. Wise, *Federal Conservation and Management of Marine Fisheries in the United States* (Washington, D.C.: Center for Marine Conservation, 1991), p. 49.

14. Ibid., p. 109.

15. Ibid., pp. 109–110, citing M. H. Belsky, "The Ecosystem Mandate for a Comprehensive United States Ocean Policy and Law of the Sea," *San Diego Law Review* 26(3) (1989): 417–495.

16. Louis B. Sohn and Kristen Gustafson, *The Law of the Sea* (St. Paul: West, 1984), pp. xix–xxx.

17. The United Nations Conference on Straddling Fish Stocks and Highly Migratory Fish Stocks was convened to explore areas for international cooperation in the conservation and management of species such as tuna, which migrate over long distances through national and international waters, and species such as cod or pollock, which straddle both fishing state EEZ's as well as international waters. The parties concluded an *Agreement for the Implementation of the Provisions on the United Nations Convention on the Law of the Sea of 10 December 1982 Relating to the Conservation and Management of Straddling Fish Stocks and Highly Migratory Fish Stocks.* It sets out a framework for and encourages regional agreements among fishing nations that taget these stocks. The elements include adoption of the precautionary principal, international cooperation, consistency in conservation measures outside Exclusive Economic Zones, enforcement provisions and dispute settlement. The Agreement also contains provisions urging nations to accomplish data collection, information sharing, and bycatch reduction.

18. Wise, *Federal Conservation,* pp. 93–103.

19. *Kokechik Fishermen's Ass'n v. Secretary of Commerce,* 839 F.2d 795 (D.C. Cir. 1988), *cert. denied,* 488 U.S. 1004, 109 S.Ct 783 (1989).

20. 16 USC §§1361–1407 (1982 & Supp. III, 1985).

21. Richard J. McLaughlin, "UNCLOS and the Demise of the United States' Use of Trade Sanctions to Protect Dolphins, Sea Turtles, Whales and Other International Marine Living Resources," *Ecology Law Quarterly* (1994):7.

22. 22 USC §1878.

23. 22 USC §1978(a)(1)–(2).

24. 22 USC §1978(a)(4).

25. McLaughlin, "UNCLOS," pp. 14–15, 25.

26. Ibid., p. 75.

27. Norse, *Global Marine,* p. 211. For a discussion of the use of the GATT response to trade restrictions in the import of tuna caught with purse seines that encircle dolphins, see Stephen Fleisher, "The Mexico–U.S. Tuna/Dolphin Dispute in GATT: Exploring the Use of Trade Restrictions to Enforce Environmental Standard," *Transnational and Contemporary Problems* 3 (1993):515.

28. McLaughlin, "UNCLOS," pp. 20, 76.

29. Ibid., pp 29, 42.

30. Ibid., pp. 65, 76–77.

31. Norse, *Global Marine,* pp. 93–94.

32. 16 USC §1822.

33. General Assembly Resolution 46/125. See also Norse, *Global Marine,* p. 94.

34. *World Development Report 1992: Development and the Environment,* Executive Summary (Washington, D.C.: World Bank, 1992), p. 6.

35. UN Environment Program, "Reefs at Risk: Coral Reefs, Human Use, and Global Climate Change," October 1993.

36. 26 I.L.M. 1529 (1987).

37. Moira L. McConnell, "The Modern Law of the Sea: Framework for the Protection and Preservation of the Marine Environment?" *Case Western Reserve Journal of International Law* 23 (Winter 1991):87.

38. For two excellent resources on laws to protect ocean diversity, see Eugene H. Buck, *Aquatic Research Laws and Treaties: Reference Guide* (Washington D.C.: Congressional Research Service Report for Congress, Library of Congress, 1989), and U.S. International Trade Commission, *International Agreements to Protect the Environment and Wildlife,* Report to the Committee on Finance, U.S. Senate, Investigation No. 332-287, January 1991.

Chapter 9

Biodiversity Conservation and International Instruments

Scott Hajost and Curtis Fish

As other chapters in this book discuss specific biodiversity initiatives evolving from the Rio Earth Summit and elsewhere, particularly the Convention on Biological Diversity (CBD), this chapter examines other international institutions related to Agenda 21 that affect biodiversity protection worldwide. Although this discussion will focus on the UN Commission on Sustainable Development (CSD) and the Global Environment Facility (GEF), we begin by examining a few other legal instruments and entities of particular importance.

Climate, Ozone, and Agenda 21

It is now well recognized that global climate change may present one of the most significant long-term threats to biodiversity, particularly natural ecosystems. For example, it is estimated that the current pace of climate change may drown or bleach coral reefs due to rising sea levels and temperatures. Moreover, increased carbon dioxide in coastal waters may act synergistically with surrounding nutrients to inflict further harm on coral health. With countless other effects on both flora and fauna, climate change poses serious and irreversible threats to biodiversity. The Climate Change Convention signed in Rio promises to address these threats directly—especially to stabilize greenhouse gas concentrations in the atmosphere to prevent human interference with the climate system. The Climate Convention defines in ecological terms that relate to the concentration of greenhouse gases. The treaty expressly states that the time frame of the objective must be sufficient to ensure the health of the world's ecosystems. This involves the identification of atmospheric concentration levels that will enable terrestrial and marine ecosystems to adapt to warming trends safely, as well as the monitoring and preservation of natural carbon reservoirs.[1] This in turn makes implementation of the Climate Convention a priority for biodiversity conservation. Indeed, the closer one examines the objectives and operation of the Climate Convention, the more the protection of biodiversity appears central to the stabilization of our climate system.

Apart from the Climate Treaty, the Montreal Protocol represents another international legal instrument of particular importance to the preservation of biodiversity. The protocol addresses the depletion and outright loss of the protective stratospheric ozone layer due to the use of chlorofluorocarbons (CFCs and other ozone-depleting substances) that allow ultraviolet radiation to penetrate the earth's atmosphere. This radiation not only endangers phytoplankton but results in marine life disruptions of unknown magnitude. Although these threats to biodiversity are currently being addressed by the Montreal Protocol, substantial action is still required to ensure a phaseout of all ozone-depleting substances including methyl bromide and Hydro-CFCs.

Agenda 21—the "charter" for the CSD and the GEF—is often described as the blueprint that resulted from the 1992 Earth Summit in Rio. There are forty chapters in Agenda 21, including a specific chapter on biodiversity protection as well as a variety of other chapters relating directly to biodiversity, such as those pertaining to oceans, fresh water, fragile mountain systems, deforestation, desertification, land use, and agriculture. Other chapters of Agenda 21 relate to biodiversity in a less direct manner: protection of the atmosphere, sustainable agriculture, and environmentally sound management of biotechnology. Agenda 21 also addresses what are known as cross-sectoral issues—issues that impact many different aspects of biodiversity protection—including women's rights, indigenous people's rights, technology transfer, international trade, and the integration of sustainable environmental policies in multilateral development financing and other international decision making. In short, all the chapters in Agenda 21 hold promise, directly or indirectly, as avenues through which to promote the conservation, sustainable use, and benefit sharing of biodiversity.

THE CSD: ORIGINS AND MANDATE

Ensuring biodiversity protection worldwide requires institutional follow-up to Agenda 21, the agreement signed in Rio, as well as other international agreements and institutions. To provide a watchdog over the blueprint that came out of Agenda 21, the countries of the world created the UN Commission on Sustainable Development. The UN General Assembly framed the CSD's guidelines, general composition, and procedure in UN Resolution 47/191. Officially the UN Economic and Social Council established the CSD as a high-level commission designed to "ensure effective monitoring, coordination and supervision of the involvement of the United Nations system in the follow-up to the [Rio] Conference."[2] Realistically, however, it remains to be seen whether the CSD will acquire the power it needs to fulfill its mandate. A checkup is due in 1997, when the General Assembly expects to review the CSD and the general implementation of Agenda 21.

The CSD had its first meeting in June 1993. At that point, the CSD outlined a thematic work program to examine resource and development issues with an eye toward implementing the goals of Agenda 21. Biodiversity, however, did not make it onto the work program for 1994. Instead, the CSD directed its attention first to human health, human habitats, toxics, and water quality. Although all of these topics relate to the protection of biodiversity—particularly water quality and protection of aquatic ecosystems—the CSD elected to focus on biodiversity as an independent topic in a later year. Thus the CSD will address biodiversity, along with land desertification and forests, with the consideration of the oceans and atmosphere in 1996.

In addition to establishing a five-year workplan, the 1993 CSD meeting also set up two subsidiary bodies to examine technology transfer and finance. These groups have prepared recommendations for providing adequate financing for developing countries to address the key Agenda 21 issues and identify technology for promotion. The group on technology has been dissolved, however, and a portion of its portfolio folded into the finance group.

Results to Date

The CSD completed its second session in May 1994 with many fearing that, without improved commitment and direction, the watchdog of Agenda 21 would develop a bark more powerful than its bite. While the CSD has been criticized for not encouraging substantive dialogue and failing to effectively present national reports submitted to the Secretariat, it should be remembered that the CSD is still quite young. Meanwhile, organizations tracking the CSD's progress remain hopeful that the commission will become an important forum for discussions regarding cross-sectoral as well as emerging issues relevant to sustainable development. Because the Convention on Biological Diversity also involves numerous cross-sectoral and emerging issues, the CSD might well assist in advancing the biodiversity dialogue in support of the Biodiversity Convention.

At its annual meeting in 1994 the CSD adopted seven decisions, some quite relevant to the conservation of biodiversity. These decisions involved consumption and production patterns, indicators for sustainable development, reporting guidelines, trade and environment, major groups (nongovernmental organizations, women, children, unions), and technology transfer—all important concerns for biodiversity. Perhaps most significant the CSD decided to create an intercessional working group to investigate the sectoral issues that the commission will be addressing, including biodiversity.

NGO Involvement

The CSD has also expanded the forum in which biodiversity and other issues are debated by encouraging and promoting nongovernmental organizations (NGOs) within the CSD process. Although the CSD is comprised of representatives of fifty-three different governments, it has also integrated NGOs. The value of nongovernmental involvement in investigatory and deliberative processes such as those the CSD pursues has been well established. NGO activities at both the initial Rio Summit and the first Conference of the Parties to the Biodiversity Convention in 1994 mark particularly effective NGO efforts in the biodiversity context alone. Moreover, the CSD may find it possible to leverage this NGO influence beyond its own parameters. For instance, if the CSD's requests for reports from relevant UN bodies, specialized agencies, and other organizations and international parties regarding their implementation of Agenda 21 are fulfilled, then, by virtue of their involvement with the CSD (here acting as a conduit of sorts), accredited NGOs might review and comment upon the reports of the numerous entities whose actions may implement or impede the objectives of the Biodiversity Convention. While many NGOs have closely monitored the activities of the CSD, others have discussed technical and procedural matters through the CSD itself. Overall the outlook for future NGO involvement is bright. Indeed, the CSD officially encourages governments and international organizations to make efforts toward strengthening NGO involvement in the implementation of Agenda 21.[3]

Relationship to UN Bodies

Another aspect of the CSD that may have a significant impact on international biodiversity efforts is the commission's eventual stature relative to other UN bodies and international organizations. Despite its broad mandate to oversee implementation of Agenda 21, the CSD is a functional commission of the United Nations Economic and Social Council (ECOSOC) and, as such, may only make recommendations to other UN bodies. This limitation, coupled with its limited resources, no doubt inhibits the powers of the CSD.

Still, the commission remains a high-level body within the UN that may one day influence major environmental and development issues at a multilateral level. In support of this evolution, the past two annual meetings of the CSD have been attended by environment ministers from many of its members. These high-level segments have greatly elevated the CSD's prominence within the world community and may advance the level of CSD activities.

Assessment of the CSD

It is perhaps in the function of impact assessment that the CSD may best champion the main objectives of the Biodiversity Convention: conservation, sustainable use, and benefit sharing. Environmental impact and policy statements play central roles in the effort to integrate environmental assessments into international economic decisions. The UN Environment Program (UNEP) has a fair amount of experience in developing environmental impact and assessment procedures at international levels. Indeed, the Biodiversity Convention itself has a requirement for environmental impact assessment regarding biodiversity. Yet there remains a need for a more effective system of assessing impacts on biodiversity. This need most certainly extends to the multilateral development banks that possess, at least on paper, environmental review procedures for natural resource impacts. The UN General Assembly has officially requested that all specialized agencies and related organizations of the UN "strengthen and adjust their activities, programs and medium-term plans . . . in line with Agenda 21."[4] Moreover, the CSD itself should receive reports from UN bodies, the World Bank, and other international finance institutions, thereby exercising its capacity to recommend specific courses of action to the General Assembly. In this manner, the CSD may promote the development of a more coordinated and more effective system of assessing the environmental impacts inextricably associated with the policies and actions of the world's financial and development institutions, as well as the member countries of the UN.

Relation to the Biodiversity Convention

The CSD's relationship with other international organizations will undoubtedly continue to evolve. In fact, one of the toughest negotiations during the initial CSD deliberations involved a possible role for the CSD in monitoring and receiving reports from the various international environmental agreements, such as the Biodiversity Convention. Many countries insisted the governing bodies of these conventions and treaties should remain independent—that is, free of reporting requirements to the CSD. This strange notion of sovereignty floated about these discussions even though the CSD's mandate falls totally within the purview of most such international agreements. Fortunately, the first Conference of the Parties to the Convention on Biological Diversity did prepare a report to the CSD. When involved with broad issues like biodiversity, however, the CSD will simply not be able to progress unless it receives reports from the wide variety of international institutions that affect biodiversity—above and beyond the Biodiversity Convention itself. In other words, international coordination has grown increasingly vital. A symbiotic relationship between these governing bodies promises to leverage their individual efforts, a key consideration given the present scarcity of environmental assistance. Accordingly, the CSD should communicate with other multilateral and bilateral entities such as the Group of Seven.

Questions and Challenges

Now that we have reviewed the CSD's potential roles in the conservation, sustainable use, and benefit sharing of biodiversity, a big question remains: what is the likelihood of such roles being fulfilled? A major concern of those who strongly support the CSD as an effective monitor for Earth Summit actions relative to biodiversity is whether the CSD will actually receive useful reports and important information from governments and international institutions. As we have seen, the CSD must have this information if it is to make effective recommendations and monitor progress. It is not clear just how effective the CSD will be: it does not have an operational capacity, it has a limited staff and resources, and the type of reporting that is required allows countries simply to reproduce all their relevant laws as a way of complying with Agenda 21. A recent U.S. response, for example, is largely a summation of all U.S. laws that relate to Agenda 21.

Another challenge for the CSD will be its ability to make recommendations on critical issues that countries will abide by—and then get adequate information on how these countries are doing. Here nongovernmental groups are likely to assume critical roles in examining national performance, as well as the effectiveness of international agreements and institutions. The Consortium for Action to Protect the Earth (CAPE) has launched an initiative to identify four critical actions governments can take to show the concrete steps they have taken to implement Agenda 21.[5] The fact remains, though, that Agenda 21 represents nothing more than a blueprint with a variety of recommendations of what governments can do on the ground. For example, one of the problems CAPE 2000 cited is water quality. Has a country listed its polluted river basins and agreed to clean them up and report on their activities? For two years this coalition has tried to produce hard information through an extensive set of questionnaires sent out to governments to see if anything concrete is happening, as opposed to ethereal speeches and presentations. Moreover, it has strongly promoted concrete policy analysis—such as its successful efforts in the 1994 CSD session that obtained U.S. and CSD endorsements of a global phaseout of leaded gasoline.

Yet another key question concerns the extent to which the CSD can influence the tremendous amount of financing that currently flows from an array of financial institutions such as the World Bank. This financing, as well as sources of private-sector financing, often has a negative impact on biodiversity.[6] It is important not only to identify financing and technology that promotes biodiversity, but also to identify the billions of dollars that are directed to regional development banks and the World Bank for projects—such as large-scale hydropower and forestry development—that prove destructive to biodiversity. The proposed Three Gorges Dam in China, for example, the largest hydroelectric project in the world, will flood an area over 400 miles long. This dam, if financed to completion, will drive an unknown number of species to extinction—among them the Yangtze River dolphin. The areas to be flooded and disrupted are also home to endangered species of alligator and tiger, not to mention well over one million people. In Nepal, a similar proposal appears likely to dam the Arun River system. Although the CSD has not tackled this type of conflict directly, large-scale energy and infrastructure projects are clearly within its portfolio. The CSD should position itself to recommend appropriate reforms to international financial policies that conflict with the goals of the Rio Earth Summit and treaties such as the Biodiversity Convention as well as the Convention on Climate Change. The timing for such reform is excellent. Many governments have already begun to review well-established international institutions such as the World Bank and the International Monetary Fund.

THE GEF GENESIS AND PURPOSE

In 1991 the UN Development Program (UNDP), the UN Environment Program (UNEP), and the World Bank created the Global Environment Facility (GEF). Developed as a pilot project to address global environmental issues, the GEF now functions as a multilateral financial institution implementing the objectives of several international treaties. To some extent the GEF represents a response to the complaint that normal bilateral and multilateral channels allow global environmental problems to continue unaddressed. Many countries have argued that traditional economic assistance suffers from insufficient funding directed at environmental issues. The four focal points for the pilot phase were climate change, biodiversity, international waters, and ozone depletion. The GEF's ozone portfolio remained very small because the Montreal Protocol already sends substantial funding to developing countries to eliminate CFCs and other ozone-depleting substances. Over half of all GEF pilot projects were directed to biodiversity, however, accounting for 43 percent of all GEF funding.

After difficult negotiations between Northern and Southern countries, both the biodiversity and the climate conventions named the GEF as an interim financing mechanism. Difficulties arose here, however, because of the North's opposition to a plethora of unrestricted funds for various climate, biodiversity, and desertification conventions. Instead, these developed countries sought a central fund to appropriate money for all such "global problems" cited in the various framework treaties. Developing countries, however, argued the GEF should assume a broader agenda that would fund projects related to the full scope of Agenda 21, whether of global or local benefit.

Process and Priorities

This fundamental tension over the criteria governing the allocation of GEF funds has remained a contentious debate. How should the GEF define global benefits as compared to local benefits? If the two overlap, who should pay for these benefits? No ready solutions appear on the horizon. For now, both the Climate and the Biodiversity Conventions employ a concept called "incremental costs." Although this approach has resisted resolution in the biodiversity context, it may, at least in theory, assist in resolving the local/global benefits and costs dispute.

Incremental costs represent those expenses incurred in efforts to achieve global environmental benefits.[7] The Biodiversity Convention established that the developing countries would pay for the "agreed full incremental costs" that the developing countries encounter in meeting their obligations under the convention. Thus incremental costs are supposed to form the basis for grant financing within the GEF. Estimating the incremental costs requires establishing a local baseline—that is, the local cost against which other costs aimed at global benefits are to be compared. Yet the benefits of biodiversity conservation continue to resist quantification, for they involve many conceptual and political questions far from resolution. Indeed, an independent evaluation of the GEF has revealed that not one of all the biodiversity projects sampled made any reference to "incremental costs." Instead of identifying that portion of a project which qualified for incremental costs, projects were funded in cases where, but for the GEF financing, the developing countries would not have undertaken the proposed activity. As a result, GEF funds were found to "often cover the total costs of the projects."[8]

GEF's Current Status

A critical point in the evolution of the GEF was the decision, in 1992, to establish an independent evaluation team. This team reviewed GEF policies and the execution of its objectives during the pilot phase. Experts from around the world were commissioned to assess the progress and potential of the GEF, its policies, and procedures, as well as their impact on the GEF's ability to achieve its objectives. Later, in the spring of 1994, the GEF was restructured. Mohamed T. El-Ashry, chairman of the GEF, hailed this restructuring and a $2 billion replenishment as "the first major financial accomplishment since Rio."[9]

The 1992 independent evaluation raised serious questions as to the GEF's capacity to provide for effective pro-biodiversity finances in the future. The central finding was that the GEF still "lacks convincing strategic framework to guide its investments in biodiversity."[10] Although the GEF played a useful role in stimulating negotiations leading to the adoption of the Biodiversity Convention, its investments have proved misguided in several respects, providing only marginal contributions to conserving biodiversity on a global scale. In the international waters sector, for example, the GEF lacks a clear strategy to define international waters and examine their relation to marine biodiversity protection efforts.

Experts responsible for reviewing the GEF confirmed what many had already found: most GEF work has failed to respond to national biodiversity priorities. The GEF's efforts to involve local communities and nongovernmental organizations have proved inadequate. The GEF has failed to bring together the appropriate UN bodies and other international agencies whose activities affect biodiversity. Furthermore, the GEF has not given sufficient attention to building national conservation capacity.[11] As a result, most GEF projects have injected large amounts of capital and expertise into national programs that often prove unable to assimilate and utilize these resources effectively. Related to this rapid influx of capital, the evaluation confirmed a problem with the long-term financial stability of the GEF's undertakings.[12] Suffering from a lack of local and national government support, normally secured via national financing of baseline project costs, the GEF's projects ironically endanger themselves. Their sole dependence on short-term donor funding presents unreasonably high risks of failure.

In an effort to address these problems, more than eighty countries participated in a fifteen-month series of negotiations to redesign the GEF's governance and structure. In March 1994, an agreement was signed in Geneva to restructure and replenish the GEF. The GEF now consists of an Assembly, a Council, and a Secretariat. The Assembly includes representatives of all participants and meets every three years. The Council, which has only thirty-two members, representing developed, developing, and newly independent states, now develops, adopts, and evaluates the GEF's activities and policies. The Secretariat works for and provides reports to both the Assembly and the Council.

NGO Involvement

Beyond the newly restructured aspects of the GEF there remains the critical independent evaluation. Admittedly, the evaluation presents a pretty tough assessment of what is supposed to be the major avenue for financing the Bio-diversity Convention and implementing projects worldwide. Despite these shortfalls, governments have decided to support a $2 billion replenishment, stipulating provisions on public access to information, including any information on associated bank loans. Several decisions made at the November 1994 GEF Council meeting also appear promising. Two in particular may prove effective in addressing the conditions placed on replenishment as well as in realigning the GEF process to promote biodiversity. Unfortunately, the meeting did not consider a guidance policy for grant approvals within the biodiversity portfolio.

The 1994 Council's first decision established a Project Development Facility to apply criteria for the selection of projects and monitor resource allocations. Although the Project Development Facility appears promising, pressure must remain on the Council to see that the facility plays a central role in project development, not a tangential one. The facility must not impede national input, however. To promote biodiversity objectives, GEF projects must be built from the ground up. The facility should foster national input on a local level. National Environment Funds could serve as effective instruments for increasing national capacity to design, develop, and implement GEF projects.

To this end, the Council reviewed the GEF Interim Project Cycle, which will direct project development for the GEF's biodiversity efforts until the Council reaches a final decision regarding this process. The Council concluded an agreement entitled "Understanding on Interim Guidance," which notes that the first priority will be the concept of "country-driven" projects. This idea is designed to ensure that "all project concepts under review for GEF funding must be endorsed and/or approved by the host government" and "must fit into a national strategic framework and be considered by government as a priority."[13] These ideas are not necessarily new to the biodiversity community. Yet their appearance in a formal understanding of the GEF Council is significant. This understanding issued by the Council also suggested that the Project Development Facility might be "utilized by national entities to prepare programs in order that GEF funded activities are clearly linked to national programs and priorities." This would appear to move the new facility in the right direction.

The Council's second major decision resulted in an advancement for NGOs within the GEF process. The CEO of the GEF was directed to invite five NGO representatives to attend Council meetings and five others to "observe" the meetings. These ten representatives will attend or observe all Council meetings except executive sessions. Furthermore, the Council directed the GEF Secretariat to provide for the costs of NGO attendees—a decision that should broaden representation of those organizations from developing countries whose budgets seldom afford such important opportunities.

The unresolved problems remain for the parties of the Biodiversity Convention to settle. The difficulties they present became clear when the first Conference of the Parties to the Convention, held in December 1994, failed to designate the GEF as the permanent financial institution of the convention, though it was designated as the temporary one.

The Small Grants Program

The Global Environmental Facility also promotes the role of NGOs by virtue of its Small Grants Program (SGP). Created in 1991 and placed under the administration of UNDP, the Small Grants Program began distributing funds to NGOs in 1992. The program emphasizes decentralized decision making and has encouraged the adoption of program strategies by many participating countries. After receiving a positive review by the independent GEF evaluation, the SGP proceeded to select 250 community-based projects. As the SGP progress report notes, grants range from less than $1,000 to as much as $50,000. So far, the majority of these projects have involved biodiversity. Representative grants have funded butterfly farming in Kenya, coastal zone management in Turkey, and a gene bank preserving indigenous medicinal plants and knowledge in the Philippines.

Challenges, of course remain. The independent evaluation cited a need to ensure that local projects align themselves with national strategies while also assuring that such community-based initiatives contribute in some manner to the GEF's goal of addressing global environmental issues. Still, the success of the Small Grants Program has attracted additional support from bilateral sources (the United States, Denmark, and Canada) as well as private sources such as the John D. and Catherine T. MacArthur Foundation. In the end, the evaluation views the SGP as a program capable of providing "critically needed insights for other GEF sponsored initiatives."[14]

The GEF in Context

The restructuring of the GEF and the follow-up to the independent evaluation may both improve the GEF's process and projects. Yet consideration of the broader trends in multilateral and private financing worldwide reveals a darker picture. A recent book tracking the activities of the World Bank, *Mortgaging the Earth,* demonstrates that we must prevent the major international financial institutions—the World Bank, IMF, IDA, and other regional development banks—from spending billions of dollars on projects that devastate both anthropological and biological diversity.[15] Compare the World Bank's $148 billion loan portfolio with the GEF's $2 billion for three years—with only half of that allocated to biodiversity—and the dilemma becomes apparent. Viewed in context, the GEF's financial support for biodiversity remains something of a voice in the wilderness. Aside from greater funding, urgent attention is still required to improve the MDB's own lending portfolios. A call must be made to fully implement policies that relate to preservation of biodiversity and to incorporate biodiversity protection into the policy core of its project cycle.

A Few Suggestions

What can the GEF do for biodiversity? First, the GEF should continue to provide strategic assistance for building capacity in developing countries. This remains a priority for the development of the national programs and the international planning process. This effort might include assisting countries in the development of a national biodiversity plan before funding other projects nationally. And because the GEF operates with the World Bank and the UNDP, major entities in development assistance, it is in a position to exemplify appropriate financial policies with respect to biodiversity among other institutions. The GEF will present an improved model for these institutions to follow if it ensures that national planning is under way, environmental assessments are undertaken, and that local communities and organizations are involved in a bottom-up process of project development.

PROSPECTS

The Commission on Sustainable Development and the Global Environmental Facility will remain key players in the global biodiversity effort. Each institution, however, must continue to strengthen its cooperation with groups in developing countries to empower them with financial and technical resources, provide them with information, support them in international meetings, and generally improve democratization. At the same time, both the GEF and the CSD should pursue policy reform among their larger sister organizations as well as economic and social reform among the Group of Seven and other industrialized countries. In turn, these nations must begin to serve as responsible financial conduits or face grave economic losses and responsibility for environmental degradation. In an effort to encourage such responsible practice in the past, the U.S. Congress has limited its approval of funds to the World Bank and asked its directors to reform its policies. Such national responses represent a powerful resource for promoting international finance reform.

Other measures central to biodiversity objectives should seek to increase communication between the many international conventions and their governing bodies. Parties to the Biodiversity Convention must continue to review the GEF's capacity to implement their objectives, while also working closely with the CSD in its preparation and follow-up to the 1995–1996 meetings dedicated to specific aspects of biodiversity.

The goals of Agenda 21 arch across borders. They address the concerns of citizens and seek to provide for the well-being of species around the world. To effectively monitor this ambitious agenda, the CSD must continue its growth and advocate its recommendations with as much force as possible. The GEF must grow, as well, assuming effective reform is achieved, and pursue the objectives of the Biodiversity Convention as if it were itself a party to the convention. Parties to the convention expect no less; and the biodiversity of the earth merits this and more.

NOTES

1. See the UN Framework Convention on Climate Change, Preamble, INC/1992/1.

2. Chapter 38, Agenda 21, UNCED.

3. E/CN.171994/L.11.

4. UN Doc. A/RES/47/191.

5. CAPE 2000 is a consortium of member NGOs, including National Audubon, Environmental Defense Fund, Friends of the Earth, National Wildlife Federation, Natural Resources Defense Council, and the Sierra Club.

6. Although it is beyond the scope of this chapter, an examination of financial institutions affecting biodiversity should consider the private sector. As a source for international funds, this sector dwarfs bilateral and multilateral funds.

7. A more thorough discussion of the incremental costs concept may be found in *Incremental Costs and Financing Policy Issues*, GEF/C.2/6.

8. Independent Evaluation of the Pilot Phase, p. 52.

9. *The New GEF* (World Bank) 6(2) (Spring 1994).

10. Independent Evaluation of the Pilot Phase, p. 49.

11. Ibid.

12. See, generally, Independent Evaluation of the Pilot Phase.

13. *Understanding on the Interim Guidance on the Implementation of the GEF Project/Program Cycle,* Joint Summary of the Chairs, GEF Council Meeting, 1994.

14. UNDP, *Progress Report No. 4, Small Grants Programme,* July 1994.

15. Bruce Rich, *Mortgaging the Earth* (Boston: Beacon Press, 1994).

PART IV

WHO OWNS WHAT?
A PUBLIC TRUST FOR BIODIVERSITY

When we survey our lives and endeavors we soon observe that almost the whole of our actions and desires are bound up with the existence of other human beings.

—ALBERT EINSTEIN

The law defines a trust as the fiduciary relationship between a trustee and a beneficiary with regard to certain property, which is called the *res*. Trusts are created by a settlor, who can be an individual, association, corporation, or government. The fiduciary duty is paramount to a trust and obligates the trustee to act for the benefit of, and not compete with, the beneficiary's granted *res*. Historically the rules governing trusts were considered "equitable," meaning they were adjudicated by courts of chancery, where rules were more flexible than in courts of law and based on principles of justice and common sense. While all trusts contain the same essential components, the *res* can be almost anything. Governmental and charitable trusts, for example, frequently involve creating a social benefit to improve the quality of human life.

The trust concept has direct and perhaps revolutionary relevance to biodiversity. Nothing but political willpower now stops society from designating a trustee to protect the biodiversity *res* for the benefit of all people. As Ralph Johnson notes in Chapter 10, this idea is not new. The public trust doctrine, a common law edifice, basically governs the public use of navigable water. Because water has always been central to human life, governments since the Roman Empire have granted themselves the power to manage it for the greater public good, even when private water rights have been adversely affected. In its more modern form, the public trust doctrine continues to reflect the intrinsic value of water to humans. There is little reason why the public trust doctrine should not be extended to biodiversity. In fact, Johnson reveals that the change may already be occurring.

It is not surprising that a public trust applies to water, the sustenance for all species. Indeed, it is not surprising that water quantity and quality are becoming major issues in the rapidly growing United States.[1] In the arid West, particularly, state legislatures and courts are rethinking the nineteenth-century prior appropriation doctrine,[2] which establishes the rule of "first in time, first in right for instream water use."[3] Where state legislatures and courts once encouraged unabridged water use and development, there is now a growing recognition that there is simply not enough water to go around.

A central legal question, equitable by nature, is determining when water use is beneficial under the prior appropriation doctrine. For most of the twentieth century, beneficial use has meant almost any use of water that resulted in traditional economic growth such as agricultural and industrial development. Only recently have ecological considerations become a factor. As a broader group of participants enter the debate over water, all citizens are becoming painfully aware that water allocation decisions are inextricably linked to clean water efforts and ecosystem health. State governments are similarly cognizant that heretofore disparate regulatory efforts relating to groundwater, surface water, water pollution, and water use must now be viewed together. In sum, changing public values over water are leading to quite a different conception of private rights, with significant ramifications for both water law and biodiversity. In many states, multiparty adjudications over water rights are forcing courts and legislatures alike to squarely face difficult choices over a central natural resource.

New thinking on biodiversity is also influencing what is commonly known as pollution law. John Pendergrass addresses this issue in Chapter 11 and concludes that federal statutes like the Clean Air Act, Clean Water Act, Resource Conservation and Recovery Act (RCRA), Comprehensive Environmental Response, Compensation, and Liability Act (CERCLA), Toxic Substance Control Act (TSCA), and the Federal Insecticide, Fungicide, and Rodenticide Act (FIFRA) are all seriously underutilized tools to combat biodiversity loss. Although pollutants have been a human health concern since at least Rachel Carson's *Silent Spring* in 1962, scientists continue to discover insidious new effects of pollutants, particularly those containing chlorine. When pollution control requirements are coordinated with traditional conservation legal hooks like species recovery plans and public land management prescriptions, the result is a new synergistic approach to biodiversity protection.

Considering that scientists have identified fewer than 20 percent of all suspected wildlife species, governments will obviously experience difficulties protecting what they are not sure exists. Effective science-based government regulation is nearly impossible without sufficient baseline information. The Biodiversity Convention recognizes this need for information by asking countries to identify and monitor their natural biological resources at all levels of diversity (genetic, species, ecosystem).[4] In the United States, this process has begun through the work of the recently established National Biological Service (NBS),[5] modeled after the Department of Agriculture's original biological survey[6] and the U.S. Geological Survey,[7] both initiated in the nineteenth century.

First funded by the FY 1994 Interior Appropriations Act, the NBS is an independent nonregulatory entity charged with gaining understanding of the United States' vast living natural resources without advocating particular management positions. Its two main objectives are to perform necessary research and to manage research information already gathered. The latter objective may actually be the more important in that it will help make vital information more universally accessible (e.g., through the Internet) and facilitate identification of further research needs. Creating a uniform system will also entail unprecedented partnerships between all levels of government, academic institutions, private organizations, and museums, which could be a building block for effective ecosystem management.

At the forefront of the NBS is the Gap Analysis Program (GAP)—a computer-based, geographic information system (GIS) that seeks to identify conservation "gaps" on all lands, public and private. GAP has been under way since 1988, when the National Fish and Wildlife Foundation provided seed money for Idaho. Since that time, Congress has appropriated additional funding for program expansion and now approximately thirty states have a GAP program at some stage of development. In Oregon, for example, GAP information is now being used for more detailed planning at the regional and watershed levels. Because of its crucial role in inventorying and monitoring biological information, GAP has been transferred from the FWS to the NBS. In fact, in many ways, the popular and nonregulatory GAP is the NBS at present. And despite the rhetoric by some anti-NBS advocates in Congress,[8] the purposes of GAP and NBS are not to increase regulations on behalf of biodiversity. Their mission is simply to give government officials a better understanding of biodiversity's components in order to protect them more rationally and effectively.

Ironically, had the NBS been operational two decades ago, one of the most infamous Endangered Species Act (ESA) conflicts might not have occurred.[9] In this case, the Tennessee Valley Authority, Interior Department, Justice Department, Supreme Court, Congress, and environmental groups all spent the better part of a decade fighting over the construction of the Tellico Dam on the Tennessee River. At issue was whether the dam would destroy the remaining habitat for the only known population of a small fish called the snail darter. Several years and many dollars later, biologists found other healthy populations of the snail darter in other waterways, effectively moot-ing much of the heated debate that the conflict had created. The moral is that it is almost impossible to expect the rational implementation of science-based laws without baseline information. The NBS can provide this information.

Once basic biological knowledge is gathered, the next step is to assess and minimize avoidable negative impacts on biodiversity.[10] In Chapter 12, Dinah Bear explains that in the United States such a policy process is probably already required of federal agency actions through the National Environ-mental Policy Act (NEPA) of 1969. NEPA, the grandparent of modern envi-ronmental law, sets the fundamental goal of a healthy environment and requires a public review of all major federal agency actions that significantly affect the environment. Although NEPA has not yet inherited specific biodi-versity regulations, agencies are beginning to scope, plan, and mitigate the effect of their actions on biodiversity beyond specific endangered species or protected areas. Furthermore, NEPA's opportunities for public comment and judicial review have, in effect, created a public trust for governmental biodi-versity information. Bear stresses that these democratic procedures, together with substantive biodiversity policy developments, have not yet realized their on-the-ground protection potential.

Nowhere are NEPA's dual roles of process and substance more vital than in managing the 191-million-acre U.S. national forest system, home to vast bio-diversity. The rationale for a public trust is particularly strong in national forests because these lands are owned by the American people and managed with taxpayers' dollars. As Walter Kuhlmann describes in some detail in Chapter 13, national forest planning is expressly bound by the requirements of NEPA, as well as by a duty to manage for natural diversity under the National Forest Management Act (NFMA). Similarly, the Federal Land Policy and Management Act (FLPMA), governing land-use practices on Bureau of Land Management (BLM) land, contains similar requirements to "weigh long-term benefits to the public against short-term benefits" and to "consider the relative scarcity of the values involved."[11] A bill designed to create organic law for the national wildlife refuge system, stalled by Senate Republicans in 1994, would have made biodiversity protection an overarching management directive for those lands.[12] Designated wilderness areas can also be important biodiversity anchors, yet they are often not as biologically important as other lands. But even with legal biodiversity authority, there are serious manage-ment challenges when it comes to establishing effective land management indicators for biodiversity that balance competing notions of sustainable resource use. Kuhlmann emphasizes that the growing science of conservation biology is a crucial component of these legal and policy questions.

Nonetheless, for many ecosystems answers are beginning to emerge. This is particularly true for forests, where intensive research is yielding biodiversity indicators for key species and ecological processes. Developing reliable indicators is, at least for now, the only practical way to gain a handle on ecosystem or ecoregional biodiversity. Some indicators, like spotted owls and salmon in the Pacific Northwest ancient forests, are relatively straightforward. But sometimes an indicator is counterintuitive—as in the case of fire, which is in fact highly beneficial for a number of forest types.

Another excellent biodiversity indicator is the black-tailed prairie dog. Long perceived as a nemesis to farmers and cattlemen, peer-reviewed science now supports the hypothesis that the prairie dog is actually the glue to the entire short-grass prairie ecosystem in the Midwest.[13] As a result of its burrowing activities, bodily discharges, and role in the food chain, the prairie dog supports over 160 other species, including the black-footed ferret, burrowing owl, ferruginous hawk, mountain plover, swift fox, bobcat, badger, bison, pronghorn, and golden eagle. In large part because of plummeting prairie dog numbers, many of these species are listed or are candidates for listing under the ESA. Perhaps most significantly, the overall health and productivity of the entire prairie ecosystem appear to be declining in almost direct proportion to the loss of overall biodiversity and, by extension, to the loss of healthy prairie dog towns.[14]

Common sense dictates that it is in the public interest to maintain healthy prairie dog populations. Yet, incredibly, at least three major U.S. policies contravene this interest. First, federal agencies like the Forest Service, Bureau of Land Management, and Bureau of Indian Affairs often actively sponsor prairie dog elimination programs on their lands, either for sport or supposed livestock grazing conflicts. Second, these same agencies frequently convey sizable economic subsidies to grazing interests that significantly damage prairie dog habitat. Third, the federal Animal Damage Control (ADC) program administered by the Animal and Plant Health Inspection Service (APHIS) frequently exterminates prairie dogs on private and public lands without any regard to biodiversity.

The ADC program, in fact, is one of the most underpublicized foes of biodiversity in the United States.[15] In the name of livestock protection, it indiscriminately kills thousands of animals such as wolves, coyotes, bears, mountain lions, and badgers, many of which are central to their respective ecosystems. Because APHIS does not even have regulations in place for the ADC program, the carnage occurs with little public monitoring and certainly without any consideration of its broader effects on biodiversity. New thinking on the ADC is long overdue, as it is for many public natural resource issues. The ADC, for example, should become much more active in combating exotic species. It should also concentrate on specific problem animals as well as nonlethal control mechanisms where feasible. Instead of responding haphazardly to incidental claims of economic hardship by those with a narrow self-interest, the U.S. government would be advised to analyze its various natural resource policies with the greater public trust in mind. Such a shift would yield immediate budgetary and biodiversity benefits.

Biodiversity's public trust is not limited by national political boundaries. While the Biodiversity Convention affirms that "the conservation of biological diversity is a common concern of humankind,"[16] it also expressly acknowledges the importance of the public/private dynamic.[17] At issue is the scientific and commercial revolution in various biotechnology products: not only is this revolution of great importance for new food varieties and medicines, but it also has forced new developments in intellectual property rights law. The biotechnical revolution raises both ethical and practical challenges. Is there a limit as to how far humans should alter life? How will national governments be able to track and enforce the infinite number of potential life patents? Can humans control the uncertain public health and natural ecosystem risks associated with genetically altered organisms capable of reproduction?

Complicating matters further in the area of intellectual property rights law is the fact that rights and obligations are governed under several overlapping and relatively ambiguous international agreements, all of which depend on domestic law for implementation. Under the Biodiversity Convention, intellectual property rights are not to "run counter" to the twin objectives of developing countries providing access to their biological resources and developed countries offering financial and technological aid. Under the GATT Uruguay Round Agreement on Trade Related Intellectual Property Rights (TRIPS), countries must provide plant variety protection either by patent rules or a *sui generis* ("its own kind") system. A patent, which by definition requires a degree of novelty and commercial value, generally allows its holder to restrict plant use from subsequent potential breeders. Conversely, a *sui generis* system is a much more flexible form of intellectual property rights protection: it protects intellectual property rights but also allows subsequent breeding rights to deserving farmers.[18]

For most developing countries, which house the bulk of global biodiversity and human population, an elastic *sui generis* intellectual property rights system for plant varieties will be preferable to a formal patent regime. It is crucial for the many small farmers in developing countries to hold broad rights in their own seeds, as a *sui generis* system allows. Not only does local seed ownership prevent small farmers from slipping into abject poverty, but it also provides the economic foundation for these farmers to conserve overall biodiversity. Indeed, most wildlife habitat in the developing world is destroyed for agricultural purposes.

There are several key legal questions, however, swirling around international intellectual property rights. Most significantly, the legal validity of individual country *sui generis* systems will ultimately be left to a closed but binding WTO arbitration panel, which will not possess any obligation to apply principles enunciated under the Biodiversity Convention. The WTO's influence over intellectual property rules, and by extension international biodiversity protection, aptly demonstrates that the relationship between trade and environment is about more than just trade sanctions. As David Downes explains in Chapter 14, a larger issue is the increasingly nuanced relationship between free market economics and the natural laws of ecology. Global agricultural practices are an ideal example. On an ever shrinking planet bound by advancing technology, Downes reminds us of the several billion indigenous people and small-scale farmers who are not necessarily advantaged by the formal international trading system. Nor is global biodiversity advantaged. The incentive for people to conserve and protect vast amounts of biodiversity in developing countries is integrally linked to how trade rules and the Biodiversity Convention are cooperatively implemented.

Similarly important in this regard is the legal status of the seventeen centers of the Consultative Group on International Agricultural Research (CGIAR), whose very mission is to collect and freely provide plant germ plasm for the world's inhabitants. Under the TRIPS agreement, these centers must now zealously protect their property rights or risk losing them.[19] It is uncertain what benefits will accrue to CGIAR or any other entity if multinational seed companies slightly alter another's original seed and then claim supreme ownership by patenting it. Considering that a large proportion of the global population still sows and trades their own seeds, the question of "who owns what" will determine not only world food security but also overall biodiversity protection.

With such weighty issues, from the global food supply to mass global extinctions, at stake, one would expect national governments and their citizenry to react with impassioned zeal. This is not the case. Most Americans, for example, do not know what biodiversity is, why it is important, or that we are losing it precipitously. According to a public survey conducted by Peter Hart and Stephen Kellert in April 1993,[20] only 22 percent of the American populace had even heard of the issue "the loss of biological diversity." In a democracy, public policy can be effective only if understood by the public it is serving.[21]

A trust on behalf of biodiversity, therefore, will only work if citizens demand it. Once demanded, a democratic state as trustee will have no choice but to respond accordingly. As Justice Oliver Wendell Holmes poignantly asserted almost a century ago: "The state has an interest independent of and behind the titles of its citizens, in all the earth and air within its domain. It has the last word as to whether its mountains shall be stripped of their forests and its inhabitants shall breathe pure air."[22]

The challenge facing countries around the world is to build a new conception of property based on ecological values.[23] It is not enough to lock away a park or a national forest and claim that biodiversity will be saved. It is not enough to grant commercial rights in a valuable gene and assume that the public interest will be guarded. Private property must somehow become part of the public biodiversity rubric. While the line between private use and public benefit might change as a consequence of such a paradigm shift, the result need not be government tyranny. Private property has always been a function of a greater social good. In other words, while free market forces may be the primary engine for biodiversity protection incentives, it should not be the rudder. Explicitly shifting private property rights in favor of a biodiversity public trust is not without its risks, but the alternative is arguably much more dangerous. The quality of human life as we know it may depend on this transformation.

NOTES

1. The United States is not alone in this dilemma. Many areas of the world are increasingly defining their security at least in part through water availability. See, for example, "Israel–Jordan: Water Dispute Central in Peace Talks," *Greenwire*, Oct. 3, 1994; from a story in *U.S. News and World Report*.

2. See also Central Valley (CA) Project Improvement Act of 1992, P.L. 102-575.

3. In the eastern United States, where water is relatively abundant, water law is based on a much more cooperative system than in the West.

4. Convention on Biological Diversity (CBD), Art. 7.

5. The Interior Department is authorized to establish the NBS under the 1956 Fish and Wildlife Act, 16 USC §742. However, House Budget Committee Chairman John Kasich (R–OH) has targeted the NBS for elimination.

6. The original survey was eventually folded into the U.S. Fish and Wildlife Service in 1939 but was subsequently abandoned.

7. 43 USC §31(a).

8. When the NBS was originally up for a vote, Rep. Jack Fields (R–TX) stated: "If you support private property rights and do not want to become an endangered species yourself, I urge you to join me in voting 'no' on final passage." Cong. Record H. 8477 (Oct 26, 1993).

9. See, generally, *TVA v. Hill*, 437 U.S. 153 (1978). As a result of this decision, Congress subsequently created the Section 7 exemption process, known as the "God Squad," which possesses the authority to allow species extinction if "the benefits of such action clearly outweigh the benefits of alternative courses of action." Congress

also eventually exempted the Tellico Dam project from all federal laws by a rider to the Energy and Water Development Appropriations Act of 1980, P.L. 96-99 (1979).

10. Article 14 of the CBD asks each party to "introduce appropriate procedures requiring environmental impact assessment of its proposed projects that are likely to have significant adverse effects on biological diversity with a view to avoiding or minimizing such effects and, where appropriate, allow for public participation in such procedures." However, local governments in several parts of the West, including Nye County (NV) and Catron County (NM), have challenged the U.S. Constitution's property clause (Art. 4, sec. 3) by "asserting" their power over federal lands. See remarks of Peter Coppelma, deputy assistant attorney general, Environment and Natural Resources Division, Department of Justice, before the National Association of Counties (May 13, 1995).

11. FLPMA, 16 USC §1712(c)(7) and (6).

12. See the bills to create a "National Wildlife Refuge System Management and Policy Act," S.823 and H.R.833, 103rd Cong. (1994).

13. Brian Miller, Geraldo Ceballos, and Richard Reading, "The Prairie Dog and Biotic Diversity," *Conservation Biology* 8 (Sept. 1994):677.

14. See David Tilman and John Downing, "Biodiversity and Stability in Grasslands," *Nature* 367 (1994):363.

15. 7 USC §§426–426b.

16. CBD, Preamble.

17. See, for example, Article 15 (Access to Genetic Resources), Article 16 (Access to and Transfer of Technology), Article 17 (Exchange of Information), Article 18 (Technical and Scientific Cooperation), Article 19 (Handling of Biotechnology and Distribution of Its Benefits), and Article 20 (Financial Resources).

18. See, for example, the 1978 and 1991 Unions for the Protection of New Varieties of Plants (UPOV). Both are still good laws and have their origins in the 1961 and 1972 UPOV agreements. The United States, conversely, operates under a strong patent system, which recognizes protection for modified living organisms. See *Diamond v. Chakrabatz;* 447 U.S. 303 (1980).

19. In order to protect its germ plasm collection, CGIAR recently signed a "trust" agreement with the UN Food and Agriculture Organization (FAO) to ensure that its collections are properly monitored and freely available to developing countries.

20. Defenders of Wildlife, "National Survey on Biodiversity," July 1993.

21. See CBD Art. 13 (Public Education and Awareness).

22. *Georgia v. Tennessee Copper Co.,* 206 U.S. 230, 237 (1907).

23. See, for example, *Just v. Marinette County,* 56 Wisc.2d 7, 201 N.W.2d 761 (1972) (a locality can use its police powers to zone an area for natural values).

References

Archer, Jack et al. 1994. *The Public Trust Doctrine and the Management of America's Coasts*. Amherst: University of Massachusetts Press.

Ausubel, Kenny. 1994. *Seeds of Change: The Living Treasure*. San Francisco: Harper-Collins.

Bogert, George. 1987. *Trusts*. St. Paul: West.

Council on Environmental Quality. 1993. *Incorporating Biodiversity Considerations into Environmental Impact Analysis Under the National Environmental Policy Act*. Washington, D.C.: CEQ.

Crucible Group. 1994. *People, Plants and Patents*. Ottawa: International Development Research Centre.

Davis, Margaret Leslie. 1993. *Rivers in the Desert: William Mulholland and the Inventing of Los Angeles*. New York: HarperCollins.

Day, Kathleen. 1995. Biotech's Other Benefits: Consumer and Industrial Products Beat the Wonder Drugs to Market. *The Washington Post*, August 27.

Epstein, Richard. 1995. *Simple Rules for a Complex World*. Cambridge: Harvard University Press.

Estes, Melissa. 1992. The Effect of the Endangered Species Act on State Water Rights. *Environmental Law* 22: 1027.

Feller, Joseph. 1991. Grazing management on the public lands: opening the process to public participation. *Land and Water Law Review* 26:571.

Frenay, Robert. 1995. Biorealism: Reading Nature's Blueprints. *Audubon* (September/October) pp.70-106.

Getches, David. 1990. *Water Law in a Nutshell*. St. Paul: West Publishing Company.

Glennon, Robert and Thomas Maddock. 1994. In Search of Subflow: Arizona's Futile Effort to Separate Groundwater from Surface Water. *Arizona Law Review* 36: 567.

Hawksworth, D. L., and J. M. Ritchie. 1993. *Biodiversity and Biosystematic Priorities: Microorganisms and Invertebrates*. Surrey, U.K.: Cab International.

Fenner, Randee Gorin. 1980. Land trusts: An alternative method of preserving open space. *Vanderbilt Law Review* 33:1039.

Hess, Karl. 1992. *Visions Upon the Land*. Washington, D.C.: Island Press.

Hodgson, John. 1989. *Biotechnology: Changing the Way Nature Works*. London: Equinox.

Hudson, Wendy, ed. 1991. *Landscape Linkages and Biodiversity*. Washington, D.C.: Island Press.

Jacobs, Lynn. 1991. *Waste of the West: Public Lands Ranching*. Tucson: Lynn Jacobs.

Lind, Michael. 1995. *The Next American Nation*. New York: The Free Press.

MacDonnell, Lawrence, and Sarah Bates. 1993. *Natural Resources Policy and Law*. Washington, D.C.: Island Press.

McNeely, Jeffrey. 1988. *Economics and Biological Diversity*. Gland, Switzerland: IUCN.

National Research Council. 1993. *A Biological Survey for the Nation*. Washington, D.C.: National Academy Press.

Pearce, David and Dominic Moran. 1994. *The Economic Value of Biodiversity*. London: Earthscan Publications.

Penny, Simon. "The Pursuit of the Living Machine" *Scientific American* (September 1995) p. 216.

Reid, Walter, et al. 1993. *Biodiversity Prospecting: Using Genetic Resources for Sustainable Development.* Washington, D.C.: World Resources Institute.

Reisner, Marc. 1986. *Cadillac Desert: The American West and Its Disappearing Water.* New York: Viking.

Royster, Judith. 1994. A Primer on Indian Water Rights: More Questions than Answers. *Tulsa Law Journal.* 30: 61.

Sax, Joseph. 1970. The public trust doctrine in natural resource law: Effective judicial intervention. *University of Michigan Law Review* 68:471.

Sax, Joseph. 1989. The limits of private rights in public waters. *Environmental Law* 19:473.

Scalia, Antonin. 1983. The doctrine of standing as an essential element of the separation of powers. *Suffolk University Law Review* 17:881.

Slade, David, ed. 1990. *Putting the Public Trust Doctrine to Work.* Washington, D.C.: Coastal States Organization.

Trust for the Public Land, The. 1995. *Doing Deals: A Guide to Buying Land for Conservation.* San Francisco: Land Trust Alliance.

U.S. Department of the Interior, National Biological Service. 1995. *Our Living Resources: A Report to the Nation on the Distribution, Abundance, and Health of U.S. Plants, Animals and Ecosystems.* Washington, D.C.: Government Printing Office.

U.S. House of Representatives. Committee on Science, Space, and Technology. 1989. *Hearings on the Natural Biological Diversity Conservation and Environmental Research Act* (June 9, 30, 1988). Washington, D.C.: Government Printing Office.

U.S. House of Representatives. Committee on Science, Space, and Technology. 1991. *Hearings on H.R. 585 and H.R. 2082, National Biological Diversity Conservation* (May 23, 1991). Washington, D.C.: Government Printing Office.

U.S. National Water Commission. 1973. *Water Policies for the Future: Report to the President and Congress.* Washington, D.C.: Government Printing Office.

U.S. Senate, Committee on Foreign Relations. 1994. *Report on Convention on Biological Diversity.* Washington, D.C.: Government Printing Office.

Vickerman, Sara. 1994. *GAP Analysis: A Framework for Ecosystem Management.* Lake Oswego, Ore.: Defenders of Wildlife.

Wilkinson, Charles. 1992. *Crossing the Next Meridian.* Washington, D.C.: Island Press.

World Resources Institute. 1995. *National Biodiversity Planning: Guidelines Based on Early Experiences Around the World.* Washington, D.C.: World Resources Institute.

Chapter 10

CAN THE PUBLIC TRUST DOCTRINE PREVENT EXTINCTIONS?

Ralph W. Johnson with William C. Galloway

Most people become more conservative as they grow older. I have just turned seventy, and I am becoming increasingly radical about preserving our environment. Humans are just beginning to understand the environmental limits of Spaceship Earth and the environmental problems we face. These problems will only become worse in the future. We have not begun to address the fundamental question of changing our philosophy of "progress" which causes so much environmental damage. We mistakenly perceive our environment as having unlimited resources and development potential, and we are damaging the environment more and more.

What we need is a fundamental paradigm shift. Humans need to adopt a "steady-state" philosophy instead of pursuing progress at unacceptable environmental costs. And the public trust doctrine can be a focal point for discourse on and catalyst for that fundamental change.

The public trust doctrine appears in constitutions and statutes in a few states, but fundamentally it is a judicial doctrine. This is interesting because the doctrine has aspects of property law, but it also protects fisheries, wildlife, and other environmental interests. This is vitally important.

Once the public trust doctrine has been adopted by a state supreme court, it becomes "property law" for that state and should be recognized and applied by all state agencies, as are other property law principles. State agencies are not just authorized but mandated to carry forward the principles of the public trust doctrine, in their own actions as well as when they issue licenses. Any action or decision of a state agency should automatically get a public trust review. Such a review should be given especially to state licensing of private water and other projects.

If a case says the public trust doctrine definitely does not apply in that state, then it clearly cannot be applied by state agencies. Courts do sometimes hold that the doctrine does not apply to a particular set of facts, but I am unaware of any state which totally denies that the doctrine applies in that state—and no case has been found where the court says the doctrine does not apply.

An example of the application of the doctrine in an administrative setting is found in California.[1] The California Water Board ruled in 1986 that irrigation withdrawals from the Sacramento River were reducing the flow of the river as it entered San Francisco Bay. Under natural conditions, the fresh water extended in a plume out into the bay. But upstream agricultural withdrawals so reduced the water quantity that the salt water now extends up into the delta, damaging the freshwater plants and animals there. The California Water Board ordered the irrigators to reduce their extractions under the public trust doctrine as pronounced in the earlier *Mono Lake* case, which held that even remote upstream uses can be enjoined to the extent that they damage public trust resources.[2]

How the Doctrine Evolved

The public trust doctrine is an ancient Roman doctrine that has been applied in both Britain and the United States. Traditionally it protected navigation, commerce, and fisheries. It has not been used explicitly to protect biodiversity, but such a ruling is only a half-step away from where the doctrine clearly already applies, so there is every possibility it will be used for that purpose in the future. The doctrine originated in view of the widespread use and acceptance of navigable freedom to the waters and beds of navigable waters. Historically it goes back to the legal system of Justinian and the Magna Carta.

In England, not even the king could act in derogation of the public trust. The geographic scope of the doctrine historically applied to the oceans in England. In the United States it also included fresh navigable waters, shore lands, and the sea up to mean high tide. Only a few cases have applied the doctrine to uplands. In Massachusetts, there was a case that involved Mount Greylock, near Williams College in the extreme northwestern part of the state.[3] It has also been extended to nonnavigable waters. Thus there are many extensions of the doctrine now.

The trust idea was formally picked up in the United States during the 1820s in a New Jersey case called *Arnold v. Mundy*.[4] But the decision that established the concept as an important resource protection doctrine nationally was a U.S. Supreme Court case, *Illinois Central Railroad v. Illinois,* decided in 1892.[5] *Illinois Central* reached the Supreme Court on the following set of facts. The legislature of Illinois conveyed to the railroad the bed of the harbor in front of Chicago on Lake Michigan. (You might suspect that a little hanky-panky was going on here.) Then, four years later, probably as a result of some investigative reporting, the legislature changed its mind and passed a law repealing the sale. The railroad said the state was taking railroad property without just compensation, violating the Fourteenth Amendment. The Supreme Court responded by proclaiming that the bed of the harbor was held by the state in trust for the public, and although the Illinois legislature might be able to convey bare legal title, the beneficial interest belonged to the state as a whole and could not be conveyed away. The Supreme Court ruled that the conveyance was at least voidable, if not void.

A second relevant case is the California *Mono Lake* decision noted earlier. In California, the state supreme court articulated its standard for review of statutes that appear to destroy public trust as applied to privately owned water rights. The California court said a statute purporting to authorize destruction of the public trust to privately owned land will be carefully scanned to ascertain whether that was the legislature's intention. That intent must be clearly expressed or necessarily implied. It will not be implied if any other inference is reasonably possible.

In *Mono Lake,* the city of Los Angeles wanted to intercept nonnavigable streams that flowed into the lake. In other words, Los Angeles would divert water under a prior appropriation permit and thus lower the water level in Mono Lake. The result would be to increase the salinity of the lake, so that the brine shrimp would probably die. That result would have a devastating impact on the California gull and other birds that feed on the brine shrimp. Furthermore, the lowering of the lake would create a causeway to the island, allowing foxes, raccoons, and other creatures access to the nesting area, which would destroy the bird population and natural diversity. For these reasons, the court said that Los Angeles could not employ its prior appropriation water permit to take this water. Moreover, the court said that the prior appropriation system has always been subject to the public trust doctrine, so there was no question of any "taking." In 1994, Los Angeles decided to stop taking any water from Mono Lake, at least until the lake level has risen by a minimum of 18 feet.

The public trust doctrine effectively restrains prior appropriation. Some people in the agricultural community say that a water right is a vested property right and, therefore, cannot be regulated. One might observe that private property acreage in Seattle, for example, can be zoned or otherwise regulated by the city. There should be no special status for water, or for the appropriation system that regulates its use.

One can also assume that biodiversity could be a basis for direct regulation, as well as a basis for application of the public trust doctrine. The public trust doctrine has slightly different goals and processes than ordinary police power regulations. Also, zoning and other police power regulations cover many more topics than the public trust doctrine, which is generally limited to navigable waters and their beds.

The Washington State Supreme Court is not known for its reckless disregard of property rights, but, even so, it has adopted the public trust concept. It has said that the doctrine has always been the law of the state, which was exemplified by the recent decision in the *Orion* case.[6] *Orion* involved about 5,000 acres of tidelands on Puget Sound, about 50 miles north of Seattle, owned by the Orion Corporation. The corporation wanted to build a high-quality housing development with canals and boat access to Puget Sound. The proposal, however, would destroy the tidelands. The area was zoned by the local county under the state Shoreline Management Act for natural uses, which prohibited the housing development.[7] Orion went to court and argued that because this zoning regulation went too far and took away virtually the full value of the property, Orion was constitutionally entitled to compensation. The state supreme court upheld the zoning, saying this tideland had always been burdened by the public trust doctrine. It could only be used for purposes that are consistent with the public trust doctrine. Housing is not a public trust purpose and therefore would not be allowed. The court said the public trust was attached to the tidelands in 1889, when the state was created, if not before, and that all tidelands and all navigable waters are subject to the doctrine. Thus *Orion* was not a question of whether the police power regulations had gone too far. This was a case where the public trust existed before any private ownership. Thus it was not a regulation per se that was at issue. It was just a question of whether the public trust burden applied.

THE DOCTRINE'S SHIFTING SCOPE

Joseph Sax is one of the key writers on this topic. In 1970, he developed a four-pronged test to identify public trust interests: first, whether public property has been disposed of at less than market value, where there is no obvious reason for a subsidy; second, whether the governmental action grants a private interest the authority to make resource decisions about broad public resource uses that benefit their private interests; third, whether an attempt has been made to reallocate the few public uses either to private uses or to public uses that have less breadth; and fourth, whether the resource is being used for its natural purposes.[8]

It is interesting that Sax and others talk about the natural purpose in public trust areas, but there is little mention of natural purposes in zoning upland areas. If an upland area were zoned for nonuse, except by wildlife, then the zoning would probably be struck down because society has a different concept about zoning uplands. If you talk about things that are wet, such as lakes, wetlands, or shores, then the courts will almost always uphold regulation. Judges apply the public trust by recognizing the special value of water areas. The public trust doctrine imposes a burden very much like an easement or covenant running with the land. If you have an easement across somebody else's property and you use the easement, you are not "taking" the subservient owner's property, you are just using what you own.

It is also interesting that there are cases in which the public trust doctrine at one time protected certain fairly narrow interests that have since been expanded. The doctrine now protects the environment, water quality, fish and animal habitat, scientific study, and recreation. The Washington State Supreme Court has stated that even this is not the entire list. Other interests may be added in the future. This is where the public interest in biodiversity can be brought in. It is an interest that should be protected.

In the 1970s there was another case in California, *Marks v. Whitney,*[9] which addressed the uses to which public trust property can be put and how such uses should be treated by the courts. One of the most important public uses of the tidelands, for instance, is the preservation of those lands in their natural state so that they may serve as ecological units for scientific study, as open space, and as environments that provide food and habitat for birds and marine life and favorably affect the scenery and climate of the area. In California, the protection provided by the public trust doctrine cannot be removed unless changes in the property make it impossible to fulfill the public trust purpose. For example, tidelands would have to be filled and built upon without court challenge before they would be free of the trust burden.

A recent addition to the public trust scope is illustrated by the California case, cited earlier, dealing with pollution caused by extractions of water from the Sacramento River for irrigation and municipal use. I realize I am treading on sensitive ground when I speak critically about water use for irrigation and municipal and industrial uses. Even so, while we generally try to control the amount of effluent that industry puts into a body of water, irrigators who remove three-fourths of a body of water and cause water quality degradation are usually exempt from regulation. But their pollution must be addressed if we are to solve the pollution problems that beset western rivers.

There are thousands of streams in the western United States that are totally dry by August or September when irrigation takes its maximum water. We are often concerned about the contaminated return flow from irrigation, which returns polluting chemicals such as pesticides, fertilizers, silt, and various other chemicals to streams. What we do not consider—usually don't even think about—is the effect of *extractions* of water on water quality and habitat. It is very difficult for fish to live in damp sand, even if it is clean.

In a 1994 decision, the U.S. Supreme Court upheld the state of Washington's instream flow requirements for a federally licensed dam.[10] In an important victory for the environment, Justice O'Connor rejected the utility district's argument that the Clean Water Act addresses only water "quality" as an "artificial distinction. In many cases, water quantity is closely related to water quality; a sufficient lowering of the water quantity in a body of water could destroy all of its designated uses, be it for drinking water, recreation, navigation or, as here, as a fishery."[11]

The public trust doctrine is not the only avenue to protect instream values. We might also consider adding fishery resources to the list of "beneficial uses" that merit a prior appropriation permit. This would bring fish protection directly into the prior appropriation system. A number of states have adopted regulations setting minimum flows to preserve fisheries. The experience of the state of Washington with these minimum flows is not very encouraging. Shortly after the minimum flows were established the state was hit by a modest drought. The political outcry by farmers who wanted water was so strong that the state legislature and Department of Ecology caved in. Minimum flow levels were largely ignored.

The public trust doctrine presents another way of protecting minimum flows and fisheries. The prior appropriation system has rules requiring efficiency in water use as well as use that is reasonable. These are pegs on which you could hang a requirement that irrigation must be more efficient and more conservation-oriented. These solutions do not get much attention because of the strong tradition in the appropriation system that says if there is any water in the stream it can be used for irrigation. Fisheries have traditionally been given a secondary role.

EXTENDING THE PUBLIC TRUST DOCTRINE'S PROTECTIONS

Although the public trust doctrine is usually considered a state law doctrine, a few cases suggest that they might uphold it as a federal doctrine as well. The *Illinois Central* case was a U.S. Supreme Court decision, but it was based on diversity of citizenship between the parties so the court was really applying the law of the state of Illinois. Usually, federal cases are decided on the basis of federal statutes. But one can argue that the federal government is, as delegatee of state powers, also bound by the public trust doctrine. From

1896 to 1979, federal courts upheld regulation of wildlife as resources held in common under *Geer v. Connecticut*,[12] which affirmed the ownership of all wildlife by the state as an incident of sovereignty. In *Hughes v. Oklahoma*,[13] however, the court overruled what is called the "legal fiction" of state ownership of wild animals but, at the same time, affirmed the legitimacy of pervasive state regulation for conservation and protection of wild animals, so long as the regulation did not impermissibly restrict interstate commerce. In *re Steuart Transportation Co.*,[14] decided shortly after *Hughes*, saw a federal court apply the public trust doctrine to wildlife, stating that "the State of Virginia and the United States have the right and duty to preserve the public's interest in natural wildlife resources."[15]

The public trust doctrine is normally limited to land that is under water or at least is wetland. An important question is whether the doctrine will protect biodiversity only where water bodies or wetlands are involved or will be expanded to protect biodiversity on dry uplands as well. Historically the doctrine has usually been limited to something wet. But the importance of biodiversity is so strong that courts may apply it to protect biodiversity even on uplands, as the *Mono Lake* decision did.

The public trust doctrine is a doctrine that can positively affect the question of biodiversity protection. There is a real opportunity for conservation organizations to make significant progress toward the preservation of biodiversity if they are selective about the cases they pursue. The doctrine is a hovering presence that could have a substantial impact on the remedies available to protect biodiversity.

NOTES

1. *United States v. State Water Resources Control Board*, 182 Cal. App.3d 82, 227 Cal. Rptr. 161 (1986).

2. *National Audubon Society v. Superior Court*, 33 Cal.3d 419, 658 P.2d 709, 189 Cal. Rptr. 346, *cert. denied*, 464 U.S. 977 (1983).

3. *Gould v. Greylock Reservation Commission*, 350 Mass. 40, 215 NE 20 114 (1966).

4. 6 N.J.L. 1 (1821).

5. *Illinois Central Railroad v. Illinois* 146 U.S. 387 (1892).

6. *Orion Corp. v. State*, 109 Wash.2d 621, 747 P.2d 1062 (1987).

7. Shoreline Mgmt. Act, Wash. Rev. Code Ann. 590.58.

8. Joseph Sax, "The Public Trust Doctrine in Natural Resources Law: Effective Judicial Intervention," *Michigan Law Review* 68 (1970):471.

9. 6 Cal.3d 251, 491 P.2 379, 98 Cal. Rptr. 790 (1971).

10. *PUD No. 1 of Jefferson County v. Washington Dept. of Ecology*, 114 S. Ct. 1900 (1994).

11. Ibid. at 1912–13.

12. 161 U.S. 519 (1896).

13. 441 U.S. 322 (1979).

14. 495 F. Supp. 38 (E.D. Va. 1980).

15. Ibid. at 40.

Chapter 11

REDISCOVERING OLD TOOLS

John A. Pendergrass

My camera is not an antique, but it is showing significant signs of wear. And it is not completely out of date, although there have been at least two generations of technology since I bought it. But I like it. I can adjust the settings without thinking about it, and I could change lenses with my eyes closed. While this familiarity allows me to concentrate more on the art than on the mechanics, it can also be limiting. I wanted to shoot extreme close-ups, for instance, but thought I could not afford to do so because the typical tool for close-ups, a macro lens, costs hundreds of dollars. Recently someone showed me how to use my normal lens to focus on an object just inches away by attaching it to the camera backwards with a piece of equipment called a reversing ring. It provided the close-up view I was looking for, and it cost only about ten dollars.

Familiarity with a tool can be both a boon and a hindrance. Efficiency is enhanced because the user spends little effort on operating the tool. But habit causes the user to not think about different ways of using the tool due to unfounded assumptions about its limitations. This country has some of the best environmental laws in the world. Yet policymakers are always trying to do more—through more legislation and regulations. Sometimes all it takes is a closer look at the existing tools.

USING OLD TOOLS IN NEW WAYS

The EPA and environmental lawyers have become quite familiar with the standard tools of their trade: RCRA,[1] TSCA,[2] CERCLA,[3] the CAA,[4] and the CWA.[5] The agency has been using them for years, so it is familiar with their provisions and mechanisms and can set a standard or review a permit "with its eyes closed." The EPA has used these tools primarily to protect public health by controlling point sources of pollution. But the EPA can also use these tools to accomplish new objectives in new ways.

What are these new goals? The EPA's Science Advisory Board (SAB) recommended in 1990 that the agency "attach as much importance to reducing ecological risk as it does to reducing human health risk."[6] Loss of biological diversity is one of the specific areas cited by the SAB in its landmark report, *Reducing Risk: Setting Priorities and Strategies for Environmental Protection,* as needing more attention from the EPA. Scientific evidence shows that pollutants threaten biological diversity in several ways. Pollution can have dramatically different effects on other species than on humans, either because they are more sensitive or because they are exposed to higher concentrations. Thus by reducing the exposure of at-risk species to certain pollutants, the EPA can contribute substantially to the protection of biodiversity. And it can do so using many of its traditional pollution control statutes.[7]

The EPA has also recently adopted a policy that makes pollution prevention the preferred method for achieving environmental policy goals.[8] Pollution prevention generally refers to the reduction or elimination of any pollutant before recycling, treatment, storage, or disposal.[9] It can be achieved through a variety of methods including substitution of raw materials, product reformulation, process changes, closed-loop recycling, and improved maintenance and housekeeping. The effectiveness of these methods is generally site-specific and depends on careful analysis of a particular source's product, customers, equipment, process, personnel, and raw materials. Again, the EPA can achieve the new goal of pollution prevention using strategies already incorporated in its traditional statutes.[10] The Clean Water Act and the Resource Conservation and Recovery Act, for example, each provide good illustrations of how familiar tools can be used to perform the tasks of biodiversity preservation and pollution prevention—even at the same time.

Congress's original statutory goals included language broad enough to encompass protection of biodiversity, though Congress used different terminology. The congressional Office of Technology Assessment defines biodiversity as "the variety and variability among living organisms and the ecological complexes in which they occur,"[11] which confirms its place as a central element of the term "environment." RCRA, like most of the statutes the EPA administers, has as its objective the "protection of health and the environment."[12] The Clean Water Act refers even more specifically to biodiversity in its objective "to restore and maintain the chemical, physical, and *biological integrity* of the nation's waters."[13]

Congress also specified pollution prevention as one of the principal methods of achieving the goals of these laws. Although the term "pollution prevention" did not have its current impact or urgency, prevention has been part of Congress's approach to solving the nation's hazardous waste problems from the initial passage of RCRA in 1976, and the strategy was clarified and emphasized in the law's amendments eight years later. In the 1984 reauthorization, Congress declared that "wherever feasible, the generation of hazardous waste is to be reduced or eliminated as expeditiously as possible."[14]

At the same time, Congress added that one of the objectives of the statute was "minimizing the generation of hazardous waste and the land disposal of hazardous waste by encouraging process substitution, materials recovery, properly conducted recycling and reuse, and treatment."[15] And one of the original congressional findings was a need for "the development, demonstration, and application of new and improved methods and processes to reduce the amount of waste."[16] The EPA eventually adopted this policy of pollution prevention and a waste management hierarchy for all programs, and Congress codified it in the Pollution Prevention Act of 1990.[17]

Pollution prevention was also among the original goals of the Clean Water Act. In that law, Congress stated its goals "that the discharge of pollutants into the navigable waters be eliminated by 1985;[18] . . . that the discharge of toxic pollutants in toxic amounts be prohibited;[19] . . . that a major research and demonstration effort be made to develop technology necessary to eliminate the discharge of pollutants."[20] Being realistic, Congress established a system of standards and permits intended to reach the goal gradually as technology improved. In the process of coping with setting, enforcing, and complying with those standards, regulators, regulated entities, and the public can easily forget that they were intended only as a means of achieving the goal of zero discharge.

The National Environmental Policy Act[21] and the Endangered Species Act are not typically thought of as EPA tools, but the agency can use its responsibilities under them to enhance the performance of its traditional regulatory tools. A principal reason for passing NEPA in 1969 was to declare a national policy to "promote efforts which will prevent or eliminate damage to the environment and biosphere."[22] Congress also made it a continuing responsibility of every federal agency to "fulfill the responsibilities of each generation as trustee of the environment for succeeding generations."[23] Since losses of biodiversity are irreplaceable, it is one of the most critical of these trustee responsibilities.

Congress was more explicit in legislating to protect biodiversity when it passed the Endangered Species Act in 1973.[24] Like all other federal agencies, the EPA has the duty of ensuring that it does not jeopardize the continued existence of any endangered species or destroy or adversely modify the critical habitat of such a species.[25] This broad mandate makes the preservation of biodiversity—at least to the extent that threatened or endangered species may be affected—an element of any action the EPA takes under any of its other statutes. But Congress provided another tool that needs no such interpretation. All federal agencies are required to "utilize their authorities in furtherance of the purposes of [the ESA] by carrying out programs for the conservation of" listed threatened and endangered species.[26] This places on the EPA a continuing affirmative responsibility to use its other statutory authorities to actively conserve threatened and endangered species. Therefore, under NEPA and the ESA, the EPA is authorized and even required to look for ways to use its familiar pollution control tools to protect biodiversity.

THE ISSUE OF DISCRETION

The EPA also has the discretion to use old tools in new ways. In *Chevron, U.S.A., Inc. v. Natural Resources Defense Council, Inc.*,[27] the Supreme Court noted that, in administering a statutory program, an agency must interpret the statute and formulate policy where Congress has left gaps. Where Congress explicitly leaves a gap for an agency to fill, the agency has express authority to interpret the statute by regulation, and the courts must uphold the agency's interpretation unless it is arbitrary, capricious, or contrary to the statute. More commonly, Congress implicitly authorizes the agency to fill a gap by being silent or ambiguous on the specific issue. In such situations, the agency may adopt its own interpretation of the statute, and the courts are required to uphold the agency's action so long as "it is based on a permissible construction of the statute."[28] This deference to reasonable interpretations of a statute provides an agency with considerable discretion to accomplish its goals. Despite the technical detail found in the statutes the EPA administers, the laws provide the agency with significant latitude for implementing their many policies.

The Clean Water Act, for instance, provides the EPA with the discretion to protect biodiversity while encouraging pollution prevention, thus accomplishing both goals with existing tools. Among the oldest tools available under the Clean Water Act, but also among the most underused, are water quality standards, which were part of the federal efforts to control water pollution before 1970. But by 1972, they were considered insufficient.[29] The 1972 amendments to the act retained water quality standards but emphasized technology-based effluent limitations and National Pollutant Discharge Elimination System (NPDES) permits.[30] Yet water quality standards, when used along with NPDES permits and effluent limitations, can make the Clean Water Act's lofty goals, including pollution prevention and protection of biodiversity, attainable.

States set water quality standards for each body of water.[31] They must designate at least one use for the body of water and must preserve the uses through water quality criteria. In setting these standards, states must consider the water body's value to fish and wildlife as well as to public water supplies, agriculture, navigation, and industry.[32] EPA regulations also require, where possible, protection of fish, shellfish, wildlife, and recreation.[33] If a state cannot achieve these protections, it must explain why.[34] The state must, at least, preserve existing uses.[35]

The law directs states to attain (or maintain) the designated uses through the technology-based effluent limitations in NPDES permits. Some bodies of water will not meet the water quality criteria, however, even when all sources comply with the limitations. Then the state must set more stringent discharge limits to meet water quality criteria.[36] These limits are established by a two-step process, working back from the water quality criteria and the volume or flow of water. First, the state determines the water body's "total maximum daily load" (TMDL), which is the amount of a pollutant it can handle in a day without exceeding its water quality criteria.[37] Second, the state allocates the load among the regulated sources (assuming that the natural sources will continue to contribute as they have in the past) and makes the individual wasteload allocation a part of the NPDES permit. Again, water quality criteria must protect the designated uses.[38]

Water quality criteria are adopted by the states, but the EPA must approve them and has a major role in developing them.[39] The Clean Water Act requires the agency to develop criteria that reflect the "latest scientific knowledge"[40] about the effects of water pollution on wildlife and on "biological community diversity, productivity, and stability."[41] These criteria can be either numerical limitations on specific pollutants or narrative criteria.[42] One common form of narrative criteria is a requirement that a body of water be "free from" specific substances or conditions. For example, the EPA's national guidance for wetlands water quality criteria includes a standard that wetlands must be "free from" activities that "would substantially impair the biological community as it naturally occurs,"[43] in other words, diversity of the ecosystem. This is a flexible standard that could be used to protect wetlands biodiversity from pollution from point sources.

The EPA has broad authority both to extend this type of biological standard beyond wetlands and also to develop pollutant-specific criteria, numerical or narrative, that protect biodiversity.[44] When statutory provisions are not explicit, courts have repeatedly upheld the agency's decisions relying on and implementing broad statutory goals—such as protecting the biological integrity of the nation's waters.

States also, when they adopt water quality standards that protect biodiversity, have an opportunity to prevent pollution. On water bodies that do not currently meet the biodiversity-based criteria, the state could use the TMDL allocations to promote pollution prevention as a method of achieving the water quality standard. For example, if the state determined that significant gains toward achieving the biodiversity-protecting water quality standard could be made by application of agricultural "best management practices," it could allocate less of the pollutant wasteload to agricultural nonpoint sources discharging into the water body. Or it could stimulate industrial and municipal pollution prevention by allocating a smaller share of the TMDL to point sources. To be successful, the state would need to carefully target such wasteload allocation efforts at sectors where there is untapped potential for pollution prevention. By providing technical assistance in conjunction with or even prior to the allocation, the state would also improve the likelihood of success.

ONE MORE TOOL

Congress recently provided an additional tool that could be used with these older ones to accomplish the new tasks. Section 304(l), added by the Water Quality Act of 1987,[45] requires states to develop lists of their waters that cannot meet their established water quality standards, including any biodiversity-based standards, due to point and nonpoint sources of all types of pollutants,[46] point and nonpoint sources of toxic pollutants,[47] and point sources of toxic pollutants alone.[48] States are also required to identify the specific point sources believed to be preventing the attainment of the water quality standard and to adopt an individual control strategy that would achieve the applicable standard within three years.[49]

When NPDES permits show that the effluent limitations are consistent with a wasteload allocation or other method which demonstrates that the standard will be met, they then become individual control strategies as defined by the EPA.[50] The agency recommends that states require sources to use "toxicity reduction evaluations" to determine how they will reduce their discharges enough to meet the more stringent effluent limitations resulting from the individual control strategies.[51] The EPA also notes that pollution prevention methods, such as product substitution and process changes,[52] may more effectively meet the new standards. Thus toxicity reduction evaluations should integrate pollution prevention assessments as a way to achieve water quality standards, including those that protect biodiversity.

The most heavily used tools of the Clean Water Act are effluent limitations and the permit system used to implement them. The analogy to the old camera is particularly apt here, since these tools need only be refocused to become instruments for preventing pollution. Under normal circumstances—when a water body meets its water quality standards, for example—the EPA establishes effluent limitations by determining how much the available pollution-control technology in each relevant industry category can handle. It then issues effluent guidelines that translate the level of technology into numerical performance standards, which are then incorporated into the NPDES permit. These effluent limitations are frequently referred to as "end-of-pipe" standards, because they are typically achieved by treatment at the point of discharge.

The EPA is required to set the effluent guidelines based on the discharge levels achievable with the specified level of technology, even going so far as describing the technology in detail in accompanying documents. This policy has had the unfortunate effect of discouraging attempts to achieve the standards through the use of other methods, such as pollution prevention. Because the actual limitations are performance standards, they do not require use of the technology identified by the EPA. A source may meet the effluent limitation by pollution prevention methods. Habit, conventional thinking, or, possibly most important, certainty of result keeps sources using the published technologies to meet their permit limits.[53] Permit reviewers may also contribute to overreliance on the published technologies by questioning nontraditional methods. The EPA and state permit reviewers should promote, rather than discourage, innovative pollution prevention techniques.

Although the effluent guidelines may be neutral with respect to whether sources use a particular technology or preventive method, the EPA could actively promote pollution prevention by using preventive methods as the basis for the guidelines. For instance, the agency has set a zero discharge limit for placer mining (mining sand and gravel deposits containing gold or other ores) based on successful methods of pollution prevention.[54] The statute gives the EPA considerable discretion in developing the guidelines by listing a number of factors to be considered, generally including the phrase "such other factors as the administrator deems appropriate."[55]

The statutory factors for the best available technology economically achievable, (BAT) guidelines specifically include one of the primary forms of pollution prevention: process changes.[56] Furthermore, a new source performance standard is defined as reflecting "the greatest degree of effluent reduction . . . achievable through application of the best available demonstrated control technology, processes, operating methods, or other alternatives, including, where practicable, a standard permitting no discharge of pollutants."[57]

Thus the EPA has a specific mandate to consider preventive methods and technologies in establishing effluent guidelines for BAT and new source performance standards. The broad discretion to consider other factors, when read in conjunction with the zero discharge goal, authorizes the EPA to establish effluent guidelines based on the best pollution prevention methods and technologies in use in each industry category.

DEALING WITH HAZARDOUS WASTE

The focal point of hazardous waste regulation has historically been the risks it poses to human health, and implementation of RCRA has for the most part followed suit. But hazardous waste also poses significant risks to the larger biological community, and Congress clearly authorized the EPA to protect the environment, including biodiversity, in implementing RCRA.[58] In fact, Congress defined as hazardous those wastes that pose "a substantial present or potential hazard to human health *or the environment*"[59] and authorized the EPA to promulgate standards "to protect health and the environment."[60] Thus the EPA has a mandate and considerable discretion to set standards for the handling, treatment, storage, and disposal of hazardous wastes—standards that protect biodiversity.

Pollution prevention could be the centerpiece of the EPA's strategy to reduce the risks posed by hazardous waste. In fact, in the 1984 amendments to RCRA, Congress placed pollution prevention first among the hierarchy of strategies to be used in coping with hazardous waste.[61] It also provided some tools to help reduce or eliminate hazardous waste generation, but they have been little used.

The waste minimization program, added by Congress in the 1984 RCRA amendments,[62] has considerable untapped potential. This program has two elements: certification and biennial reporting. The certification requirement itself has two interlocking pieces—requiring generators of hazardous waste who ship wastes off-site to certify that they have a waste minimization program in place, as well as requiring a corresponding annual certification by generators who must obtain permits for on-site treatment, storage, or disposal.[63] All generators must also submit biennial reports detailing not only their efforts to reduce waste but their actual results.[64]

The certification program has been limited to simply requiring generators to sign the appropriate form; the EPA has not required them to provide any information about how they minimize wastes or the results of their efforts. In fact, the legislative history indicates that Congress intended that the EPA should not look behind the certification to the substance of the generator's program.[65] Nevertheless, the statute does not explicitly preclude the EPA from collecting such information. Under *Chevron*, as long as the agency's action is based on a reasonable interpretation of the statutory language, including the purposes sections, the courts should defer to the agency and uphold its action. For example, the EPA could inspect generators to verify the existence of certified programs.[66] Alternatively, the agency could request such information under Section 3007,[67] which contains broad information-gathering authority. This would be a minimal addition, but it might provide further incentive to generators to develop effective waste minimization programs.

Under the biennial reporting provision, the EPA has more explicit authority to encourage generators to prevent pollution. The statute requires the report to include information about specific efforts toward pollution prevention and waste reduction, progress made, and comparison to previous years.[68] More important, this section authorizes the agency to "promulgate regulations establishing such standards, applicable to generators . . . as may be necessary to protect human health and the environment."[69] This is broad authority that could be used to develop a comprehensive program to ensure that generators engage in serious efforts to minimize waste.

The required information gives the EPA a means of evaluating each generator's waste minimization efforts. The agency could add requirements that the generator's efforts follow the waste management hierarchy established in the statute's objectives.[70] This places preventive techniques, such as process substitution, first. Rather than simply accepting whatever efforts generators describe in their biennial reports, the EPA could guide those efforts by requiring them to engage in facility planning. Facility planning has emerged as a well-accepted and flexible tool that facility managers can use to identify methods of preventing pollution. It relies on facility-specific analysis rather than top-down imposition of techniques. The EPA could require generators to prepare waste volume and toxicity reduction plans based on this type of analysis and could then evaluate their progress through the biennial reports. Such requirements fit within the agency's discretion to establish standards to protect human health and the environment, particularly when read in conjunction with the emphasis Congress placed on waste minimization in its statement of RCRA's policy and objectives.[71]

The EPA could also impose similar facility planning and waste volume and toxicity reduction plan requirements on generators required to obtain permits for on-site treatment, storage, or disposal of hazardous wastes. The permit section authorizes the permit issuer (the EPA or the authorized state) to include terms and conditions necessary to protect human health and the environment.[72]

Just a Question of Implementation

Environmental law is often criticized for requiring the same end-of-pipe approach to all problems. It has also been described, with both approval and disapproval, as primarily protecting public health rather than the environment. To the extent that these descriptions are accurate, they are based less on the law than on its administration and implementation.

Biodiversity protection and pollution prevention are two instances where existing statutes provide tools that can be used much more extensively than they are now to protect ecological values. The occasion of the twenty-fifth anniversary of the passage of NEPA, inaugurating the modern era of environmental law, is symbolically the perfect time for the EPA and the rest of the environmental profession to take a fresh look at the authority provided under existing law to find better solutions to environmental problems.

The EPA has an opportunity to refocus the lenses it already owns and to experiment with new ways of using some of those old tools. It should not be timid about being creative; nor should it be timid about reinterpreting statutory provisions that are vague, ambiguous, or silent on certain issues. The Supreme Court has made it clear that the courts should defer to the agency's reasonable interpretation—that the EPA has considerable discretion and can use it to prevent pollution and protect biodiversity without new statutory authority. The EPA should seize the opportunity to live up to its name by using its existing tools in creative and different ways.

NOTES

The author thanks Ashley Bale for research assistance on this chapter. Thanks also to Robert L. Fischman for his thorough research on biodiversity and to Bradley C. Bobertz for his thorough research on pollution prevention. An earlier version of this chapter appeared in *The Environmental Forum,* May/June 1993.

1. 42 USC §§6901–6992(k) (1988).

2. 15 USC §§2601–2671 (1988).

3. 42 USC §§9601–9675 (1988).

4. 42 USC §§7401–7626 (1988).

5. 33 USC §§1251–1387 (1988).

6. Science Advisory Board, U.S. EPA, *Reducing Risk: Setting Priorities and Strategies for Environmental Protection* (1990), p. 6.

7. For a more complete discussion of biodiversity and EPA's authorities, see Robert L. Fishman, "Biological Diversity and Environmental Protection: Authorities to Reduce Risk," *Environmental Law Journal* 22 (1992), p. 435.

8. EPA Pollution Prevention Policy Statement: "New Directions for Environmental Protection" (June 15, 1993).

9. 42 USC §§13101(b) and 13102(5)(A) (Supp. IV 1992).

10. For a full discussion of how the Clean Water Act and RCRA may be used to achieve pollution prevention, see Bradley C. Bobertz, "The Tools of Prevention:

Opportunities for Promoting Prevention Under Federal Environmental Legislation," *Virginia Environmental Law Journal* 12 (1992):1.

11. Office of Technology Assessment, U.S. Congress, *Technologies to Maintain Biological Diversity* (1987), p. 3.

12. 42 USC §6902(a) (1988).

13. 33 USC §1251(a) (1988) (emphasis added).

14. 42 USC §6902(b) (1988).

15. 42 USC §6902(a)(6) (1988).

16. 42 USC §6901(a)(4) (1988).

17. 42 USC §§13101–13109 (Supp. V 1993).

18. 42 USC §1251(a)(1) (1988).

19. 42 USC §1251(a)(3) (1988).

20. 42 USC §1251(a)(6) (1988).

21. 42 USC §§4321–4370(c) (1988).

22. 42 USC §4321 (1988).

23. 22.42 USC §4331(b)(1) (1988).

24. 16 USC §§1531–1544 (1988).

25. ESA §7(a)(2), 16 USC §1536(a)(2) (1988).

26. ESA §1536(a)(1) (1988).

27. 467 U.S. 837 (1984). See also Administrative Procedure Act, 5USC §§551–559.

28. 467 U.S. 837, 843 (1984).

29. See, generally, William Rogers, *Environmental Law* (St. Paul: West Publishing Co., 1977) pp. 354–369; *Shanty Town Assocs. Ltd. Partnership v. EPA,* 843 F.2d 782–85 (4th Cir. 1988).

30. P.L. 92-500, 86 Stat. 816. Amended in 1977 and 1987, the current law, also referred to as the Clean Water Act (CWA), is codified at 33 USC §§1251–1387 (1988).

31. 33 USC §1313(a) (1988).

32. 33 USC §1313(c)(2)(A) (1988).

33. 40 CFR §131.2 (1994) (promulgated pursuant to 33 USC §1251(a)(2) (1988)).

34. 40 USC §131.10(g) (1994).

35. 33 USC §1313(d)(4)(B), 40 CFR §131.1(h) (1994). Recently the U.S. Supreme Court upheld the state of Washington's use of water quality criteria to protect specific species of fish even though the condition was not directly related to the discharge that led to the need for a permit.*PUD No. 1 v. Washington Dept. of Ecology,* 114 S. Ct. 1900, 128 L.Ed. 2d 716 (1994). In upholding the use of state certification requirements under the CWA to ensure biodiversity protection, even when not directly related to the discharge that initiated the need for a permit, the Supreme Court has revitalized on of the oldest tools available under the CWA. It noted that the applicable river's

designation as fish habitat is consistent with the CWA's goal of preserving "chemical, physical and biological integrity of the Nation's waters." 114 S.Ct. 1910.

36. 33 USC §1313(d) (1988).

37. 33 USC §1313(d)(1)(C) (1988).

38. 40 CFR §131.10(h) (1994).

39. 33 USC §1313(e)(3)(C) (1988).

40. 33 USC §1314(a)(1) (1988).

41. 33 USC §1314(a)(1)(C) (1988).

42. 40 CFR §131.11(b)(2) (1994), 33 USC §1313(c)(2)(B) (1988) (numerical criteria for toxic pollutants).

43. U.S. EPA, "Water Quality Standards for Wetlands: National Guidance" (1990), pp. 18, 6.

44. 33 USC §1313(c)(3) (1988).

45. P.L. 100-4, Sec. 1(a), codified at 33 USC §1314(*l*).

46. 33 USC §1314(*l*)(1)(A) (1988)(*l*).

47. 33 USC §1314(*l*)(1)(B) (1988)(*l*).

48. 33 USC §1314(*l*)(1)(C) (1988)(*l*).

49. 33 USC §1314(*l*)(1)(D) (1988)(*l*).

50. 33 USC §1314(*l*) (1988)(*l*).

51. U.S. EPA Guidance Documents: "Generalized Methodology for Conducting Industrial Toxicity Reduction Evaluations" (EPA/600/2-88/070); "Methods for Aquatic Toxicity Identification Evaluations" (Phase 1 Toxicity Characterization Procedures (EPA/600/3-88/034), Phase 2 Toxicity Identification Procedures (EPA 600/3-88/035), Phase 3 Toxicity Confirmation Procedures (EPA 600/3-88/036).

52. "Implementation of Requirements Under §304(*l*) of the Clean Water Act as Amended" (1988), p. 34, reprinted in *Environmental Law Institute Clean Water Deskbook,* pp. 289, 340 (1st ed. 1988).

53. See Office of Technology Assessment, "Serious Reduction of Hazardous Waste" (1986), pp. 177–178.

54. See *Rybachek v. U.S. EPA,* 904 F.2d 1276 (9th Cir. 1990).

55. 33 USC §1314(b) (1988).

56. 33 USC §1314(b)(1)(B), §1314(b)(4)(B) (1988).

57. 33 USC §1316(a)(1) (1988).

58. 42 USC §§6901–6992(k) (1988).

59. 42 USC §6903(5)(B) (1988) (emphasis added).

60. 42 USC §6902(a) (1988).

61. 42 USC §6902(b) (1988). See also Fred Krupp, "High Court Decision Should Spur Pollution Prevention," *Environmental Defense Fund Letter,* July 1994, p. 3. For a discussion of how the U.S. Supreme Court has recently furthered this policy see *City of Chicago v. Environmental Defense Fund,* 114 S. Ct. 1588, 128 L.Ed. 2d 302 (1994).

62. 42 USC §6925(h) (1988).

63. 42 USC §6925(h)(1) (1988).

64. 42 USC §6922(a)(6) (1988), 40 CFR §264.75 (1993).

65. S. Rep. 284, 98th Cong., 1st Sess. 6 (1983).

66. 42 USC §6927 (1988).

67. 42 USC §6927(a) (1988).

68. 42 USC §6922(a)(6) (1988).

69. 42 USC §6922(a) (1988).

70. 42 USC §6902(a) (1988). See also 59 *Fed. Reg.* 41,442 (1994) (EPA is soliciting comments on criteria to be considered in setting priorities for a national waste minimization plan) and "EPA Proposes Public Participation Rule, Updates Combustion, Minimization Plans," *Environment Report* 25(4) p. 147 (May 26, 1994) (summary of the companion draft waste minimization plan press release).

71. 42 USC §6902(a)(6) (1988).

72. 42 USC §6925(c)(3) (1988).

Chapter 12

THE PROMISE OF NEPA

Dinah Bear

The National Environmental Policy Act (NEPA) is this country's charter for environmental policy.[1] It contains the fundamental environmental policy for us and for future generations. It is the statute that mandates the development of ecological sciences in a manner that allows us to understand more about the impacts we are having on our earth.

NEPA's broad and prescient policies are not widely known. NEPA Title I declares: "It is the continuing policy of the Federal Government, in cooperation with State and local governments, and other concerned public and private organizations, to use all practicable means and measures, including financial and technical assistance, in a manner calculated to foster and promote the general welfare, to create and maintain conditions under which man and nature can exist in productive harmony, and fulfill the social, economic, and other requirements of present and future generations of Americans."

NEPA says that it is the "continuing responsibility of the Federal Government to use all practicable means, consistent with other essential considerations of national policy, to improve and coordinate Federal plans, functions, programs, and resources" so that the United States may:

1. fulfill the responsibilities of each generation as trustee of the environment for succeeding generations;

2. assure for all Americans safe, healthful, productive, and aesthetically and culturally pleasing surroundings;

3. attain the widest range of beneficial uses of the environment without degradation, risk to health or safety, or other undesirable and unintended consequences;

4. preserve important historic, cultural, and natural aspects of our national heritage, and maintain, wherever possible, an environment which supports diversity and variety of individual choice;

5. achieve a balance between population and resource use which will permit high standards of living and a wide sharing of life's amenities;

6. enhance the quality of renewable resources and approach the maximum attainable recycling of depletable resources.

NEPA covers every creature that we know about today and that we are going to discover tomorrow. It covers mushroom fairy rings as well as megafauna, plants that are listed as threatened or endangered under the Endangered Species Act (ESA) as well as those that are not. It requires the analysis of cumulative effects and encourages monitoring once an action has been approved. NEPA also established the Council on Environmental Quality (CEQ) as an agency to advise the president on environmental matters, to prepare an annual environmental quality report, and to oversee the implementation of NEPA throughout the government. In February 1993, President Clinton proposed that CEQ be abolished and its functions be transferred to a new Department of the Environment. Once people started thinking through the consequences of that proposal, objections began to arise. Key members of Congress, such as Congressman Dingell (an original author of NEPA), Congressman Studds, Senators Chafee and Baucus, and more than thirty public interest organizations expressed opposition to abolishing the statutorily based environmental agency within the Executive Office of the President. Thus, in September 1994, the administration announced that CEQ would be staying. During this period, Congress did not amend NEPA's requirements or CEQ's authority.

So NEPA is still on the books. The Council on Environmental Quality remains with a very small staff; the NEPA regulations are in place; and the administration has asked for appropriations for CEQ. Nonetheless, there is no question that we are in serious trouble in terms of NEPA, not to mention the CEQ. In my view, there has been a serious failure of political will to interpret NEPA and to implement it anywhere near its full potential. Part of that failure is due to an exclusive emphasis on the NEPA process as opposed to NEPA's policies.

One of NEPA's strengths, from an ecological point of view, is its integrated approach. This substantive strength has been a political weakness, however, because it has not led to the formation of a political constituency. Another NEPA strength, or something that people thought was a strength, has been NEPA's permanent authorization. But again, ironically, this fact has meant Congress has not had to focus on NEPA and has led to casual monitoring of

NEPA's implementation and a failure to allocate adequate resources for NEPA oversight and implementation.

While I have painted a fairly dismal picture, NEPA is still around and even kicks up from time to time. And I think there is a lot of potential for making it much more alive. Here I want to discuss seven factors that could invigorate NEPA. None of these can be achieved overnight. Some certainly come with formidable obstacles, either in the political world or in the judicial world. But we need to try some new approaches to implementing this old but important law. Although it may not be as glamorous or as fun as writing a new bill, we really need to look at the laws we have and figure out how to use them.

Before I make my seven points, I want to include a caveat. I think that the basic NEPA process—as a process—has a great deal of value. If all that happens as a result of NEPA is that an agency—kicking and screaming—gets forced to go through it, that itself is a benefit. I just think there are some improvements that can be made to the way we think of this process and its relationship to policy and, specifically, to the policy goal of protecting biological diversity.

POINT 1: PROCESS WITH A PURPOSE

First, we should consider using the NEPA process as a process with a purpose—the protection of life, that is, biodiversity. Too many people, on both sides of the debate, view the NEPA process as an end in itself. I recommend rethinking our view of the process and viewing it as a dispute resolution tool designed to implement NEPA's policies. In suggesting that we think of the NEPA process as an alternative dispute resolution (ADR) mechanism, I am not suggesting that litigation should be abandoned. Litigation is an essential tool for resolving legal disputes or forcing recalcitrant agencies to begin complying with the law. But it is a less useful method for resolving factual disputes about the adequacy of analysis and for forcing the ultimate decision that you advocate. The Supreme Court has interpreted NEPA throughout the years in such a way that only the procedural requirements are enforceable in federal court.

Suppose you are concerned about the impact of a proposed federal action on biological diversity. As you begin participating in the NEPA process for a particular action or as you initiate the NEPA process (if you are in a federal agency), consider developing an up-front agreement for minimizing the impact on biological diversity in the area—taking into account the views of affected and interested persons and institutions—and then develop the NEPA process for that proposed action with that end in mind. You may want to consider hiring an expert in ADR techniques. Obviously, the context is much different than ADR used to resolve disputes between private parties: everyone is entitled to participate in the NEPA process. Often there are certain parties who are intensely interested in the proposed action who may be willing to invest much more in the process than simply reviewing and commenting on documents if they believe their participation will really make a difference in the outcome. I am not suggesting that the goal should be a better process or a better document (although both are obviously desirable)—but, rather, a satisfactory outcome of the decision-making process. This approach will not work in every situation. There are legal issues in NEPA that still need to be resolved, such as the application of NEPA to actions abroad. These issues are not going to be amenable to this approach: they are going to have to be resolved at the policy level or in federal court. But NEPA litigation today is viewed by people in and out of government with a great deal of cynicism and disdain.

In the government, there are very good people located in the agencies who understand how NEPA is supposed to be used and consequently want to begin the process at a much earlier point in the planning process or policy development. But they are not allowed to do that because lawyers in the agency's general counsel office say, "It's not absolutely clear that we're required to do this and as long as we can make a good faith argument that it's not required, we don't want to do it and set a precedent." The result, of course, is that the agencies end up not doing anything at all—or disguising it as much as they can so it does not look or smell like NEPA.

In the environmental community, many groups are frustrated by the results of NEPA litigation. Most of the time they lose. And even when they win the case they don't really win because they don't attain their substantive goal. When you look at the track record, it is very hard to win a NEPA case today (which makes one wonder why government agencies are so frightened of it). Nonetheless, the threat of litigation seems to discourage creative use of NEPA in the agencies and dampen enthusiasm for the NEPA process in much of the environmental community.

If an agency decides to consciously use the NEPA process as an ADR tool, it may run into obstacles. There are resource problems—inadequate staff in many government agencies and nongovernmental organizations. Compliance with the Federal Advisory Committee Act[2] may be a real or imagined hurdle due to requirements that advisory committees be chartered by the General Services Administration, as well as the requirements for notice and public access to meetings. But if agencies and affected parties show sufficient interest in trying this approach, I believe these obstacles can be addressed in a constructive manner.

POINT 2: MEETING THE TITLE I GOALS

The goals in Title I of NEPA are eloquent and far reaching, but they are very, very broad. They have yet to be adopted into many agencies' actual policy and planning program processes. But there is a little-known requirement in the NEPA regulations that requires the agencies, in an environmental impact statement (EIS), to explain how each alternative meets or does not meet the policy goals of Title I. The agency also has to identify the "environmentally preferable alternative" at the end of the NEPA process in a record of decision (ROD).

The requirement to include this analysis in the EIS itself is news to a lot of people, both in and out of government. They are not accustomed to looking for that information in the alternative analysis. CEQ did a survey several years ago and, not surprisingly, a lot of the EISs did not have a Title I analysis in them. One factor that appears to make a difference is whether the agency adopted a substantive environmental policy goal specific to its mission activities—that is, what level of protection did it seek with respect to certain habitats or what level of degradation did it define as unacceptable? If the agency did articulate these standards, it was much more likely to relate its alternative analysis in the EIS to NEPA's policies. Yet very few agencies do this. Many agencies still go through the NEPA process without giving thought to the relationship between the alternatives and the policies of NEPA and the decision before them.

Indeed, sometimes the NEPA process is engaged without any thought of making a real decision. This appears particularly true when an agency decides to prepare an EIS at the broad program level. A good example pertains to the program EIS for the National Fish and Wildlife Refuge System. Several years ago, a Fish and Wildlife Service (FWS) official brought the draft EIS to CEQ's attention. I took a look at it and was pretty appalled. It was devoid of any meaningful analysis in terms of alternatives. I met with FWS officials and asked, "Why are you really doing this EIS?" They looked at me in shock and said, "CEQ always says you should do an EIS. Why would you be critical of that?" Finally, someone else said, "Well, to be honest, we are just doing this because somebody in the Solicitor's Office said we had to update the last one." And that is exactly how the EIS came across. There was no thought about how it really related to management decisions, let alone to the agency's policies or to NEPA's policies. In fact, it was not even clear that any management decisions were going to be made.

In recent months, however, there has been real debate about how the National Wildlife Refuge System will be managed. Policy direction is emerging. As Director Beattie said recently, "We have a ten-year plan disguised as an EIS." And this is where I suspect you are going to see the linkage between meaningful environmental policy goals and NEPA.

If you have an interest in a particular agency's programs, check to see whether that agency has articulated a policy related to biological diversity. If it has, look to see how that policy is or is not incorporated into the agency's NEPA analysis. If it hasn't articulated a biodiversity policy, you may want to encourage the agency to develop one.

POINT 3: SET SENSIBLE STANDARDS FOR SCIENCE

My third point concerns the desirability of developing standards for scientific analysis that are compatible with good science but do not require the complete cessation of action until comprehensive knowledge about a certain impact is obtained. Ideally, such standards would be used in courts during the inevitable battle of the experts. This shows up in the Wisconsin Forest Service cases, discussed in Chapter 13 by Walter Kuhlmann,[3] where the judge says in his opinion, "But there is one biologist in the country, at least one, that disagrees."

Well, I am sure there is. One can probably find at least one biologist in the country that disagrees with just about any analysis of impacts. This, it seems to me, is not a very good way of judging the adequacy of analysis. The legal community and the scientific community need to do some further thinking about how to describe, how to analyze, and how to deal with ever-evolving scientific standards in a courtroom setting—and, if possible, develop criteria that can be referenced by all parties concerned, even in litigation. I realize this is not a new topic and no one has yet come up with the perfect answer. And, no, I am not advocating the establishment of a "science court." But I do not think we possess a satisfactory answer today—particularly when we are dealing with topics as broad as biodiversity and with statutes as broad as NEPA.

POINT 4: GET THE INFORMATION

NEPA is a statute that requires the development and acquisition of ecological information. Several years ago, CEQ held a series of regional conferences and agency, state, and public interest representatives from Atlanta to Alaska discussed the subject of NEPA and biodiversity. Following the conferences, CEQ published a report entitled "Incorporating Biodiversity Considerations into the Environmental Impact Analysis Under the National Environmental Policy Act."[4] I encourage you to obtain a copy of this report.

The most frequent comment from the agency representatives at these conferences, repeated time and time again, was: "We don't have the information. We hear you, but we do not have the environmental baseline data, let alone the capacity to make predictions about future impacts." Even allowing for a certain amount of exaggeration or lack of data coordination, there is considerable evidence pointing to our lack of information about the biological resources in the United States.

Yet the statutory sections and regulations under NEPA relevant to the problem of biological information have not received much attention. One of NEPA's three major purposes is "to enrich the understanding of the ecological systems and natural resources important to the Nation";[5] and under the act, agencies are obligated to "initiate and utilize ecological information in the planning and development of resource-oriented projects."[6] In the CEQ regulations, there is a specific regulation that deals with an agency's obligations in the face of incomplete or unavailable information.[7]

The original CEQ regulation mandated a "worst case analysis" in the absence of available information. After several controversial judicial decisions interpreting that requirement, CEQ amended the regulation in 1986. In my opinion, the amendment retained the substance of that regulation—that is, the examination of low-probability "catastrophic consequences"—but eliminated the words "worst case."

Amazingly, after spending three years hearing a number of impassioned pleas on all sides of the issue, I have not had a single phone call about that regulation from anybody. Now, I do not think that all NEPA analysis problems have been resolved since the amendment of that regulation. I think everybody was geared up for a fight about those two words and then everybody went away.

Almost totally ignored during that debate was the requirement contained in Section 1502.22(a)—the provision that says if you do not have the information you are supposed to, then go get it. There is legal wiggle room in the regulation, particularly with regard to whether the costs of obtaining such information are "exorbitant," but you would be amazed at how few times people have asked agencies to get missing information under the rubric of that regulation. And fewer yet go to CEQ and say, "We have asked the agency for information, they will not do it, and we think it is available. Help us get it." Remember that NEPA is premised on the idea that science should drive the policy process. And be sure to use those statutory and regulatory provisions that mandate the acquisition of ecological information to protect biological diversity. If you are concerned about a proposed action that may affect biological diversity, be sure to bring this regulation to the agency's attention and ensure that it acquires the information needed to develop the best possible analysis.

POINT 5: THE ISSUE OF SCOPE

My fifth point goes to the question of the geographic scope of NEPA—that is, do federal agency obligations under NEPA cross U.S. boundaries and extend into areas such as the high seas and foreign nations? This is one of the major NEPA policy disputes that must be resolved. At present, an executive order issued by President Carter directs agencies to develop an environmental impact assessment in certain limited situations, but it does not cover most U.S. actions in other countries and it omits requirements for public involvement throughout the process.[8] It is also specifically written in a way to avoid any enforcement of the order.

This issue has been controversial since NEPA's passage, and it is no less so today. The Clinton/Gore administration took the first step in applying NEPA to federal action outside the United States by declining to appeal a case holding that NEPA applies to U.S. actions in Antarctica.[9] However, it now appears that its consideration of whether NEPA applies to U.S. actions outside the United States is bogged down in what has become the customary interagency fight over this issue.

Meanwhile, the rest of the world is moving ahead to endorse environmental impact assessments (EIA).[10] The UN Environment Program (UNEP) has issued principles and guidelines based on our environmental impact assessment, and Agenda 21, the document developed and blessed through the UN Conference on Environment and Development (UNCED), supports the use of EIAs. Many international environmental conventions, including the Convention on Biological Diversity, support EIAs.[11] Article 14 of the convention obligates signatory nations to develop EIA procedures for proposed projects "that are likely to have significant adverse effects on biological diversity with a view to avoiding or minimizing such effects . . . to ensure that the environmental consequences of programmes and policies that are likely to have significant adverse impacts on biological diversity are duly taken into account; and to promote the exchange of information and consultation on activities which are likely to have a significant adverse effect on the biological diversity of areas beyond a party's control." Once the Senate ratifies the convention, attention needs to be paid to ensure that this provision is effectively implemented under NEPA.

The United States also has signed an international convention for Environmental Impact Assessment in a Transboundary Context; however, the United States has not ratified this convention because of the lingering controversy over NEPA's extension abroad. Ironically, a much more direct type of EIA legislation is found in the U.S. law, commonly known as the Pelosi Amendment,[12] which requires the U.S. government not to vote affirmatively for a multilateral development bank (such as the World Bank) project unless it is accompanied by an EIA at least 120 days ahead of the vote. This law seems to have a salutary effect in at least stimulating the development of EIA procedures and public access to information in areas of the world that have not yet fully embraced the process. Remember to use the Pelosi Amendment if you are concerned about the impacts on biological diversity from an action that may be funded by a multilateral development bank.

POINT 6: EPA's REVIEW OF EISs

Another critical but underused component of the NEPA process is the review of EISs by EPA. Many people are not familiar with this function. During the authorization of the original Clean Air Act in 1970, EPA was directed to review environmental impact statements and to refer unsatisfactory proposals to CEQ. Based on this authority, EPA now rates EISs for adequacy as well as judging the acceptability of a proposed action's impact. This function is housed in the Office of Federal Activities (OFA), the one office in EPA that pays attention to NEPA.[13] The Office of Federal Activities has just begun to issue guidance for specific activities to assist its EIS reviewers.

The first example of this guidance, available through OFA, addresses habitat evaluation and includes a discussion on biological diversity. It has a lot of good technical information in it. It tells their reviewers what things to look for and what kinds of ecosystems are in the United States. If you are concerned with a proposed action in a particular ecosystem that may affect biological diversity, you may wish to obtain this guidance to inform your involvement in the NEPA analysis.

The guidance does not contain EPA's own policy determinations about what level of degradation or mitigation is acceptable. Ultimately, of course, specific action guidance is the lead agency's bailiwick, not EPA's. Nonetheless, the rating and review of EISs plays a valuable role in the NEPA process. Agencies often modify their analysis to conform with EPA's recommendations; courts may also cite EPA's criticisms in their deliberations.[14]

POINT 7: THE QUESTION OF REMEDIES

My seventh point goes to the question of remedies. NEPA litigation is still a very necessary tool. One of the problems, however, is that there is not a cause of action under NEPA itself. As those who litigate know, NEPA causes of action are always brought under the Administrative Procedure Act (APA).[15] Currently, the standing requirements under the APA are interpreted in a manner that runs counter to the philosophy and direction of NEPA compliance.

For example, many observers believe that NEPA needs to be used at a policy and program level much more than it is today. This is particularly relevant for impacts on biological phenomena such as biological diversity, where the focus is on the interrelationship of living organisms in an ecosystem. Presently, some potential plaintiffs are precluded from bringing lawsuits until the action is at the site-specific level. (Instead of being able to challenge the adequacy of an EIS for a forest plan, for example, at least one court has held,[16] and the government is arguing in subsequent cases, that plaintiffs must wait until a proposal for a particular timber harvest is made.) Another potential problem is the courts' insistence on a final agency action under the APA—whereas with NEPA the whole point is getting some action *before* there is a final agency action.[17] In short, it may be time to develop a specific standing provision for NEPA suits that reflects and reinforces the goals of NEPA, rather than relying on the much more general APA provision.

In conclusion, I urge reconsideration of NEPA's potential to address ecological issues such as biological diversity when dealing with a matter related to U.S. government action.

NOTES

This chapter was written prior to the author's reappointment as general counsel of the Council on Environmental Quality. The material contained herein does not necessarily reflect the policies of the Clinton Administration.

1. 42 USC §§4321–4347.

2. 5 USC App. II.

3. *Sierra Club v. Marita,* 845 F.Supp. 1317 (E.D. Wis. 1994).

4. The report was published in 1993 and is available at CEQ.

5. 42 USC §4321.

6. 42 USC §4332(H).

7. 40 CFR §1502.22.

8. Executive Order 12114 (1979).

9. *Environmental Defense Fund v. Massey,* 986 F.2d 428 (C.A.D.C. 1993).

10. The term "environmental impact assessment" is generally used in the international context as a generic term for what is referred to in the United States as "the NEPA process."

11. Convention on Biological Diversity, done at Rio de Janeiro, June 5, 1992. The U.S. Senate has not yet ratified the convention.

12. 22 USC §262m-7.

13. EPA has declined to comply with NEPA for its pollution control activities. Depending on the particular statute, EPA has statutory relief from NEPA compliance, has been found to be exempt from NEPA by the courts, or has declared itself exempt

from NEPA compliance. However, in a "Policy Statement on the National Environmental Policy Act and EPA Programs" issued in February 1994, Administrator Carol Browner "reaffirm[ed] the Environmental Protection Agency's commitment to the goals of NEPA in its programs and operations" and stated that EPA, within the framework of its enabling legislation, will strive to fully meet NEPA's goals in carrying out its programs.

14. See, for example, *Conservation Law Foundation and Town of Newington v. Department of the Air Force* (LEXIS 12916 1994, D.N.H. 1994), a case dealing with the EIS for the disposal and reuse of Pease Air Force Base. The court cited criticism from EPA's comments on the draft and final EISs.

15. 5 USC §706(2)(A). Under this provision, an agency action may be set aside if it is shown to be "arbitrary, capricious, an abuse of discretion or otherwise not in accordance with the law."

16. *Sierra Club v. Robertson*, No. 92-3701 slip op. (8th Cir. June 23, 1994).

17. See Judge Randolph's concurring opinion in *Public Citizens v. USTR*, 5 F.3d 549 (D.C. Cir. 1993).

Chapter 13

WILDLIFE'S BURDEN

Walter Kuhlmann

Why are legal institutions having such a difficult time comprehending and assimilating the strong movement in the scientific community toward an ecological approach to the conservation of our native biological heritage? As federal agencies fall in step behind the banner of "Ecosystem Management" and the literature promoting core reserves, buffers, corridors, and other biogeographic perspectives expands exponentially, we must ask how the law is reacting to this ecosystem perspective. Even though the "law of ecosystems" is in its infancy, we can already perceive a number of hurdles standing in the way of establishing legal duties with respect to communities or ecosystems.

My purpose is not to criticize the Endangered Species Act (ESA) for its current limitations in solving community/ecosystem or landscape-level problems,[1] nor is it simply to call for an endangered ecosystem act.[2] Major new legislative mandates to protect ecosystems are not likely to be well received by Congress these days, due to a growing antienvironmental sentiment in that institution since the early 1990s. Equally important as a deterrent to new broad ecosystem legislation is the growing realization among scientists, as well as activists on all sides of the public lands debate, that effectively protecting ecosystems will require a much greater commitment in sheer magnitude of protected acreage than had been imagined when the Endangered Species Act was passed.[3] Thus, setting aside for now the possibility of more expansive legislation, we need to confront the problems that courts have had, and will continue to have, in fulfilling a meaningful role in protecting public lands from threats to biological diversity that operate on a community/ecosystem or landscape scale.

A number of factors have conspired to create an imposing "burden of proof" for anyone seeking to obtain relief from harms to what Aldo Leopold called the land organism.[4] I use the term "burden of proof" in a broad sense. It encompasses the difficulties in assembling proof of harm on the ecosystem and landscape scales, overcoming the uncertainties of scientific predictions, making these predictions of harm palpable to a judiciary raised in a culture that has never questioned the beneficial nature of engineering (and which, at best, held to single-species thinking), and overcoming the problem of deference to agency expertise (far more a judicial construct than a reality). Can such burdens on the parties and scientists who wish to protect ecosystems be overcome?

WHY USE AN ECOSYSTEM APPROACH IN STATING LEGAL CLAIMS?

The plaintiffs in the cases challenging the management of the Wisconsin National Forests elected to employ an ecosystem approach for a variety of reasons. The activists were knowledgeable about plants (small home range), and there was no grizzly or spotted owl as a keystone or umbrella species to use as a surrogate for protecting those rare plants of concern. Others in the plaintiff group were birders, who saw anecdotal evidence in the field that interior-forest songbirds were declining. Both the plant and bird people had little inventory data, not to mention a lack of long-term data, to constitute real monitoring of perceived population declines. Yet the scraps of data, first-order studies, field observations, deer exclosure information, and theoretical predictions from conservation biology all came together to support a consistent pattern of serious declines in interior-forest habitat and species.

The Forest Service wished to take what Leopold called a "prevailingly local" approach to these problems,[5] yet the Wisconsin activists knew that the causes of the decline in observations were broad ecosystem and landscape dysfunction. With the help of conservation biologists who also had extensive field experience in the Northwoods, we thought we could prove several key ecologically based facts about the loss of structure and function, addressing underlying threats to processes in the forests, and, in doing so, cover scores of species at once.

First we looked at the Endangered Species Act for an umbrella—such as the wolf, a wide-ranging listed species. But protecting habitat does not necessarily protect biodiversity if one is managing habitat with a narrow focus on one listed species to the exclusion, perhaps, of others. Indeed, maximizing management for the benefit of the timber wolf has caused the Forest Service in northern Wisconsin to create scores of aspen openings—thereby boosting deer populations and creating more forest fragmentation in the name of a listed species. Even leading wolf biologist David Mech agreed (in a letter in the administrative record of the Nicolet Forest case) that the timber wolf population in Wisconsin was not limited due to an inadequate prey base, yet he was reluctant to pull back from an intensive management program to enhance deer populations throughout suitable wolf habitat. His aim was to give every advantage to the wolf and ensure the best chance for a "successful" wolf recovery program.

Thus we used our ecological perspective to claim that the agency needed to disclose threats to diversity under the National Environmental Policy Act (NEPA) and its supporting regulations,[6] as well as the diversity language in the National Forest Management Act (NFMA) and its supporting regulations.[7] These provisions, coupled with NEPA's hard look doctrine, led us to believe that the federal district court would surely hold that in order to perform a competent environmental impact statement (EIS) for a large block of public land, the Forest Service would be required to examine and disclose the environmental consequences of forest fragmentation predicted by well-accepted conservation biology.

Apart from our practical reasons for choosing this approach, the strong conservation biology background of the activists persuaded them that focusing their critique on ecological problems would be of considerably greater long-term value than attacking the management prescriptions for a few sensitive species. Indeed, unless the government protected large habitat blocks designed under the concepts of conservation biology, we believed that any subset of listed species dependent on interior forests would remain subject to overwhelming threats.

THE COMPLEXITY AND SCALES OF ECOSYSTEM WORK AGAINST SUCCESSFUL CLAIMS

Although an ecosystem approach has the advantage of addressing the root causes of biological decline, and doing so for many species at once, it has its disadvantages. First, the structure and function of affected ecosystems are terribly complex. Much is unknown about how ecosystems work.[8] But frank admissions regarding our ignorance about ecological processes simply undermine the effectiveness of litigants and their experts.

Not only are ecological processes difficult to describe, but the forces of change affecting the structure and function of ecosystems operate on broad spatial and temporal scales.[9] When arguing for reductions in human-caused disturbance to a region, one faces tough questions: How large an area must we examine in order to capture the relevant environmental effects the agency should have considered? Why should we consider these environmental effects legally actionable when you predict they might not be visible, or reach irreversible proportions, for decades?

When scientific predictions are saddled with admissions of limited data, limited understanding, and long-term effects subject to a considerable range of outcomes, all dependent on the geographic scale chosen for the analysis, it becomes difficult to persuade a court that the issues are sufficiently palpable and that there is any urgency to the plaintiffs' claims. There are no carcasses to point to, no pictures of structure or function to show the court what might be lost in the absence of a sound management approach, and no easy way to articulate the future species composition of an area subject to edge, area, and isolation effects.

As witnesses, scientists are predisposed to caution. Most are careful not to draw conclusions beyond what is clearly shown from the data. And, given the long-term nature of the impacts on ecological processes, such caution is warranted. Nonetheless, it is yet another impediment to advancing strong claims about why we need to protect ecosystems now. Scientific caution played a direct role in the rulings of the district court in the Wisconsin cases. In evaluating the importance of the principles of conservation biology to the EISs in the Wisconsin cases, the district court looked to the report from the Committee of Scientists who assisted the Forest Service in promulgating the NFMA planning regulations. That committee singled out the issue of diversity as one so prone to complexity and confusion that the scientists, in the late 1970s, refused to make any general statements about how diversity might be assessed or managed.[10] The district court seized on this hesitancy as a key reason for refusing to hold the agency to any particular level of scientific rigor and deferring to the agency's methods—despite the fact that those methods led to conclusions about the fate of ecosystems under stress from fragmentation that were directly at odds with those predicted by well-accepted conservation biology.

CAN THE COURTS GRASP THE CONCEPT?

While understanding ecosystem structure and function is a task difficult enough to humble the finest scientist, it seems even more daunting to the finest legal minds. In several respects, courts seem ill-equipped to grasp what scientists consider as evidence, how science deals with problems of uncertainty, and the scale of the ecosystem problem.

Of course, courts are presented with scientific testimony all the time in medical malpractice cases, construction litigation, and warranty and intellectual property cases, to name just a few areas. But there is a difference between these cases—in which the universe is reduced to a small set of relationships, calculations, or tests—and ecosystem analysis, which is more theoretical, probabilistic, and still largely based on little data or experience. (The landscape changes we have worked upon the face of the earth are just a snap of the fingers in evolutionary terms.) In describing ecological matters, the ignorance of courts about the scientific method and the role of uncertainty and prediction in scientific work becomes an acute problem.

Conservation biologists Dennis Murphy and Barry Noon point out that lawyers and scientists think of evidence and proof in very different terms:

> Our experience . . . suggests that lawyers do not understand how science is done. They perceive that we do science like criminals build successful alibis. Alibis are built of evidence that must stand in total, akin to a structure built from so many metaphorical bricks. The structure, it is often argued, is no stronger than the weakest brick used in its construction. The lawyer's job is then to find that weak brick and, in doing so, bring down the structure. In other words, lawyers view our conservation plans as having been built from bricks of data. Such plans would thus be as weak as the weakest data or empirical generalizations used to construct them. Such plans, they argue, are fatally flawed given a paucity of observations, a poorly constructed theoretical model, or even a calculation error.
>
> What scientists do—or should do—to bring science to conservation planning is quite different. Biologists do not construct conclusions from data; they construct hypotheses that are tested with data. A conservation plan is not built from bricks of hard data, but is loosely constructed with pertinent information on distributions, abundances, natural history observations, and habitat associations. The resultant structure is tested with statistical analysis of empirical data, prediction from ecological theory and population models, and inferences drawn from studies of related species. In essence, we fling bricks of data at a structure—our plan, our hypothesis— as a means of identifying its weaknesses. Drawing inferences from the results of these tests, we adjust and reshape the structure to strengthen it.[11]

The process of trying to *falsify* hypotheses—and, if repeatedly unsuccessful, concluding that the hypothesis is robust—eludes many legal scholars, including Chief Justice William Rehnquist. In dissenting from the majority opinion in *Daubert v. Merrell Dow Pharmaceuticals, Inc.,*[12] the chief justice criticized Justice Blackmun's use of falsifiability as a criterion for determining scientific reliability: "I defer to no one in my confidence in federal judges; but I am at a loss to know what is meant when it is said that the scientific status of a theory depends on its 'falsifiability' and I suspect some of them will be, too."

In the Wisconsin cases, the district court found uncertainty of application to be a critical weakness in the plaintiffs' case. The court was quite concerned about scientists' admissions in the record that the precise outcomes of prolonged and ubiquitous unnatural disturbance regimes were difficult to predict. The court concluded that the impacts of forest fragmentation were "still open to debate." But in refusing to hold the Forest Service to the well-accepted conclusions of conservation biology, at least as to general principles regarding the impact of habitat patch size on long-term threats to diversity, the district judge let stand the agency's methods, which had none of the indicia that courts typically use in judging the scientific reliability of evidence or opinions.

In an amicus curiae brief filed by the Society of Conservation Biology and the American Institute of Biological Sciences, their counsel Nathaniel Lawrence succinctly pointed out the error in this conclusion:

> Plainly, the literature and administrative record of this case also reveal considerable uncertainty and disagreement about how large forest reserve blocks should be to ensure conservation of the biodiversity currently found in, for example, national forests in Wisconsin. From a scientific viewpoint, however, nothing in this continuing debate supports abandoning the basic theory so thoroughly as to designate no large blocks at all for diversity purposes. *In particular, it would seem inappropriate to treat scientists' candor about uncertainty, and the scientific dialogue through which uncertainty is reduced, as a reason to reject the superior reliability gained through scientific inquiry, on those points that are generally accepted.*[13]

Even if one is before a court that is literate in the scientific method—a court that understands notions of scientific evidence, theory, and reliability and will prefer conclusions based on those methods to conclusions appearing more definite but arising from a lack of comprehensive treatment of prevailing science—there remains another level of burden that is perhaps more sociological than intellectual. Judges, like the rest of society, have been fed a steady diet of single-species strategies as the key to conservation. Our society has been told for decades that through a combination of hunting restrictions, protecting small Research Natural Areas or Nature Conservancy lands, and the Endangered Species Act, we could meet our goals if only we devoted enough time and money to the problem. In short, the desired level of biological diversity was ours to determine and control, one species at a time.

With great confidence in minor engineering fixes that would not disrupt our way of life, judges, like the rest of society, respond with disbelief when confronted with the habitat prescriptions now regularly voiced by conservation biologists. When faced with the question whether Congress intended to include loss of habitat within the definition of "take" under the ESA, the District of Columbia Circuit Court of Appeals balked at the implications of recognizing habitat loss in the case of the grizzly bear. Noting that grizzly might

need 35 to 42 million acres of reserved lands, the court argued that the vast-
ness of the habitat approach made it obvious that Congress could not have
intended such a result.[14] Courts may simply not be sociologically ready for
the new biogeographic prescriptions flowing from conservation biology—
they are too "improbable," to use the language of the D.C. Circuit Court.

THE SUBSTANTIVE LAW OF DIVERSITY REMAINS LESS SPECIFIC IN ITS STANDARDS THAN THE MINIMUM VIABLE POPULATION REGULATION

Many lawyers I have talked to feel that the diversity language in NFMA is too
vague and discretionary to be enforceable.[15] While it has long been the strategy of the Forest Service to make its governing laws as vague as possible in
order to confer maximum discretion and minimum standards for judicial
review, the diversity language has been particularly susceptible to this criticism. Beyond the ubiquitous multiple-use gloss that permeates all federal law
on forestry, it has been argued that to "provide for diversity" is a mandate
without specific performance standards.

The minimum viable population standard of the NFMA wildlife regulation
is a good deal more specific.[16] While scientists may disagree on the methods
to be used to make that determination, they have a much narrower target at
which to aim their data and opinions than the broad diversity language.
Indeed, some population biologists have asked me why the Wisconsin plaintiffs did not simply opt for a population viability analysis of a critical species
or two, rather than taking the murkier community and landscape approach.
One scientist speculated that it would be much more difficult to prove
ecosystem harm than doing the population viability work for an important
species or two.[17] The success of the northern spotted owl litigation in the
Pacific Northwest supports this comment.

Furthermore, if we are concerned about ecosystems we must find a basis
to argue for recovery. After all, further decline or recovery seem to be mutually exclusive options with no middle ground or safe harbor. While the concept of recovery is explicitly recognized in the ESA, it is not clear from the
statutory language in NFMA whether the requirement to provide for diversity is intended to mean the level of diversity that is present at the outset of
a planning cycle or some sustainable level tied to historical conditions to
which species have adapted, conditions that would need to be restored. Of
the two diversity regulations under NFMA, the latter includes a requirement
that the goal is diversity "at least as great as that which would be expected in
a natural forest."[18] Notably, this reversal from Gifford Pinchot's goal of reduc-

ing wilderness to regulated growth is one the agency has sought to strike from its regulations.[19] If they are successful, this would leave us with even less guidance on the substantive requirements for biological diversity.

Although the NEPA regulations define "effects" to include the effects on the "composition, structure, and functioning of affected ecosystems,"[20] NEPA does not impose substantive requirements on agency action, refusing to require that agencies make environmentally protective decisions, only informed ones.[21] At present, then, there is no clear standard for what behavior will be considered adequate and lawful performance of ecosystem protection and what behavior will fall below that legally required minimum and be actionable. This ambiguity is another hurdle for the plaintiff seeking to articulate that a certain agency action is a violation of a legal duty to conserve ecological processes.

SHOULD COURTS DEFER TO AGENCY METHODS?

Lawyers who have experience challenging the government under the Administrative Procedure Act (APA) are familiar with the deference that courts grant to agency decisions and underlying methods. There are sound reasons, grounded in the separation of powers among the branches of government, why the judiciary does not undertake to review agency decisions de novo, based on the arguments that reviewing courts find most persuasive. The courts assume that the agency has done its job rationally, using the expertise it has developed over the years, and will only overturn an agency's decision if it can be shown that the agency's action was arbitrary, capricious, or contrary to law.

This standard has often been restated as requiring a plaintiff to show that there is no rational basis for the agency's action. Another facet of the rule is that the agency is presumed to have expertise in the area for which the agency was formed. These rules keep the judiciary in a review capacity rather than allowing the judiciary to substitute its judgment for that of the agencies and, in effect, doing the job of the Executive Branch. While this principle of comity to the Executive Branch has a sound constitutional basis, its practical effect is to elevate agency work that is often outdated and substandard while discounting the value of science that is well accepted outside the agency.

A review of federal court rulings since the early 1980s reflects a clear predisposition in agency cases to refuse to take a close look at an agency's scientific work or hold the agency to minimal standards of scientific competence. In the Wisconsin cases, it was impossible to find criticism of the agency's methods in the literature because the agency's methods had never been peer-reviewed or addressed in the literature in any other way. Yet in quickly adopting the usual standard of deference, the court did not first ask whether the agency's work met a standard of minimum reliability (for example, under the indicia of reliability set out in the *Daubert* case discussed earlier).

So powerful is the concept of deference to the agency that in the Wisconsin cases—despite thirteen nationally known experts supporting the plaintiffs and the court's acknowledgment that the agency had not rebutted the central points from the plaintiffs' scientific record—the court nonetheless refused to find that the agency's methods were sufficiently irrational as to be inadequate as a matter of law.[22]

The heavy presumption in favor of agencies is even more troublesome for its implications for future biodiversity claims. If, for example, in future planning rounds the Forest Service contends that it had plausible reasons for protecting small habitat patches in a few blocks of 1,000 hectares each, embedded in moderately logged but highly fragmented "matrix" areas, while rejecting recommendations from scientists outside the agency to be more conservative by protecting 50,000-hectare patches with significant buffer areas around them, courts will be hard pressed not to defer to such judgments.

If the issue becomes, as it may, what level of protection is needed given the uncertainty of environmental consequences (no matter how grave or irreversible the "worst case" might be), it is very unlikely that courts will discount agency judgments and compel measures with a reasonable probability of protecting ecosystems. That is to say, where the scientific issue is probabilistic and relies on admittedly uncertain predictions, it may be all but impossible to ask courts to take a fresh look at their legal obligation to defer to agency judgments and instead make the kind of searching inquiry needed to understand scientific weaknesses that may be at the foundation of those judgments.

The irony is that community and ecosystem dysfunction is perhaps more grave and irreversible than many threats to single species. Yet due to the large-scale, complex, and probabilistic nature of the issues, it is less likely to receive the kind of close scrutiny from the courts that would be warranted by the importance of the problems.

THE PRECAUTIONARY PRINCIPLE—IS THIS AN ANSWER?

For problems of large scale and considerable uncertainty, international environmental law has developed a doctrine known as the "precautionary principle." In essence, the principle shifts the burden to those who propose a use or development to show that the proposed action is harmless, rather than requiring those who oppose the use to show it would be harmful.[23] Often seen as an express response to scientific uncertainty,[24] the precautionary principle has received greatest acceptance in matters of large-scale and complex environmental consequences such as global warming, ozone depletion, and ocean dumping.[25]

Some consider the concept to be a repudiation of science's ability to gauge environmental impact, viewing science as the tool of the "assimilative capacity approach" to environmental protection. The assimilative capacity paradigm assumes that nature can absorb considerable disturbance or pollution, that we can calculate how much disturbance can be tolerated, and that we can do so in time to reverse adverse impacts. Yet science, I would argue, is the first step in defining not only what we know, but what we do not know, and articulating even if in narrative rather than quantitative terms the risks of being wrong. In this sense, science can equally serve the precautionary approach by defining the limits of our knowledge. But then, admittedly, we must move beyond the calculations of biological science and economics to make a policy judgment about how to address the growing realization of the uncertainty of our impacts on the future biotic content of the forests and other ecosystems.

The linkage between a precautionary approach and protection of biological diversity was recognized in the 1992 Convention on Biological Diversity drafted at the Earth Summit in Rio de Janeiro. The preamble noted that "where there is a threat of significant reduction or loss of biological diversity, lack of full scientific certainty should not be used as a reason for postponing measures to avoid or minimize such a threat." The exposition of the precautionary approach, and the development of arguments for its use in the field of conserving biological diversity, could fill many additional chapters. Can it be implemented in some fashion without major new legislation that would create explicit ecosystem protection language or make NEPA's concern for ecological effects a substantive mandate in agency decision making?

The best answer in the short term may be to consider the development of joint scientific and legal analysis that would target this issue and bring test cases in appropriate jurisdictions and on appropriate facts. In doing so, the scientific testimony will have to be well developed. Moreover, scientists and lawyers must recognize the tremendous burdens they face and construct their testimony and arguments accordingly. We will have to explicitly address questions of scientific uncertainty and take the time to make a full record on questions of scientific method, the importance of scientific prediction, and the role of scientific theory. We must forcefully argue that courts should utilize conservation science, despite its uncertainties, because it is a vastly superior guide to saving our native diversity than the methods that often survive judicial challenge, not because of their merit, but because of the inherent pre-sumptions running in their favor due to deference and the high burdens placed on competing science.

One might say that our planet's accelerating loss of diversity should be proof enough that traditional, judicially administered burdens of proof and deference ought to be cast aside in conservation cases in favor of a more pre-cautionary approach. In a sense, it is just this argument that we must make. But it must be explicated through the particulars of how science works, and how we must understand and respond to the predictions of that science.

THE BEST ROUTE TO REAL PROTECTION

At present, conservation biology is just finding its way into the proceedings of administrative agencies and court decisions reviewing those agency actions. When we convince courts and agencies that this science must be part of a competent EIS, we then turn to the more difficult question of what sub-stantive standard will ultimately be applied to hold agencies to a real duty to take action to protect biological diversity.

To succeed in that endeavor, we must face the practical burdens of proof that will be encountered. We must begin by confronting the questions of sci-entific uncertainty, scientific method, and scientific theory and explaining them to the courts as a foundation for their opinions on the future fate of ecosystems. Building a strong scientific record, openly admitting the role of uncertainty and dealing with it, stressing the critical nature of communities, ecosystems, and landscapes, not taking for granted any understanding by the court of how science works—these are important steps in this course.

Assuming no major legislative changes in the near term, probably the most imposing legal hurdle that remains is judicial deference to agency expertise. On this crucial burden, I would argue for a two-tiered approach to the pre-cautionary principle. Once conservation science establishes a prima facie case that adverse impacts on native biodiversity are significant, using 40 CFR §1502.22 and the overall NEPA process, then the burden of scientific proof should shift: the agency should be obligated to show the harmlessness of its activities.

A similar argument for biological diversity and procedural burdens can even be made under the Endangered Species Act. Even though it is now largely a species-by-species statute, there are areas where the ranges of a number of listed species overlap and broader habitat needs can be identified in community/ecosystem or landscape terms. Here, using current tools under the ESA, such as recovery and habit conservation plans, we may be able to convince a court that we cannot effectively perform our obligations on a single-species basis and that an integrated ecological strategy is the only viable approach.

If we can focus on the methods, strengths, and limits of science, and adequately explain those concepts to the judiciary, we may be able to fashion a common law precautionary approach to ecosystem protection. This will be difficult to do if we continue to choose cases mainly for their likelihood of success in the short term, deferring the day when major litigation forces the judiciary to understand these difficult issues for ecosystem survival over the long term. Building a strong scientific record—with an understanding of the real legal burdens that are faced in making a scientific case—is the best non-legislative route to gaining real protection for ecosystems and landscapes.

NOTES

1. S. Winckler, "Stopgap Measures," *Atlantic Monthly* 269 (1992):74–81.

2. K. A. Kohm, ed., *Balancing on the Brink of Extinction* (Washington, D.C.: Island Press, 1991).

3. R. F. Noss and A. Cooperrider, *Saving Nature's Legacy* (Washington, D.C.: Island Press, 1994); M. Bader, "A Northern Rockies Proposal for Congress," in *Wild Earth,* Special Issue: The Wildlands Project: Plotting a North American Wilderness Recovery Strategy" (Canton, N.Y.: Cenozoic Society, 1992); D. Foreman, *Confessions of an Eco-Warrior* (New York: Harmony Books, 1991); D. Foreman, "The New Conservation Movement," *Wild Earth* 2 (1991);6–12; R. Barker, *Saving All the Parts* (Washington, D.C.: Island Press, 1993); R. E. Grumbine, *Ghost Bears* (Washington, D.C.: Island Press, 1992).

4. A. Leopold, "Wilderness as Land Laboratory," in *The River of the Mother of God and Other Essays* (Madison; University of Wisconsin Press, 1991).

5. Ibid.

6. See 40 CFR §1508.8.

7. See 16 USC §1604(g)(3)(B), 36 CFR §§219.26 and 219.27(g).

8. W. S. Alverson, W. Kuhlmann, and D. M. Waller, *Wild Forests: Conservation Biology and Public Policy* (Washington, D.C.: Island Press, 1994).

9. Noss and Cooperrider, *Saving Nature's Legacy.*

10. USDA Forest Service, "Proposed Guidelines for Land and Resource Management Planning in the National Forest System" (including the "Final Report of the Committee of Scientists," Feb. 22, 1979, p. 26599); 44 *Fed. Reg.* 26554 et seq., May 4, 1979.

11. D. D. Murphy and B. D. Noon, "Coping with Uncertainty in Wildlife Biology," *Journal of Wildlife Management* 55(4) (1991):773–782.

12. 509 U.S. ___, 125 L.Ed.2d 469 (1993).

13. N. S. W. Lawrence, "Brief of Amici Curiae the Society for Conservation Biology and the American Institute for Biological Sciences," *Sierra Club et al. v. Marita et al.,* Case No. 94-1736, U.S. Court of Appeals for the Seventh Circuit, San Francisco: Natural Resources Defense Council. Emphasis added.

14. *Sweet Home Chapter v. Interior Department,* 17 F.3d 1463, 1465 (D.C. Cir. 1994). As noted earlier, this decision was overturned by the Supreme Court in June 1995.

15. 16 USC §1604(g)(3)(B).

16. 36 CFR §219.19.

17. R. Lande, personal communication.

18. 36 CFR §219.27(g).

19. USDA Forest Service, "Advance Notice of Proposed Rulemaking," 56 *Fed. Reg.* 6508 et seq., Feb. 15, 1991.

20. See 40 CFR §1508.8.

21. *Robertson v. Methow Valley Citizens' Council,* 490 U.S. 332, 351 (1989).

22. See *Sierra Club v. Marita,* 845 F. Supp. 1317 (E.D. Wis. 1994), and companion case at 843 F. Supp. 1526 (E.D. Wis. 1994). These decisions were upheld by the Seventh Circuit in January 1995.

23. P. W. Birnie and A. E. Boyle, *International Law and the Environment* (Oxford: Clarendon Press, 1992); E. Hey, "The Precautionary Concept in Environmental Policy and Law: Institutionalizing Caution," *Georgetown International Environmental Law Review* 4 (1992):303–318; B. A. Weintraub, "Science, International Environmental Regulation, and the Precautionary Principle: Setting Standards and Defining Terms," *N.Y.U. Environmental Law Journal* 1 (1992):173–223; J. M. Van Dyke, D. Zaelke, and G. Hewison, *Freedom for the Seas in the 21st Century* (Washington, D.C.: Island Press, 1993); D. Bodansky, "Scientific Uncertainty and the Precautionary Principle," *Environment* 33 (1991):4–5, 43–44; E. Christie, "The Eternal Triangle: The Biodiversity Convention, Endangered Species Legislation and the Precautionary Principle," *Environmental and Planning Law Journal* 10 (1993):470–485.

24. Bodansky, "Scientific Uncertainty."

25. Van Dyke, Zaelke, and Hewison, *Freedom for the Seas,* pp. 316–317.

Chapter 14

GLOBAL TRADE, LOCAL ECONOMIES, AND THE BIODIVERSITY CONVENTION

David R. Downes

The Convention on Biological Diversity represents one of the international legal system's initial efforts to unite economic and environmental issues in a relatively balanced way within a single legal instrument.[1] In fact, the Biodiversity Convention is one of the most ambitious attempts in any legal system to integrate environmental goals with a wide range of economic sectors.

The Biodiversity Convention's provisions on trade in "genetic resources"—one of the economically valuable aspects of biodiversity—embody an innovative approach to the interplay of trade and environmental concerns. These provisions are based on the principle that trade in genetic resources must take place within a framework of rules which ensure that not only the trade but the overall production process of which it is part are sustainable. Thus while the convention is ordinarily considered a part of international environmental law, it can also be viewed as a sustainable trade agreement. As such, it should be a useful reference point and precedent in the future evolution of trade law.

Particularly innovative are the Biodiversity Convention's provisions requiring countries to take special measures to protect customary resource uses and local and indigenous communities' traditional knowledge, innovations, and practices, where they carry on sustainable traditions. These provisions reflect an understanding that local economies—especially local economies where long-standing residents use natural resources according to customary rules that take into account ecological constraints—can be more sustainable than the expanding global economy. They also help to affirm indigenous peoples' moral and political claims to lands, natural resources, and knowledge.

International trade law has given almost no consideration to environmental protection, sustainable use and development, or the rights and needs of indigenous communities within nation-states. A great American legal theorist once argued, however, that there is an inherent drive—however "sluggish" or "faint-pulsed"—that pushes even the most "wrong-headed and arbitrary legal system" closer to an "ideal of justice."[2] In the Biodiversity Convention, international law takes a step, however tentative, toward justice in the fields of economic and environmental regulation—justice with ecological and economic dimensions. The future challenge for activists, lawyers, and governments is to put the convention's innovative ideas into practice, in both international and national law.

THE BIODIVERSITY CONVENTION

The Biodiversity Convention is one of the crop of international agreements on sustainable development harvested at the Earth Summit at the close of the UN Conference on Environment and Development in Rio de Janeiro in June 1992.[3] The convention has been signed by over 170 countries and ratified or acceded to by over 120, plus the European Economic Community.[4]

The convention defines biodiversity as "the variability among living organisms from all sources, including, inter alia, terrestrial, marine and other aquatic ecosystems and the ecological complexes of which they are part; this includes diversity within species, between species and of ecosystems." This broad definition encompasses the diversity of life found in all natural habitat as well as habitat modified by humans. It also includes the genetic diversity of varieties and breeds of domesticated species, such as wheat, apples, or cattle.

The convention recognizes "the importance of biological diversity for . . . maintaining life sustaining systems of the biosphere" and also acknowledges that "conservation and sustainable use of biological diversity is of critical importance for meeting the food, health and other needs of the growing world population." The convention defines biodiversity's "value" broadly. It recognizes that biodiversity has intrinsic value and that biodiversity "and its components" have "ecological, genetic, social, economic, scientific, educational, cultural, recreational and aesthetic values."

The Biodiversity Convention has three objectives: the conservation of biodiversity; the sustainable use of its components; and the equitable sharing of the benefits from the use of genetic resources (including both technologies and financial benefits). The convention provides for three interrelated types of action to accomplish its objectives: implementation by parties through national law and policy; creation of an international structure to support national implementation and international cooperation; and establishment of a new set of rules for international transfers of genetic resources.

National implementation. The Biodiversity Convention requires parties to take a comprehensive set of broadly defined actions at the national level to achieve conservation and sustainable use. For example: parties must create national plans, strategies, or programs for biodiversity conservation; inventory and monitor the biodiversity within their own territories; identify destructive human activities, monitor their effects, and regulate them to reduce the impact on biodiversity; and integrate consideration of biodiversity conservation into national decision making.[5] Because some threats to biodiversity transcend national frontiers, the convention also requires parties to cooperate on "matters of mutual interest" relating to conservation and sustainable use, such as conservation of biodiversity in areas outside national jurisdiction like the high seas. Recognizing that biodiversity conservation and loss will vary widely among and within countries, the convention defines most obligations in general terms to give parties flexibility in how they implement them.[6]

International structure. The Biodiversity Convention sets up an international structure to support national implementation and to promote continued international cooperation. The convention has a permanent secretariat and a Subsidiary Body on Scientific, Technical, and Technological Advice (SBSTTA). It will have an information clearinghouse to support scientific and technical cooperation. The parties meet periodically in Conferences of the Parties to elaborate the convention—for instance, by negotiating protocols (follow-up treaties on specific issues). Each party must submit reports to the Conferences of the Parties on the steps it has taken to implement the convention.

The international structure also includes a multilateral fund, funded by contributions from developed countries, that will help finance implementation of the convention in developing countries.[7] Conservation of biodiversity benefits the entire world, but achieving conservation will be more difficult for developing countries, where most known biodiversity is found. In the convention, developed countries agreed to shoulder a heavier share of the financial burden of achieving the shared benefits of biodiversity conservation.[8]

Genetic resources trade. The Biodiversity Convention sets up a new regime for the international transfer of "genetic resources," which are defined as "genetic material of actual or potential value."[9] The convention affirms each party's sovereign right to control access to its genetic resources, but requires each party to take steps to facilitate access for other parties to its genetic resources. It also requires the users of genetic resources to share equitably the benefits, including technologies, with the providers of those resources.

The genetic and chemical structures found in diverse species, and varieties of species, are an extremely valuable source of products such as pharmaceuticals, biotechnology products and processes, and new varieties of crops.[10] Scientists discovered the anticancer drug taxol in the bark of the Pacific yew, a tree previously considered to have no commercial value, that grows in the Northwest ancient forests. The hybrid varieties that yield bumper corn crops in the United States depend on traditional varieties or wild relatives of corn found in Mexico for resistance to disease or drought. The aggregate value of biodiversity as a present and future source of genetic and chemical information is difficult to measure, but clearly immense.

The convention uses the term "genetic resources" to refer to this aspect of biodiversity—biodiversity as a source of valuable information.[11] Previously, biodiversity information was considered a "common heritage" of humankind, exchanged freely among the countries of the world and owned by none. A number of developing countries became concerned, however, that they were donating their wealth of genetic resources freely but were receiving in return a disproportionately small share of the benefits from its use.[12]

The outcome of ensuing international discussions was the Biodiversity Convention's new rules for the transfer and use of the information content of biodiversity. The convention affirms that each country has control over access to its genetic resources—a step toward ownership of property, although in legal terms not precisely the same thing. It also provides for a measure of local community control over access to certain resources. The convention does not, however, abandon entirely the principle that there should be a degree of freedom of access to genetic resources. Thus parties agree to take steps to facilitate access to genetic resources by other parties. Articles 15, 16, and 19 require parties to ensure that users of genetic resources share the benefits, including technologies, with the providers of the resources.

One rationale for the shift to the new regime is that it is just and equitable for countries to own their genetic resources in the same way they own other natural resources such as oil or timber. Adding to the weight of this argument, there is strong evidence that individuals and communities in many societies have labored to conserve, modify, and improve genetic resources. In other words, many genetic resources are not just "found" in developing countries; they were made there, through human effort.

Finally, the new regime is also intended to help achieve sustainable development that uses biodiversity without depleting it. Agricultural scientists have collected seeds from Third World farmers' fields in gene banks, but the most reliable way to conserve them is on site. Tropical rain forests and coral reefs are treasure troves of yet-undiscovered species of value that will not survive if their habitat is destroyed. Increasing the benefits to those who possess biodiversity is necessary to create an economic incentive for them to conserve it.

AN INTEGRATED APPROACH TO TRADE AND ENVIRONMENT

The Biodiversity Convention is innovative in that it is simultaneously a conservation agreement and a trade agreement. Conventional trade agreements treat the environment or conservation as marginal concerns when they mention them at all.[13] They tend to view international trade in isolation from other human activities and detached from its environmental consequences.[14] They show almost no regard for other considerations, such as environment, conservation, labor rights, human rights, public health, or worker safety. Indeed, trade agreements are drafted as if trade were not just the optimal means but the sole means of improving human welfare. Compounding the problem, the international legal system lacks mechanisms for linking trade agreements with instruments that cover these other issues.

A number of previous multilateral environmental agreements do link environment and trade, generally by restricting certain categories of trade to accomplish environmental or conservation goals. The Convention on International Trade in Endangered Species (CITES), for instance, provides for special treatment of certain products on environmental grounds.[15] It sets up a system in which parties to the treaty agree to ban substantially all trade in products made from species that are listed as being in danger of extinction because of that trade. Consistent with this, CITES parties have banned the ivory trade because it led to huge declines in populations of African elephants. CITES and other multilateral environmental agreements demonstrate broad-based international understanding that trade must be controlled in certain circumstances to ensure that it does not damage the environment or natural resources.[16] In sum, then, trade agreements treat environmental concerns as marginal and view them with suspicion, as potential obstacles to the overarching goal of free trade, whereas multilateral environmental agreements like CITES tend to place limits on trade that menaces environmental goals such as preservation of endangered species.

The Biodiversity Convention takes a different approach to trade and environment.[17] In contrast to the neoclassical economic view of past trade agreements, the convention recognizes the principle of ecological economics that "the ecosystem contains the economy."[18] Thus the convention places trade squarely within its ecological context. While affirming the value of the genetic resources trade, the convention insists that trade be sustainable within the context of a sustainable process of production. Genetic resources are the raw material for "a process of production that extends from rainforests and coral reefs to drugstores, factories, and supermarkets."[19] The Biodiversity Convention establishes basic rules for each stage of that process, rather than banning it altogether.

The first stage of commercial use consists of "prospecting" for useful genetic resources in the wild or in farmers' fields. This stage is covered by Article 10(b), which requires parties to take measures, "as far as possible and as appropriate," to avoid or minimize harm to biodiversity from "the use of biological resources." Biological resources under the convention include genetic resources and any other living component of ecosystems that is valuable for humanity, such as fish or timber. As we shall see, Article 8(j) also requires prospectors to involve local and indigenous communities.

In later stages in the process, a company or government in one country gains access to the genetic resources in another country and then uses them in research and development. Under Article 15(2), a convention party must take steps to facilitate access to its genetic resources, but only for "environmentally sound uses." In other words, the intended end use—in biotechnology, pharmaceuticals, or crop breeding—must not harm the environment, a key tenet of sustainability. As the power of biotechnology to create radically new organisms increases, this tenet will grow in importance. It is becoming easier and easier to transfer genes among widely different organisms that would never interbreed in nature. Corporations are now developing tomatoes that include genes and traits from flounders, for example. While the range of resulting products have tremendous productive potential, they also pose unprecedented environmental risks. To deal with these risks, parties must comply with the convention's requirement that uses of genetic resources be environmentally sound.

LOCAL ECOSYSTEMS AND THE GLOBAL ECONOMY

Genetic and biological resources, as they exist today in the hands of farmers, pastoralists, hunters, and gatherers, are not only valuable as raw materials for the manufacture of new commercial commodities. They are also essential as the means of production and reproduction in local economies that are relatively well integrated into local ecosystems.[20]

Local people in these economies depend on a wide range of ecological and economic values of genetic and biological resources. Their gardens, farms, and surrounding areas include many different species and many varieties of species, which provide long-term stability in the face of climactic variation, crop diseases, and other changes, while also producing a range of valuable products. Often they manage these local biological resources under traditional rules and institutions that take into account ecological constraints. For local economies, diversity is "the basis and foundation of production and economic activity, not merely an 'input.'"[21] Diverse biological resources produce not only for subsistence and local markets but also for equally important nonmarketable ecological services (such as protection of water quality and flood control) as well as aesthetic, cultural, and spiritual values.

Larger scale markets generally do not capture the value of genetic and biological resources to local economies and tend to overstate the net benefits of long-distance trade.[22] Similarly, most trade agreements, such as the General Agreement on Tariffs and Trade (GATT) and the North American Free Trade Agreement (NAFTA), are deliberately intended as legal tools for maintaining and expanding the field of operations for the global economy, regardless of the costs to local economies, however sustainable they may be. They help corporations move commodities to the most lucrative market for consumption and move capital to the cheapest site for production. Values of the environment and the community that are not commodified receive no consideration. Indeed, under the logic of free trade, a country gains a "comparative advantage" if it can produce goods more "efficiently" by lowering its environmental standards so that producers do not have to go to the expense of curbing pollution.

This conventional approach to trade is also inherently unsustainable in that it depends on constantly expanding extraction of resources and consumption and production of goods, which brings it up against fixed ecological constraints.[23] At the global level, this increase in extraction, consumption, and production correlates with an increase in the distance between consumers and producers.[24] When consumers and producers are separated by thousands of miles, the social connection between them is reduced to a minimum. It consists primarily of the economic relationship of the transfer of a commodity for value plus a legal connection through a trade law regime that requires nothing except deregulation of trade. International law and institutions lack the rich array of procedures, standards, and concepts needed to create links of communication and responsibility. Thus it is nearly impossible for one party to hold others accountable for environmental costs.

In contrast, many local economies are accustomed to operating within the constraints of local ecosystems and have evolved methods for dealing with them. Producers and consumers are more likely to live close to the means of production and thus are less able to "externalize" costs onto others. Sometimes they are the same individuals, or have bonds of kinship or marriage, and in any case they tend to live close together in the same community, all of which tends to increase accountability. While some of these communities may have engaged in long-distance trade for centuries, they often have developed traditions that minimize its impact on their environments.

This discussion is not intended to romanticize non-Western or nonindustrial cultures. Those cultures, too, cause biodiversity loss, especially as their populations grow. And they, too, often seek some of the benefits of the industrial economy. But their traditional economies and styles of life are in many cases far more consistent with conservation than those of industrial society. As we shall see, the Biodiversity Convention could lead the way to legal recognition of this fact—which would be a major sustainable step forward in the context of international trade law.

PROTECTING LOCAL ECONOMIES AND ECOSYSTEMS

The Biodiversity Convention's treatment of local and indigenous communities is perhaps the most innovative aspect of the attempt to synthesize trade and environment. These provisions of the convention could lead to the recognition in international law of the value that cultural—and economic—diversity may have for sustainable development. Here two provisions are particularly relevant to the role of local traditional economies under pressure from the expanding global economy: Articles 8(j) and 10(c).[25] The discussion of Article 8(j) focuses on implementation of these provisions in the context of the genetic resources trade. Article 10(c) discusses an analogous analysis of how it should be integrated into regulation of the use of other biological resources (such as fisheries, forests, and farms).

Article 8(j). Article 8(j) of the Biodiversity Convention requires parties, "as far as possible and as appropriate," to take measures to "respect, preserve and maintain knowledge, innovations and practices of indigenous and local communities embodying traditional lifestyles relevant for . . . conservation and sustainable use."[26] Parties must also "promote [the] wider application" of such knowledge, innovations, and practices.[27] Article 8(j) also requires that governments obtain the indigenous and traditional communities' approval for this wider application and that they encourage fair sharing of benefits with those communities.

These requirements are relevant to the genetic resources trade, because many of the world's genetic resources are themselves innovations of indigenous and local communities. Their existence and conservation today are the result of the long-term application of traditional knowledge and practices by indigenous or local communities. For generations up to the present day, these communities may have husbanded and modified the genetic resources used to create a patented plant.[28] In other cases, traditional knowledge may have provided a lead to discovery of a valuable patented product.[29]

Those who take genetic resources under Article 15 from the territories of indigenous and local communities must therefore ensure the communities' prior approval and involvement. Governments must also encourage equitable sharing of the benefits with those communities whenever they encourage the wider application of the use of genetic resources—for instance, when they encourage or enforce "biodiversity prospecting agreements" with pharmaceutical companies seeking leads to new products.

There are a number of specific ways to implement these general requirements. First of all, governments should recognize the legal right of communities to make and enforce contracts for access to resources with commercial firms, so that the communities have a chance to reap a larger share of the benefits.[30] Moreover, they should consult with these communities on establishing minimum standards for such transactions. Governments should also explore whether to create new types of intellectual property rights (IPRs) to be held by indigenous and local communities over their genetic resources and knowledge about them.[31] Governments could also consider affording legal protection to trademarks or certificates of origin for sustainably produced traditional products. This would permit communities to profit from sustainable use without facing unfair competition from misleadingly similar products that are not traditional and may not be sustainable. Another option would be to provide grants to local and indigenous communities to conduct (possibly in partnership with scientists) assessments of the sustainability of traditional practices or to develop small-scale sustainable enterprises based on traditional uses that are sustainable. Finally, governments could also implement these provisions by reforming systems of national accounting to account for a larger proportion of the value of nonmarket ecological values as well as local market and subsistence values of biodiversity-rich ecosystems.

Article 10(c). Article 10(c) requires parties, "as far as possible and as appropriate," to "protect and encourage customary use of biological resources in accordance with traditional cultural practices that are compatible with conservation or sustainable use." To satisfy the mandate of Article 10(c), governments should extend legal recognition and protection to traditional systems of resource management where they effectively promote sustainable use. These systems should have protection against incursions from competing users of resources, for instance by giving villages and citizens the legal right to enjoin outside users and recover damages from them for violations. Management systems warranting protection could include, for example, traditional land tenure or usufruct rights or village taboos on use of sacred groves.

Particularly worthy of attention are communal systems for regulating access to common resources. Privatization, which is often offered as the solution to the "tragedy of the commons" caused by open-access regimes, is not a sure route to sustainability. (Private ownership of midwestern farms has not stopped soil erosion.) Indeed, it can worsen environmental problems as well as increasing inequities of wealth and power. Traditional community regulation of access to common resources offers a range of effective models for sustainable management that resolve the problems of open-access regimes and may be better suited than privatization to local social structures. The Biodiversity Convention mandates that parties give these models priority.

Defining new terms. The terms "indigenous and local," "community," "customary," "traditional," and "sustainable use" do not have established meanings in international environmental law. Thus an essential task will be to develop rigorous definitions of these terms to prevent governments from using them as loopholes that permit unsustainable exploitation. One critical step will be to put the Biodiversity Convention in the hands of local and indigenous communities themselves, through training, education, and (where requested) legal assistance, so that they can interpret and enforce the terms of the convention.

In defining these terms, it might be worth investigating whether the protection in Articles 8(j) and 10(c) for "local" communities, "traditional" lifestyles, and "customary" uses could also be applied to centralized industrial economies in order to protect remnants of nonmarket or local uses. In the United States, for example, the household garden or the family farm might qualify as traditional, and the farmers' market might be a "customary" use in the "local community." To a significant extent, such activities may be associated with greater biodiversity, not to mention their other values for health, food cost and security, and social ties in local communities.[32]

From this perspective, the Biodiversity Convention could help society move closer to sustainability through what Ivan Illich terms "modern subsistence."[33] Through economic activity supplementary to markets, society could reintegrate ecological values currently externalized by the market economy. The Biodiversity Convention offers the opportunity to explore these possibilities.

RECOMMENDATIONS

An obvious first step for the United States is to ratify the Biodiversity Convention. The Clinton administration supports the convention, and in the early stages of Senate discussions there was bipartisan support, but the Senate could not conclude the advice-and-consent process during the months of partisan struggle leading up to the November 1994 elections. The Senate should return to a bipartisan approach and give advice and consent, so that the United States can join the great majority of nations as a convention party.

Meanwhile, at the international level, governments will need to cooperate to develop some common ground for implementing the Biodiversity Convention's provisions on access to genetic resources and benefit-sharing. Implementation will raise complex legal questions as well as challenging political issues. The process should be inclusive and open. It must include the various interested groups, especially local communities, so that they have a chance to shape the outcome. When governments publish national reports on implementation as required by Article 26, they should make sure that the reports detail plans and actions for the convention's provisions on genetic resources and communities. At every stage, the involvement of nongovernmental organizations will be critical.

Successful implementation of the convention's provisions on genetic resources and communities could create a model for sustainable trade in other resources. This underscores the fact that the Biodiversity Convention is not the only forum in which governments should consider these issues. The progressive provisions of the convention should serve as minimum standards for measures to promote sustainable development within international trade law. To implement their obligation to cooperate on "matters of mutual interest," convention parties should raise this point in current discussions in the World Trade Organization (WTO) committee on trade and environment. The WTO must ensure that its elaboration and application of trade rules are consistent with the convention's guidelines. The convention should also guide negotiations on regional trade agreements, such as the proposed expansion of the North American Free Trade Agreement to other countries in such as Chile.

While there are good legal grounds for these proposals, it will be politically difficult to advance them. In general, trade experts and officials are unaccustomed to looking beyond conventional concepts of trade issues and trade policy for guidance, and it is unlikely that they will turn to the Biodiversity Convention unless environmentalists press for them to do so. Nevertheless, achieving sustainability requires precisely this kind of integration of environmental and economic principles.

NOTES

The author is grateful to Dana Clark for her helpful comments. Support for research came from the John D. and Catherine T. MacArthur Foundation and the Moriah Fund.

1. Convention on Biological Diversity, open for signature June 5, 1992, 31 I.L.M. 818 (1992).

2. See Karl Llewellyn, *The Bramble Bush* (1930), p. 9.

3. In Rio, over 160 countries signed the Biodiversity Convention and the Framework Convention on Climate Change, both of which are legally binding. Governments also signed a set of "non-authoritative, non-legally binding forest principles," the Rio Declaration on Environment and Development, and Agenda 21, a several-hundred-page-long plan for achieving sustainable development by the twenty-first century.

4. See UN Environment Program, Conference of the Parties to the Convention on Biological Diversity, 1st Meeting, UN Doc. UNEP/CBD/COP/1/Inf. 4 (1994).

5. See Art. 6(a), 7(a)–7(c), 8(1), and 10(a).

6. Most of the obligations are qualified by the phrase "as far as possible and as appropriate." This phrase gives countries flexibility to fit implementation to their particular economic, social, cultural, and other conditions. It does not give them complete discretion; if it were a complete escape clause, it would have the absurd effect of erasing the obligation to which it applied.

7. Other recent multilateral environmental agreements, such as the Montreal Protocol on Substances That Deplete the Ozone Layer and the Framework Convention on Climate Change, also establish such financial mechanisms to support implementation by developing countries.

8. As of December 1994, it appeared that funding from developed countries under the Biodiversity Convention would amount to about $40 million per year over the following three years.

9. "Genetic material" is defined in turn as "any material of plant, animal, microbial, or other origin containing functional units of heredity," that is, genes.

10. Ultimately all of our food, as well as most of our other daily needs, derive from the diversity of technologies that plants and other photosynthetic organisms use to tap the energy of the sun. The blueprints for these technologies are stored as genetic information. "If our ultimate natural resource is the solar flow of low entropy, then our ultimate capital is the gene pool in which evolution has evolved and stored technologies for tapping this basic flow for life generation." See Herman E. Daly and John B. Cobb, Jr., *For the Common Good* (Boston: Beacon Press, 1991), p. 205.

11. In general, most samples of biodiversity transferred internationally will probably include some genetic material and thus will qualify as genetic resources, although some chemical extracts from species may be exceptions. See David R. Downes, "New Diplomacy for the Biodiversity Trade: Biodiversity, Biotechnology and Intellectual Property in the Convention on Biological Diversity," *Touro Journal of Transnational Law* 4 (1993):14; David R. Downes and Chris Wold, "Biodiversity Prospecting: Rules of the Game," *BioScience* 44 (1994):382; Lyle Glowka et al., *A Guide to the Convention on Biological Diversity* (Gland, Switzerland: IUCN, 1994), p. 22.

12. The controversy over control of biodiversity information is analogous to conflicts over other types of information in several respects. As a practical matter, it is more difficult for someone to be the sole and exclusive owner of information than of

physical property, because information is relatively cheap to reproduce and easy to move. As an ethical matter, there is less agreement about who is the rightful "owner" of information than of physical property, and it is less clear how far rights of ownership over information extend. Democratic principles argue for strict limits on private rights over information in order to maximize freedom of debate and the free exchange of ideas and information and to guard against domination by the government or other powerful actors. Yet there are moral grounds for existing ownership rights such as copyrights or patents: they help creators and inventors obtain the recognition and reward for their efforts that they deserve. Such intellectual property rights (IPRs) also create economic incentives to innovate, which benefit society as a whole. Analogously, there are both moral and incentive arguments for giving countries, communities, or individuals property rights over biodiversity information.

13. NAFTA, for instance, relegates most environmental issues to a side agreement, which provides for consideration of environmental aspects of trade policy only in very narrowly defined circumstances. GATT mentions the environment only insofar as Article XX provides for narrowly defined exceptions from general trade rules for measures "necessary to protect human, animal or plant life or health" or "relating to the conservation of exhaustible natural resources if such measures are made effective in conjunction with restriction on domestic production or consumption." The Uruguay Round agreements concluded by GATT parties at the end of 1993 follow essentially the same approach.

14. In this respect, trade agreements reflect the neoclassical economic view that the economy contains the ecosystem. See Herman E. Daly and Kenneth N. Townsend, "Introduction," in *Valuing the Earth: Economics, Ecology, Ethics* (Cambridge, MA: The MIT Press, 1993), pp. 1, 3. Thus "the ecosystem is not the containing natural matrix of the economy but just one more sector within the all-inclusive economy waiting for its due allocation of resources according to individual willingness to pay for its service or product."

15. Other multilateral environmental agreements that regulate trade to accomplish environmental goals are the Basel Convention on the Control of Transboundary Movements of Hazardous Wastes and Their Disposal and the Montreal Protocol on Substances That Deplete the Ozone Layer.

16. See Robert Housman et al., eds., *The Use of Trade Measures in Selected Multilateral Environmental Agreements* (Geneva: United Nations Environment Programme, 1995).

17. For a detailed analysis of the relationship between the Biodiversity Convention and GATT see David R. Downes, "The Convention on Biological Diversity and the GATT," in Housman et al., *The Use of Trade Measures.*

18. See Daly and Townsend, "Introduction." The ecosystem supplies the economy with "a throughput of matter-energy," without which the economy could not survive.

19. See Downes and Wold, "Biodiversity Prospecting," p. 383.

20. See for example, Charles Victor Barber et al., *Breaking the Log Jam: Obstacles to Forest Policy Reform in Indonesia and the United States* (Washington, D.C.: World Resources Institute, 1994), John A. Dixon and Paul B. Sherman, *Economics of Pro-*

tected Areas: A New Look at Benefits and Costs (Washington, D.C.: Island Press, 1990), pp. 186–188.

21. See Vandana Shiva, "Biodiversity, Biotechnology and Profits," in Vandana Shiva et al., eds., *Biodiversity: Social and Ecological Perspectives* (London: Zed Books, 1991), pp. 43–44.

22. For instance, large-scale markets do not reflect the tremendous value of biological resources at the local level through subsistence use and local market exchange. The monetary rewards of international trade are increased because those engaging in trade pass on many environmental costs of trade to others. Examples of these costs include the damage from introduction of alien species and greenhouse gas emissions from fossil-fuel-powered transportation.

23. See Herman E. Daly, "Introduction to Essays Toward a Steady-State Economy," in Daly and Townsend, *Valuing the Earth*, pp. 11, 14–15, 38; see also Herman E. Daly, "Problems with Free Trade: Neoclassical and Steady-State Perspectives," in D. Zaelke et al., eds., *Trade and the Environment: Law, Economics and Policy* (Washington, D.C.: Island Press, 1993), pp. 147, 151.

24. See for example, Madhav Gadgil and Ramachandra Guha, *This Fissured Land: An Ecological History of India* (Berkeley: University of California Press, 1992), p. 52.

25. Other relevant provisions are Article 10(d) (requiring parties to help local populations develop and implement projects to restore biodiversity in degraded ecosystems) and Article 14(1)(a) (requiring parties to institute environmental assessment procedures that include "appropriate" public participation).

26. Article 8(j)'s obligation is "subject to [each party's] national legislation." As with other qualifying language, this phrase does not give the party complete discretion in implementation. See note 6 above. Rather, this caveat makes clear that parties can maintain the legal concepts and structures they use to govern indigenous affairs in particular, such as legal definitions of indigenous tribes. See Melinda Chandler, "The Biodiversity Convention: Selected Issues of Interest to the International Lawyer," *Colorado Journal of International Environmental Law and Policy* 4 (1993):141, 154 (noting that the clause "preserves the U.S. relationship with Native American tribes as well as other national laws governing that relationship").

27. This clause implies that governments are to bring local resources into large-scale trade. It illustrates the dynamic tension between global trade and local sustainability expressed in the Biodiversity Convention; the Convention does not entirely abandon the trade policy principle of promoting global trade. As has been explained, however, the convention does require that trade and the overall production process be sustainable.

28. Informal innovation and continuing conservation have resulted in myriad "folk varieties" or "land races" of crops, vastly improving crop productivity and enriching plant genetic resources over millennia. See Jack R. Kloppenburg, Jr., *First the Seed* (Cambridge: Cambridge University Press, 1988), pp. 185–186.

29. Indigenous and local communities have "sophisticated and detailed knowledge of the uses of local biota" that can provide leads for discovery of valuable compounds. See Downes and Wold, "Biodiversity Prospecting," p. 382; see also Walter V.

Reid et al., "A New Lease on Life," in Walter V. Reid et al., eds., *Biodiversity Prospecting: Using Genetic Resources for Sustainable Development* (Washington, D.C.: World Resources Institute, 1993); Mark J. Plotkin, "The Outlook for New Agricultural and Industrial Products from the Tropics," in E. O. Wilson, ed., *Biodiversity* (Washington, D.C.: National Academy Press, 1988).

30. Since biodiversity is frequently associated with indigenous and traditional communities, when a country sets up a system for regulating access to genetic resources pursuant to Article 15 it is in effect "promoting wider application" of traditional knowledge, innovations, and practices within the terms of Article 8(j). In such cases, Article 15 access regulation must incorporate the consent and benefit-sharing requirements of Article 8(j).

31. Regardless of whether they create new IPRs, governments must ensure that existing IPR systems are applied consistently with Article 8(j). A number of national IPR systems allow for patents over modified plants or animals, IPR-like "plant breeders' rights" over crop varieties, or patents over chemicals derived from living organisms. If the proprietary organism, variety, or chemical is derived in part from genetic resources or traditional knowledge, then the existing IPR system has "promoted the wider application" of traditional knowledge and innovations, in the terms of Article 8(j). The legal system must therefore ensure that the source community gives its prior approval before IPRs are granted. It must also provide for "respect" of the community's contribution (which could be accomplished by requiring the patent applicant to make acknowledgment in the application) and encourage sharing of benefits. See Frederic Hendrickx, Veit Koester, and Christian Prip, "Access to Genetic Resources," in V. Sanchez and C. Juma, eds., *Biodiplomacy: Genetic Resources and International Relations* (Nairobi, Kenya: ACTS Press, 1994).

32. See for example, Wendell Berry, *The Gift of Good Land* (San Francisco: North Point, 1981), p. 167.

33. "The term 'subsistence economy' is now generally used only to designate group survival which is marginal to market dependence and in which people make what they use by means of traditional tools and within an inherited, often unexamined, social organization. I propose to recover the term by speaking about modern subsistence. Let us call modern subsistence the style of life that prevails in a postindustrial economy in which people have succeeded in reducing their market dependence, and have done so by protecting—by political means—a social infrastructure." See Ivan Illich, *Toward a History of Needs* (New York: Pantheon Books, 1978), p. 52.

CONCLUSION

I will prescribe regimen for the good of my patients according to my ability and my judgment and never do harm to anyone. To please no one will I prescribe a deadly drug, nor give advice which may cause his death. . . . In every house where I come I will enter only for the good of my patients, keeping myself far from all intentional ill-doing and all seduction.

—THE HIPPOCRATIC OATH

The policy of biodiversity protection is remarkably similar to the art of medicine. Both contain strong doses of science, yet both are laden with judgments and values of educated humans who seek merely to do the right thing. The difference between the two, of course, is that biodiversity protection by definition covers a much broader spectrum of life, thereby causing inevitable human error to reverberate more widely. As conservation biologists Reed Noss and Allen Cooperrider observe: "Science is a kind of understanding, albeit incomplete, and a kind of problem solving. The number of problems that need solving in the field of conservation are not becoming any fewer. Science in the form of conservation biology is a set of principles, empirical generalizations, and techniques for protecting nature—a toolbox for saving the earth. It is not a perfect toolbox . . . but it is the best we have."[1] It is not a coincidence that the Hippocratic Oath's reference to "house" (*oiko* or "eco") can be replaced by its Greek linguistic cousin "ecosystem" and still maintain its meaning.

Yet, increasingly, good faith stewardship of biodiversity is being met with fierce resistance by those powerful interests who have always opposed government interference with the market economy and by those smaller interests who are scared by their economic future. To both groups of people, the Constitution's Fifth Amendment "takings" clause, which has always required difficult public/private balancing, means protecting everything and anything

217

they own, damn the cost to society. Most disturbing are the growing number of murders, rapes, bombings, arsons, beatings, and associated threats of violence now linked to antienvironmentalists, many of whom operate under the "Wise Use" and "Private Property" banners.[2] While allegedly only rhetorical, it is telling that one of this movement's prominent leaders, Ron Arnold, has publicly stated: "We're out to kill the fuckers. We're simply trying to eliminate them. Our goal is to destroy environmentalism once and for all."[3] With emotions running this high, those who desire good medicine for the earth will not be able to sit quietly.

Indeed, the metaphoric words of author Robert Wright have taken a hauntingly literal meaning: "Our ethereal intuitions about what's right and what's wrong are weapons designed for daily, hand-to-hand combat among individuals."[4] Driving the social tensions over biodiversity protection are two inescapable future trends: the scientific limits of present consumption patterns and the brewing revolution in environmental law.[5] While past economic growth policies are undeniably unsustainable and perhaps suicidal, the modern practice of reflexively slapping additional regulations on new problems has often proved to be inefficient, ineffective, and costly. Somehow the legal system must be geared to create human incentives for biodiversity protection as it simultaneously affirms core human values such as biodiversity. Certain moral issues defy "the calculus of the market" by falling outside the premises and value judgments of formal economic study.[6] Biodiversity is, or should be, one of these moral issues.

Conservationists, Congress, and all other citizens would benefit from greater attention to the relationship between economics and ecology. One tack is to simply follow federal money: what direct biodiversity protection do our tax dollars buy—and where do tax dollars for other activities needlessly harm biodiversity? These questions, if honestly asked, will discomfort a number of vested interests on both sides of the policy debate, but they just might lead to enhanced biodiversity protection. The result might be greater flexibility for private property owners but greater accountability for private users of public resources. The winner would be biodiversity itself.

But the inescapable solution to our extinction crisis, of which biodiversity budgetary politics are only one part, is the potential genius of human adaptability. Unlike any other species, humans possess the unique capacity to create and destroy. The challenge for our species in this era of unprecedented economic and social specialization is to understand the surrounding natural world, and to build a harmonious spot within it. This will entail more than recycling bottles and cans, more than direct mail donations for the rain forest, and more than eloquent speeches by members of Congress. It will entail us thoroughly assessing our impact on the biotic community.

The cultural shift necessitated by a more intimate relationship to biodiversity will not be easy. Some of the requirements for the shift are familiar virtues pushed strongly in other contexts: diligence, responsibility, compassion, honesty, patience, humility, and teamwork.[7] Others, such as respect for the diversity of people, will be no easier to achieve for biodiversity than they have been for civil rights.[8] Still other prerequisites will involve accepting new and potentially radical theories of economics and science. All the requirements for a cultural shift on behalf of biodiversity, however, will raise, not lower, qualitative human living standards.

From a wholly legal perspective, the biodiversity shift may already be occurring. An international treaty now directly addresses biodiversity. Endangered Species Act implementation now seeks to protect it. Public land managers now regularly attempt to conserve biodiversity. Even historic common law doctrines are creeping toward the concept of biodiversity.

But are these changes being outpaced by the looming crisis of biodiversity loss? Only time will tell. Clearly, however, the legal system could be improved to protect biodiversity. As Defenders of Wildlife president Rodger Schlickeisen explains in the Epilogue, no less than a constitutional amendment may be needed to steer our massive body of laws toward a sustainable future. This amendment would not seek to replace fundamental American values, but would supplement them. It would not seek to deny American citizens their hard-won gains, but would seek to secure them. It would vividly show the Constitution to be the living document its framers intended.

Biodiversity law is the law of life. Its protection will require multifaceted and unprecedented cooperation between humans and nature, rich and poor, public and private. To be effective, biodiversity law must ultimately depend on the affirmative values of all citizens, not just "experts." Although these values will be influenced by sophisticated tenets of science and economics, their strength will be grounded in common sense and the eternal hope that humans can, indeed must, do better in cherishing the gift of life.

NOTES

1. Reed F. Noss and Allen Y. Cooperrider, *Saving Nature's Legacy* (Washington, D.C.: Island Press, 1994), p. 340.

2. See, generally, David Helvarg, *The War Against the Greens* (San Francisco: Sierra Club Books, 1994).

3. Ibid., p. 8.

4. Robert Wright, *The Moral Animal* (New York: Pantheon, 1994), p. 328.

5. See, for example, Lester Brown et al., *State of the World 1994,* (New York: Norton, 1994). See also Jessica Mathews, "Scorched Earth: Why the Hill Has Become an Environmental Disaster Area," *Washington Post,* Dec. 18, 1994, p. A25.

6. Robert Heilbroner, *Behind the Veil of Economics* (New York: Norton, 1988), pp. 50–51.

7. See, for example, William Bennett, *The Book of Virtues* (New York: Simon & Schuster, 1993).

8. See, for example, "Elder's Wish Outweighs Law, Hunters Say: Protected Whale Slaughtered So That 94-Year-Old Can Taste It Again Before He Dies," *Globe and Mail* (Toronto), Sept. 26, 1994; David Halberstam, *The Fifties* (New York: Ballantine Books, 1993), pp. 412–436, 667–684; Lani Guinier, *Tyranny of the Majority* (New York: Free Press, 1994).

EPILOGUE

THE ARGUMENT FOR A CONSTITUTIONAL AMENDMENT TO PROTECT LIVING NATURE

Rodger Schlickeisen

Granting that the earth is for man—there is still a question: What man?

—ALDO LEOPOLD

For thousands of years, successive human generations have passed onto their descendants a fundamentally undamaged living natural estate. Now, however, this precious inheritance is under serious threat. Natural areas in many parts of the world are being supplanted or drastically altered by human activities, and the earth's biological wealth is rapidly being depleted. Scientists have predicted that a significant portion of the world's plant and animal species will become extinct within the next several decades despite present conservation efforts. This trend has serious implications for the future of humans. Species losses not only impair life-support systems essential to human existence but also deprive the world of valuable foods and medicines.

To meet this threat effectively, more is required than humankind has attempted to date. Ordinary laws and conservation programs have proved insufficient. Relying on statutes alone is insufficient because normal legislative processes are systemically biased in favor of current benefits as opposed to the long-term future. Common law is insufficient as well. It falls far short of addressing the comprehensive need for protecting species and habitat. As for the United States Constitution, as currently written and interpreted, it overwhelmingly favors other values, especially private property rights.

This epilogue proposes an amendment to the U.S. Constitution that explicitly imposes upon the government an obligation to protect the right of all people, including future generations, to the benefits of our living natural resources. A properly written constitutional amendment would protect against both legislative and administrative actions that significantly harm natural systems and biological diversity. It would guarantee a citizen's right to sue against questionable government actions in this matter. It would bolster the public welfare as an offset to the present overemphasis on private property values. Above all, it would serve as a catalyst prompting the nation to embrace an ecological morality to complement its social morality. This is a necessity if America is to sustain and maximize its benefits from nature over the long term.

SOCIETY'S NEED AND DUTY TO PROTECT LIVING NATURE

In the late 1960s and early 1970s there were proposals in the U.S. Congress for a constitutional amendment establishing every citizen's right to a decent and healthful environment. One reason why these proposals failed is that success in winning enactment of environmental protection statutes fostered arguments that a constitutional amendment was unnecessary. This thinking now needs reassessment. The majority of our environmental protection laws were enacted as people became increasingly worried about pollution threats to human health and the loss of aesthetic and recreational opportunities. Not only were many of these environmental problems easily seen by the naked eye, but it was clear to the public that the problems were intensifying. People communicated their concern to elected officials and a series of statutes was passed, usually by a Democratic congress and a Republican president.

Since the 1970s, significant advances have been made toward solving many of these problems. The Clean Water Act ensures that today rivers are not catching fire, as the Cuyahoga once did. Emission controls on automobiles have reduced some types of air pollution, and the use of certain toxic pesticides such as DDT has been curtailed. The worst stream-polluting municipal and industrial activities are being reduced. Thanks to the Endangered Species Act (ESA), some of our most charismatic endangered species are recovering, including the alligator, gray whale, and bald eagle.

This progress has given the public the impression that all of our critical environmental problems are being solved. In fact, the contrary is true. Most disturbing are problems that were not targeted by the early legislation, most of which have only been recognized since the early 1970s. These problems involve subtle, long-term ecological degradation. They include global warming, ozone depletion, industrial chemicals that enter the food chain and disrupt hormones in humans and other animals,[1] and, perhaps most important, the loss of biodiversity, which is uniquely menacing because of its accelerating speed and its irreversibility.

By 1980, the problem of ecosystem deterioration and accompanying species extinction began impinging on the national consciousness. In that year, the *Global 2000 Report to the President,* prepared by the Council on Environmental Quality (CEQ) and the Department of State, predicted that as many as 600,000 species—perhaps 20 percent of all species on earth as then estimated—would be lost by the year 2000. Another 1980 report, CEQ's *Environmental Quality,* called this projected loss "unprecedented in the last 65 million years." The *Global 2000* report was followed by a set of recommendations to the president, *Global Future: Time to Act,* including a proposal to "establish a federal Interagency Task Force on Conservation of Biological Diversity to develop a comprehensive long-term strategy to maintain biological diversity."[2]

Although the reports' recommendations were largely ignored by the Reagan administration, scientific attention was beginning to focus on biodiversity loss. The new field of conservation biology was growing into a comprehensive and sophisticated scientific discipline. Satellite imagery was used to gather estimates of rain-forest loss. Research teams penetrated deep jungle and high mountains in search of areas rich in species. Sophisticated mathematical modeling enabled better estimates of species loss. With advanced genetic analyses and habitat models and a wealth of on-the-ground studies of altered habitats, researchers showed that small, fragmented populations face greater probabilities of extinction and that most nature reserves are too small to save all the species in them.

This research led to growing recognition among scientists that species loss is even greater than had been feared—and the rate of loss is accelerating. In 1990, the EPA's thirty-nine-member independent Science Advisory Board reported that species extinction and habitat loss, along with ozone depletion and global climate warming, pose the gravest risks to the global environment and human welfare.[3] New data suggest that there may be 30 million or more species in the world—and that 6 million or more may be lost by the year 2000.[4] Moreover, losses will continue to accelerate: one estimate projects that 66 percent of Amazon plant species and 69 percent of Amazon bird species will disappear.[5]

Attention was at first focused on tropical rain-forest diversity. Now scientists have recognized that other ecosystems are also at risk. Entire U.S. ecosystems are being threatened with extinction. A new Defenders of Wildlife report, *Endangered Ecosystems of the United States,* lists twenty-one types of critically endangered ecosystems, among them Pacific Northwest old-growth forest, tallgrass prairie, South Florida pine rocklands, and midwestern wetlands. Seven of the twenty-one have already lost more than 98 percent of the area that was present when European settlers arrived.[6] The overriding message is clear: poorly planned development and other human activities are rapidly destroying the biodiversity on which human well-being depends.

The human harm from continued biodiversity loss will come in many forms.[7] Yet the vast majority of citizens do not recognize the seriousness of this threat.[8] For one thing, even highly disturbed ecosystems may give the illusion of being healthy. In California, for example, although valley hills in the San Francisco Bay area appear covered with healthy oaks, closer inspection reveals that there are no saplings. Because ecological processes have been interrupted and cattle and deer are eating acorns and young seedlings, there has been little regeneration for decades, and the old oaks are beginning to die. Moreover, the native flowers and bunchgrasses that once covered the hills beneath the oaks are gone, replaced by European weeds.[9]

Some prominent critics, such as Julian Simon and Aaron Wildavsky, neither trained in the biological sciences, have argued that the rate of biodiversity loss is exaggerated and we do not need to be concerned about extinctions.[10] This argument is easily answered. Although there is indeed uncertainty about the exact rate at which species are becoming extinct, there is no doubt among mainstream scientists that we have entered the greatest episode of mass extinction since the loss of the dinosaurs.[11] Quibbling about the exact rate misses the point—when someone drives their car headfirst into a wall, arguing about whether the dead driver was traveling at 80 miles per hour or 90 miles per hour is academic.

Another argument is that even if extinction estimates are correct, technological advances, such as genetic engineering, will allow human beings to flourish even if we lose many of the species that presently support human life.[12] This argument deserves inspection. It is true that technology provides daily advances in many areas and may help solve certain environmental problems, such as acid rain, ozone depletion, and heating of the atmosphere. For these pollution problems, at least partial solutions exist in the form of alternative energy sources and industrial chemicals.[13] Implementation will depend on cost and political will.

But how useful is technology when it comes to repairing damaged ecosystems or replacing the services they render? Unfortunately for those who pin their hopes on ecological engineering, natural ecosystems are so complex and so little understood that once destroyed it would be impossible to rebuild them on a large scale. Despite decades of trying, skilled specialists have found it virtually impossible even to restore damaged U.S. saltwater wetlands— some of the simplest ecosystems in the world in terms of their species composition.[14] We barely know enough to introduce a single new species into a functioning ecosystem with safety, and the ecological literature is full of horror stories of ecosystems severely damaged by such attempts.[15] Ecosystems are so incredibly complex that a team of biologists with a billion-dollar budget could not begin to rebuild a tropical forest.[16]

If we cannot rebuild destroyed ecosystems, can we replace their functions with technology? Can we artificially create new soil for all the world's agriculture and filter all the water currently purified by wetlands through treatment plants? Can we farm all our seafood in enclosures, as we now do some salmon? Can we sustain our agricultural base without the addition of new genes from wild plants to confer disease resistance? Can new "virtual reality" experiences provide psychological benefits equal to those we gain from actual contact with nature and its many magnificent species? Can we invent from whole cloth the pharmaceuticals and genetic models upon which modern medicine and genetic recombination technology depend? The obvious answer is no. We depend on the natural world for our well-being, and if we destroy it, we destroy our children's patrimony. We thus have certain knowledge that future generations are not only being placed at risk but will in fact experience significant harm. As Edward O. Wilson has written: "There is no way in sight to micromanage the natural ecosystems and the millions of species they contain. That feat might be accomplished by generations yet to come, but then it will be too late for the ecosystems—and perhaps for us."[17]

Scientists are not alone in demanding that contemporary society address the long-term environmental damage being caused. A growing number of moral theorists are now making the same argument. Before scientific evidence proved otherwise, moral philosophers generally accepted the comfortable assumption, embedded in Western economic and political institutions, that technological advances and economic growth are synonymous with progress and hence desirable. If such progress nonetheless presaged diminution of some aspect of the quality of life, it was confidently believed that the loss would be more than offset by gains elsewhere and in overall wealth. That assumption fits comfortably with the concept of utilitarianism that is so influential in the United States. Utilitarianism offers the goal of "the greatest happiness for the greatest number." It views all human obligations as being limited to, and satisfied by, consideration only of individuals alive today or anticipated in immediate human posterity. Economic well-being is seen as the key to human happiness. Economic growth is seen as progress that by definition will benefit posterity.

For an influential and growing number of theorists, however, traditional utilitarianism is no longer adequate because of scientific evidence that society is causing substantial long-term environmental damage. Gone is the confident belief that since all growth and change represent progress, life in the future will necessarily be better than life today. It is of course impossible to predict the values future generations will hold, but common sense forces us to anticipate the continued validity of the basic human needs now recognized to be at risk. Moreover, utilitarianism's excessive reliance on "present-value" discounting techniques is ludicrous. These techniques, which discount future impacts back through time to determine a much lower present value, could eliminate even future catastrophe from having any bearing on current decisions.[18]

Some moral philosophers claim that no individualistic ethical framework can adequately conceptualize living humanity's obligations to future generations.[19] They propose use of ethical frameworks consistent with the ideas of eighteenth-century political philosopher Edmund Burke that treat our obligations to the future as extending not to individuals but to organic human society as a whole. And some are prepared to go further—to replace today's anthropocentrism with a more holistic, ecosystemic approach to valuing nature and thus to grant moral consideration even to nonhuman entities.[20]

While such a challenge to anthropocentrism may have merit, the desirability of a wholly ecosystemic reordering of moral philosophy is not the subject of anything approaching consensus among moral theorists. Nor is acceptance of such a major reordering necessary to support legal protection for biodiversity. It is necessary only to accept the scientific reality that current policies are certain to harm future generations and that we have a moral obligation to modify those policies in the interest of intergenerational equity:

> In order to define what intergenerational fairness means in using and conserving our common patrimony, it is useful to view the human community as a partnership among all generations. . . . The purpose of human society must be to realize and protect the welfare and well-being of every generation. This requires sustaining the life-support systems of the planet, the ecological processes, environmental conditions, and cultural resources important for the survival and well-being of the human species, and a healthy and decent human environment. . . . This requires that each generation pass the planet on in no worse condition than it received it and provide equitable access to its resources and benefits.[21]

A critical feature of this intergenerational obligation is its recognition that the living are at once trustees of the environment for future generations and beneficiaries of that environment. This dual role means we are not required to forsake using natural resources in order to preserve them. We have both a right to use those resources and an obligation to conserve them to protect future options and welfare. The obligation it imposes on us is not to forgo use of natural resources but only to ensure that they will last.

This foregoing proposal incorporates a strong recommendation for being fair in decisions having impacts across generations. As such, it reinforces philosopher John Rawls' classic decision model intended to eliminate temporal bias by requiring that self-interested decision makers not know when they make decisions in which generation they themselves will live. Although such an idealized decision model cannot be duplicated in the real world, it helps to conceptualize the objective viewpoint society should take if it is to extend its moral horizon and assure intergenerational equity.

Theorist Bryan Norton of the Georgia Institute of Technology has modified Rawls' rational decision model on the basis of the holistic Leopoldian view that ecosystem health will be assured only if "the sum total of species and the variety of associations in which they exist are preserved over time."[22] He employs the modified model to evaluate alternative strategies for natural resource use. To acknowledge and balance society's two roles of resource trustee and resource beneficiary, Norton proposes a "naturalist-preservationist" strategy assuring great attention to the utilitarians' favored economic criteria. But he rejects exclusive reliance on such criteria. He proposes a two-step decision process that first considers "ecological information on the biotic systems in question, its strength and redundancy, its vulnerability to stress" and, second, uses economic considerations "to determine which of the permissible models of exploitation will maximize human material well-being in the present."[23]

Our sense of moral obligation to future generations should focus our attention primarily on policies that we know threaten unrecompensable harm to posterity. As for biological diversity, these are policies that seriously harm species, habitats, and ecological processes. Norton aptly describes these policies as requiring preemptive constraints limiting the manner in which society's immediate economic objectives may be pursued. This is where our moral duty is inescapable—for the welfare of our successors is profoundly at stake and we can no longer claim to be ignorant of that fact. Because we have knowledge of the consequences of our actions, the options available, and the capacity to choose those options, we also have the moral responsibility to act.

Norton also has devised a conceptual tool that he calls a "risk decision square" to identify subjects that warrant society's undivided attention because of their intergenerational aspects. A typical square looks like this:

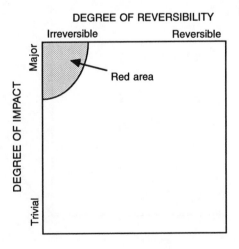

Subjects requiring decisions because of their effect on the future are located by plotting the potential magnitude of their impact against their degree of reversibility. Subjects falling in the far upper left quadrant, the "red area," are those threatening maximum impact on the future with the least possibility of reversal. These are decisions that cannot be compensated for by increases in wealth or in any other manner. They risk unrecompensable harm to the future and must therefore be "constrained by a moral principle of sustainability" or even be "morally forbidden."[24]

With modification, the risk decision square can also be a useful tool for evaluating proposals to protect future generations and identifying those that truly warrant a constitutional amendment. The new tool might be used to evaluate not only the environmental amendment proposed here but others, such as the currently popular proposal for an amendment to require a balanced federal budget. Norton uses the x and y axes in his decision squares. If a z axis is added, the square becomes a decision cube. Using a third dimension, it is now possible to plot proposals for amendments to protect the future based not only on their degree of expected impact and reversibility, but also on the level of governmental constraint required to assure the desired outcome. For example:

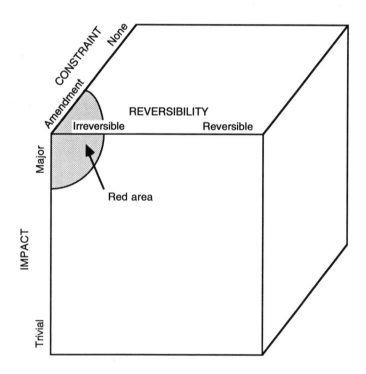

Beginning at the most remote point on the z ("constraint") axis and moving inward, the level of constraint rises and becomes more legally formal. At first there is no formal constraint—a libertarian reliance on voluntary action by private individuals and entities. Next come increasing levels of constraint imposed by common and statutory law. These are followed by increased constraint from new judicial interpretations of constitutional law. And finally—closest to the intersection of the x and y axes—there is a new constraint imposed at the highest possible level via amendment to the Constitution.

Using this "constitutional amendment decision cube," suppose a specific subject threatens high and irreversible impact on future generations. If it nonetheless can be satisfactorily dealt with by lower-level constraints—whether imposed by voluntarism, common law, statutory regulation, or even constitutional judicial interpretation—it falls outside the three-dimensional red area and does not merit elevation to explicit constitutional expression. But if the subject falls within the red area—that is, if it is found to be fraught with danger for the future, lacks any significant opportunities to reverse the trend or otherwise compensate for it, and is impervious to effective attack through other means—then a constitutional amendment is required.

A moral perspective leads one to conclude that any policy destroying essential biodiversity is unethical and must be morally forbidden. The magnitude and certainty of the future harm society is causing with policies that entail the loss of biodiversity has led many moral philosophers to use biodiversity loss as a prime example when discussing the responsibility of the living to the unborn. There should be no question that a proposal to deal with the biodiversity loss problem falls in the red area of Norton's risk decision cube and that a solution is possible only by constitutional amendment.

LAWMAKING PREJUDICED AGAINST THE FUTURE

To look to elected politicians to legislate a solution to biodiversity loss is probably futile. Our political and legislative process currently reflects the conviction that the best life for ourselves—and by extension for our descendants—maximizes current economic benefits. Thirty years after Stewart Udall forcefully condemned our "myth of superabundance," most voters continue to favor candidates promising the quickest improvement in our material standard of living while ignoring evidence that long-entrenched policies must be changed if the nation's material gains are to be sustained over the long term. It is hardly surprising, then, that our actions to protect biodiversity are woefully inadequate.

Despite numerous surveys showing strong public support for saving endangered species and for the ESA itself,[25] political opponents have managed to impede the act's implementation and most administrations and Congress have starved the program for funds.[26] Largely on this account, many listed species do not have approved recovery plans, and few of those plans are being properly administered.[27] In many cases, courts have found the ESA being violated by the government itself. Until recently, use of ESA provisions reaching beyond single species to promote ecosystem health and prevent endangerment was essentially untried. And the congressional climate has been so unfavorable that whenever the act has come up for periodic reauthorization, its backers have felt compelled to concentrate primarily on simply protecting the inadequate program rather than seeking its expansion.

Now the ESA faces its most serious challenge ever. Supporters worry that it may be shredded by congressional opponents who seize upon the act's every shortcoming and inconvenience to economic activity as reasons to emasculate it.[28] Of particular significance, some opponents propose to repeal the requirement that species be listed as endangered or threatened exclusively on the basis of objective science. Instead, they would make listing conditional on favorable cost/benefit analysis. In that case, "present-value" discounting could result in essentially all negative impacts projected beyond two or three decades having no influence at all on current listing decisions. Such a policy would ignore both the scientific significance of species loss and the ethical issue of harm to future generations.

One of the most effective political attacks on the ESA uses the Constitution itself. So important did our founding fathers consider private property rights that they assured their protection by including them in the Bill of Rights. They could not have foreseen that this action would someday result in the use of that value to undermine another important American value—fostering our descendants' well-being by protecting biological diversity. It was of course also impossible for the drafters of the Constitution to anticipate that within a mere two centuries an exploding population with nature-devouring technology would fundamentally threaten the future welfare of the nation. Now, our legislative process is facilitating the accelerated loss of nature, sacrificing the welfare of future generations in order to maximize immediate economic benefits. Without a major catalyst, legislation is unlikely to be effective in protecting biodiversity and thus averting serious harm to future generations.

LIMITATIONS OF THE TRADITIONAL LEGAL SYSTEM

Historical and contemporary interpretations of the Constitution are at odds with the objective of providing effective stewardship of valuable natural resources and ecological processes. That our founding fathers could not have foreseen our contemporary environmental problems is obvious. Still, to those not schooled in the development of our legal system, it is discouraging to learn that something as basic as society's need to assure the sustainability of our living natural resources is not included in the U.S. Constitution or common law, even though the Constitution's drafters unquestionably intended to provide for the welfare of future generations. The Preamble makes this clear: We the People of the United States, in Order to form a more perfect Union, establish Justice, insure domestic Tranquility, provide for the common defence, promote the general Welfare, and secure the Blessings of Liberty to ourselves and our Posterity, do ordain and establish this Constitution for the United States of America.

The Preamble, then, clearly states "and our Posterity." Yet in the original articles and amendments there is nothing explicitly providing for posterity's welfare by protecting nature. Attempts to establish an environmental fundamental right through new interpretation of various provisions of the Constitution have all been unsuccessful.[29]

Wildlife law in the United States has traditionally viewed wildlife as a common resource. Although the boundaries separating federal and state government responsibilities for wildlife stewardship remain imprecisely defined, by common law practice and the Tenth Amendment the primary responsibility resides with the states.[30] The states, in turn, exercise that responsibility by considering themselves "as the owners of their wildlife resources, and as trustees holding wildlife in custody for the benefit of their citizens."[31] But state government has a long history of concentrating its wildlife stewardship activities on regulation and management of a comparative handful of sport species valued almost exclusively for their direct consumptive uses.[32] Moreover, the ecologically arbitrary boundaries of the states, and thus the limits of their responsibility and authority, are inconsistent with the cross-border dimensions of the many ecological processes society needs to preserve.

Environmentalists intent on stemming biodiversity loss want appropriate protection for all living organisms—even the insects and microorganisms responsible for such life-supporting services as decomposing waste and providing fertile soil. But little in current law protects the myriad life forms and their interactions that provide such services. The common law doctrine of nuisance has evolved to redress a wide variety of injuries to private property and public rights, including pollution or other harm to the environment. But even the concept of public nuisance, which by definition involves harm to an interest common to the general public, has not been extended to a subject so complex as conserving biodiversity for human benefit. The other common law doctrine that might be available is the public trust doctrine. But this doctrine, which establishes state government's common law responsibility for certain water resources, still demonstrates insufficient application to the much more comprehensive task of protecting biodiversity.[33]

As things stand, we have no practical alternative but to try to protect bio-diversity as incidental to the regulation of pollution as an immediate health threat and, especially, the use of land as property. Again we are confronted by the formidable reality of the Constitution's silence on stewardship of natural resources. Conversely, the Fifth Amendment places heavy emphasis on pro-tecting the right of the individual owner to do as he wishes with his property, even though, in the case of land, it may be home to much of the biodiversity upon which society's welfare ultimately depends. So ingrained in the Ameri-can culture is our notion of private property rights that it has given rise to "one of the more bizarre notions of Anglo-American property law [that there is an] asserted right of an owner to destroy what he owns, even if in doing so he deprives the world of something valuable and unique."[34]

Unless this constitutionally protected value is appropriately balanced with the even more fundamental value of preserving nature's benefits, landowner-ship can be interpreted to convey to a present tenant a unique and legally protected power to destroy species and habitats important to the continued welfare of society. This at least appears to be the practical import of Supreme Court decisions giving deference to individual owners to decide the fate of the wildlife species and natural biodiversity associated with their land.

Joseph Sax, a noted authority on public land law, has analyzed the unprecedented challenge that biodiversity preservation poses to traditional property rights concepts. Sax has concluded that the Supreme Court has rejected the challenge, opting purposely to limit severely the legal foundation for protecting land for its ecological value. He notes that Justice Antonin Scalia's majority decision, in the landmark *Lucas v. South Carolina Coastal Council*,[35] effectively leaves historical common law nuisance principles as the only source of state authority to regulate private land in favor of ecological processes—but simultaneously says those processes are not covered by nec-essary "background principles of nuisance and property law."[36] Similarly, Richard Lazarus has said that in *Lucas* "the Court [apparently assumes] that the common law of nuisance is the sole legitimate basis for a restriction that eliminates all economic value."[37] And Dan Tarlock asserts that Scalia's opin-ion "reflects an unjustified contempt for all levels of environmental regula-tion, no matter how clear the scientific link between a land use activity and harm to other land in the area, and a lack of appreciation for the extent to which the teachings of ecology have altered our conception of harmful land use practices."[38] All three scholars conclude that recent majority opinions err in their approach to protecting ecological processes and biodiversity because they ignore the fact that definitions of property have always been elastic.

To the legal scholar it is no doubt fascinating to contemplate how, through the complex and sometimes tortured evolution of judicial interpretation, our legal system might eventually do the unprecedented and find creative means to integrate into court decisions a broader doctrine of ecological protection.

But why should we gamble the welfare of our children and future generations on this possibility? When we are dealing with a value as fundamental as providing for the future welfare of our own species, should we not opt for a stronger, more direct remedy? Should not biodiversity be considered a commons benefiting all society and appropriately protected for that purpose in the Constitution?

Another justification for a constitutional amendment safeguarding nature's living legacy has to do with the problem of legal standing to sue when the object of a lawsuit is to prevent future harm.[39] Consider this hypothetical situation: Against the odds, Congress has enacted a comprehensive law protecting biodiversity. Relying on that law, a plaintiff is in court with unimpeachable evidence that a proposed federal agency action will cause immediate significant loss of biodiversity and thereby inflict serious human harm, but not until one hundred years in the future. The plaintiff's objective is to protect present generations' unborn descendants and all subsequent human life. The plaintiff's attorney knows that unless the plaintiff argues some other purpose that clearly involves harm to himself and living humanity, precedent suggests that the court will find insufficient injury for him to sue. The plaintiff's attorney therefore presents instead a potentially more salable argument that advances a separate purpose involving harm to living humanity. This, the attorney determines, might lead to a finding that the plaintiff has standing and can therefore pursue the real objective.

At best, the outcome on standing in this case would be uncertain when by any reasonable moral standard it should be assured. Why, moreover, should it be necessary to find a back door into court when the plaintiff's noble purpose is to advance one of society's most fundamental values? Why should not the Constitution itself assure U.S. citizens legal standing for such a worthwhile purpose in which society has great interest? Not only does the Constitution not assure such standing, but a number of legal scholars have interpreted recent court cases as indicating that the courts are *purposefully* making it more difficult for opponents of damaging natural resource use to bring lawsuits. And, it is claimed, Congress is abetting the move by enacting legislation that serves the same end.[40] Only an amendment that guarantees citizens a constitutional right to protect biological resources important to future generations will be able to resolve all doubt about the standing of a citizen to sue to enjoin government actions that endanger those resources.

A PROPOSED CONSTITUTIONAL AMENDMENT

How should we structure a constitutional amendment to protect biological diversity for future generations? At one extreme might be a simple statement of public policy and at the other an extensive declaration of right combined with specific directives to official bodies to secure that right, along with some description of the process to be followed.

The following suggestion, which relies primarily upon stating an environmental right, includes a basic policy statement. It is concise and fundamental in order to accommodate the goal of maintaining the Constitution as a living document. It purposely leaves to statutory law and judicial interpretation the task of determining the complex details. It is that:

> The living natural resources in the United States are the common property of all the people, including generations yet to come. All persons and their progeny have an inalienable, enforceable right to the benefits of those resources for themselves and their posterity. The United States and every State shall assure that use of those resources is sustainable and that they are conserved and maintained for the benefit of all the people.

Whatever the wording and length, the language should establish the right to the benefits of living nature and explicitly extend that right to future generations as a class. Nothing less can guarantee the fundamental values at issue and guarantee that those values receive at least the same legal deference the Supreme Court now gives to other values of no greater merit. The result should be that future conflicts between sustainable use of our living natural resources and other constitutionally embedded values will shift in favor of sustainability. This should mitigate the traditional political bias maximizing immediate benefits at the expense of assuring their continuation over the long term.

A. E. Dick Howard has noted that the provision of a constitutional environmental right "might result in a broader definition of what constitutes a nuisance, private or public. Moreover, the existence of a constitutional right could alter the balancing technique which courts use in nuisance cases to weigh the social and economic benefits of the defendant's activity against the harm which that activity is doing to the plaintiff."[41]

The wording is intended to make the amendment self-executing. It provides for citizen participation by guaranteeing that citizens will have standing to sue to enforce its provisions, both for themselves directly and for future generations as their guardians, whether or not there is supporting statutory law. In its most direct application, this will provide a direct means of bringing a cause of action to prohibit legislative or other government action that violates government's obligation to protect living nature's benefits for all people, including future generations. The language also imposes an obligatory duty on all levels of government to take positive action to secure the stated right. It recognizes traditional state management responsibility for resident fish and wildlife within a constitutionally mandated framework of sustainability. And it encourages legislative and administrative approaches to utilizing our natural resources so that all adopt the same common framework.

By constitutional recognition of environmental sustainability, the amendment should powerfully, albeit informally, promote in a way otherwise unavailable a paradigm shift in America's traditional culture of natural resource exploitation. Because the Constitution is the most fundamental expression of society's values,

> constitutional provisions promote a model character for the citizenry to follow, and they influence and guide public discourse and behavior. On a practical level, the public tends to be more familiar with constitutional provisions than specific statutory laws. Citizens tend to identify with, and in turn are identified by, the form of their national constitution. Thus, establishing . . . environmental protection in a national constitution results in the identification of environmental protection with expressions of national pride and character. The establishment process itself further informs the nation's consciousness.[42]

CONSTITUTIONAL PROVISIONS ELSEWHERE

It is likely to be argued that environmental values and nature conservation simply do not deserve elevation to constitutional status.[43] Constitution writers all over the world have tended to accept the precept that constitutions should be limited to only the most basic and necessary fundamentals of government. Thus it is instructive to note the recent appearance of environmental constitutional provisions elsewhere.

Since the 1960s, numerous international legal documents have been negotiated with the explicit intent of advancing protection of the environment for the future, most recently the Convention on Biological Diversity. Many other nations now have environmental provisions in their constitutions. So do some of our states.

Edith Brown Weiss notes that thirty-three national constitutional provisions, nearly all of them recent, require government, private citizens, or both to provide such protection. Following are excerpts from three national constitutions that provide both a fundamental environmental right and a complementary statement of public policy:[44]

- *Brazil:* Ch. VI, Art. 225: "Everyone has the right to an ecologically balanced environment. . . . This imposes upon the Public Authorities and the community the obligation to defend and preserve it for present and future generations. . . . It is incumbent upon the Public Authorities . . . to preserve and restore essential ecological processes and to provide for the ecological management of species and ecosystems."

- *Portugal:* Pt. I, Sec. III, Ch. II, Art. 66: "(1) All have the right to a humane, healthy, and ecologically balanced human environment and the duty to preserve it."
- *Turkey:* Article 56: "Everyone has the right to live in a healthy, balanced environment. . . . It is the duty of the State and the citizens to improve the natural environment and to prevent environmental pollution."

Moreover, no fewer than twelve U.S. states include in their constitutions explicit provisions requiring government to conserve nature.[45] Four of these—Hawaii, Illinois, Montana, and Pennsylvania—incorporate references to future generations and five—Hawaii, Illinois, Massachusetts, Pennsylvania, and Rhode Island—establish a fundamental environmental right. Following are relevant excerpts:

- *Hawaii:* Art. XI, Sec. 1: "For the benefit of present and future generations, the State and its political subdivisions shall conserve and protect Hawaii's natural beauty and all natural resources." Art. XI, Sec. 9: "Each person has the right to a clean and healthful environment. . . . Any person may enforce this right against any party, public or private, through appropriate legal proceedings."
- *Illinois:* Art. XI, Sec. 1: "The public policy of the State and the duty of each person is to provide and maintain a healthful environment for the benefit of this and future generations." Art. XI, Sec. 2: "Each person has the right to a healthful environment. Each person may enforce this right against any party, governmental or private, through appropriate legal proceedings."
- *Massachusetts:* Amend. Art. XLIX: "The people shall have the right to clean air and water, freedom from excessive and unnecessary noise, and the natural, scenic, historic and esthetic qualities of their environment; and the protection of the people in their right to the conservation, development and utilization of the agricultural, mineral, forest, water, air and other natural resources is hereby declared to be a public purpose."
- *Montana:* Art. IX, 1: "(1) The state and each person shall maintain and improve a clean and healthful environment in Montana for present and future generations."
- *Pennsylvania:* Art. I, Sec. 27: "The people have a right to clean air, pure water, and to the preservation of the natural, scenic, historic and esthetic values of the environment. Pennsylvania's public natural resources are the common property of all the people, including generations yet to come."
- *Rhode Island:* Amend. Art. XXXVII, Sec. 1: "The people shall . . . be secure in their rights to the use and enjoyment of the natural resources of the state with due regard for the preservation of their values."

It should also be recalled that in 1972 Supreme Court Justice William O. Douglas, supported by Justices Harry Blackmun and William Brennan, gave serious consideration in *Sierra Club v. Morton*[46] to the proposition that someone or some human institution should be permitted standing to sue on behalf of nonhuman nature. In fact, so close was the vote by which the proposal lost that Garrett Hardin, writing in the foreword to Christopher Stone's book, *Should Trees Have Standing? Toward Legal Rights for Natural Objects*, commented optimistically:

> In a way, the trees lost, albeit narrowly—and perhaps temporarily. Had they won, the Mineral King decision would no doubt have been called "a watershed decision." . . . I submit that it is a good bet that we are near the ridge of a watershed. It is not merely the closeness of the decision (4-to-3) that leads to the suspicion; it is also the tone of the majority opinion—which is not unfriendly to the trees—as well as other evidences of a changing climate of opinion in this country.[47]

If three Supreme Court justices and other scholars believed legal standing should be granted on behalf of nonhuman nature based on nature's own intrinsic values, then a suggestion that the Constitution should protect living nature explicitly for humans is certainly not out of bounds.

DOES THE PROPOSED AMENDMENT GO FAR ENOUGH?

To many committed environmentalists, the proposal to protect living nature for its value to present and future generations will seem inadequate. They no doubt will be joined by the moral philosophers who reject traditional anthropocentric ethical frameworks in favor of ecocentric ones that grant moral consideration to elements of nonhuman nature. They may even consider the idea of protecting nature for merely human purposes to be moral anathema.

It is possible to be sympathetic to this perspective and still conclude that, because of the inherent legal and systemic constraints of our anthropocentric culture, it actually offers little benefit to the cause of protecting nature. Moreover, a number of moral philosophers categorically reject the proposition that because there are important values inherent in nature, one must conclude that all nonhuman nature (such as a tree) has "rights." Bryan Norton has noted that Aldo Leopold himself, although including in his "land ethic" specific obligations of humans to nature, nonetheless stuck to an anthropocentric approach when it came to determining policy.[48] As a practical matter, and in light of the legislative process and trend of judicial interpretation of the Constitution, it is extremely unlikely that our legal system in the foreseeable future will follow Justice Douglas's suggestion and grant legal consideration without first confirming the existence of moral consideration.

Perhaps the amendment proposed here will turn out to be but a way station on the road to granting legal consideration to nonhuman nature. In the meantime, the approach entailed by this amendment—establishing a guardian-protected right of future human generations to the continued benefits of nature's biodiversity—should offer better prospects of acceptance because it relies only on anthropocentric moral arguments with which our legal system should be comfortable and for which it was created. The Constitution already guarantees to "our Posterity" legal rights to go along with their moral rights to such fundamental values as liberty, religious freedom, and freedom of speech. What is necessary is the fairly straightforward task of persuading society that posterity has an equal moral right to benefit from living nature, and that this moral right should be similarly and equally protected by a legal right stated in the Constitution.

While the proposed amendment does not go as far as some would wish in protecting nature from human impact, to my mind it goes as far as possible considering current and foreseeable constraints. Also, while the amendment's direct purpose is to promote human welfare, the result nonetheless should be a significant degree of otherwise unattainable protecton for the natural environment. Biological diversity in this context is potentially a very big umbrella under which numerous environmental values should find shelter.

Toward a True Land Ethic

Scientists are warning that losses of species and natural habitats, together producing the loss of biological diversity, have already reached a crisis stage. Because these losses are the result of human activities that harm future generations even while benefiting current material standards of living, present generations have a compelling moral obligation to prevent this biocrisis from ending in catastrophe. There are ways for Americans to live more sustainably and opportunities to choose them, but the political will to do so is missing. Elected officials align themselves with beggar-the-children policies that maximize short-term economic gain without heed to the need for sustainability. Biological diversity is destroyed to provide immediate economic benefits for current constituents, to the detriment of future generations unable to defend themselves against the political assault on their welfare.

To the extent that elected officeholders do enact statutes giving greater protection to species and natural habitats, their efforts, unless supplemented by a constitutional amendment, will probably be so slow and unwieldy that they will result in serious, permanent, and unnecessary additional losses of biodiversity. Even with the requisite set of statutes, judicial interpretation of standing and private property rights probably would defeat meaningful implementation and enforcement. It is time for the United States to treat the Constitution as the living document our forefathers intended and amend it to protect a value that its drafters undoubtedly would have embraced had they possessed the knowledge and foresight. That value merits constitutional expression because it is one of society's most fundamental: to provide for proper stewardship of the natural estate upon which human life depends.

Properly worded and interpreted, a constitutional amendment will help our nation protect nature both by law and by culture. It will assure that citizens have a legal right to continue to receive the benefits of living nature. It should provide at least equal legal footing for biodiversity with other values already in the Constitution. And it should help stimulate throughout society a change from resource exploitation activities that give priority to short-term economic benefits, at the expense of the future, to ones that emphasize current well-being within a framework of assured continued environmental health that permits maximization of long-term benefits. Ultimately, such an amendment may point the way to our adoption of the "land ethic" first propounded by Aldo Leopold, an ecological morality in which humans see themselves not as conquerors of nature but rather as partners in our shared land community. Paradoxically, it is only by adopting this perspective that we can maximize nature's benefits to human society over the long term.

NOTES

1. Theo Colborn, Frederick S. vom Saal, and Ana M. Soto, "Development Effects of Endocrine-Disrupting Chemicals in Wildlife and Humans," *Environmental Health Perspectives* 101 (October 1993):1.

2. U.S. Council on Environmental Quality and U.S. Department of State, *The Global 2000 Report to the President,* 2 vols. (Washington, D.C.: Government Printing Office, 1980), and *Global Future: Time to Act* (Washington, D.C.: Government Printing Office, 1981); U.S. Council on Environmental Quality, *Environmental Quality—1980: The Eleventh Report of the Council on Environmental Quality* (Washington, D.C.: Government Printing Office, 1980), p. 31.

3. U.S. Environmental Protection Agency, *Reducing Risk: Setting Priorities and Strategies for Environmental Protection,* 1990.

4. R. L. Peters and T. E. Lovejoy, "Transformations in Terrestrial and Freshwater Fauna During the Past 300 years as the Result of Human Actions," in B. L. Turner II et al., eds, *The Earth as Transformed by Human Action* (Cambridge: Cambridge University Press, 1991), pp. 353–369.

5. D. Simberloff, "Are We on the Verge of a Mass Extinction in Tropical Rainforests?" in D. K. Elliott, ed., *Dynamics of Extinction* (New York: Wiley, 1986), pp. 165–180.

6. Defenders of Wildlife, *Endangered Ecosystems of the United States* (Washington, D.C.: Defenders of Wildlife, 1995).

7. See Eric Chivian, "Species Extinction and Biodiversity Loss: The Implications for Human Health," in Eric Chivian et al., eds., *Critical Condition: Human Health and the Environment* (Cambridge, Mass.: MIT Press,1993), pp. 197–218; Ernest Partridge, "Nature as a Moral Resource," *Environmental Ethics* 6 (Summer 1984):101–130; Edward O. Wilson, "Is Humanity Suicidal?" *New York Times Magazine,* May 30, 1993), pp. 24–29; Reed F. Noss and Allen Y. Cooperrider, *Saving Nature's Legacy: Protecting and Restoring Biodiversity* (Washington, D.C.: Island Press, 1994), pp. 19–23; Stephen R. Kellert and Edward O. Wilson, *The Biophilia Hypothesis* (Washington, D.C.: Island Press, 1993); Mark J. Plotkin, "The Outlook for New Agricultural and Industrial Products from the Tropics," in E. O. Wilson, ed., *Biodiversity* (Washington, D.C.: National Academy Press, 1988), pp. 106–116; J. Trevor Williams, "Identifying and Protecting the Origins of Our Food Plants," in Wilson, *Biodiversity* pp. 240–247; Paul R. Ehrlich and Harold A. Mooney, "Extinction, Substitution, and Ecosystem Services," *BioScience* 33(4) (April 1983):248–252; Walter E. Westman, "How Much Are Nature's Services Worth?" *Science* 197 (2 Sept. 1977):960–963; Paul R. Ehrlich, "The Loss of Diversity: Causes and Consequences," in Wilson, *Biodiversity* pp. 21–27.

8. Defenders of Wildlife, "National Survey on Biodiversity," Peter D. Hart Research Associates and Dr. Stephen R. Kellert, April 1993.

9. M. Barbour, B. Pavlik, F. Drysdale, and S. Lindstrom, *California's Changing Landscapes* (Sacramento: California Native Plant Society, 1993), p. 244.

10. Julian L. Simon and Aaron Wildavsky, "Extinction: Species Loss Revisited," *Endangered Species Blueprint* 5(1) (Fall 1994).

11. Wilson, "Is Humanity Suicidal?" p. 29.

12. Simon and Wildavsky, "Extinction," pp. 6–9.

13. Dean Edwin Abrahamson, *The Challenge of Global Warming* (Washington, D.C.: Island Press, 1989), p. 224; James J. MacKenzie, *Breathing Easier: Taking Action on Climate Change, Air Pollution, and Energy Insecurity* (Washington, D.C.: World Resources Institute, 1988), pp. 17–23; James J. MacKenzie and Mohamed T. El-Ashry, *Ill Winds: Airborne Pollution's Toll on Trees and Crops* (Washington, D.C.: World Resources Institute, 1988), pp. 56–57.

14. William R. Jordan, Robert L. Peters, and Edith B. Allen, "Ecological Restoration as a Strategy for Conserving Biological Diversity," *Environmental Management* 12(1) (1988):61–62.

15. Charles S. Elton, *The Ecology of Invasions by Animals and Plants* (London: Chapman & Hall, 1958), pp. 15–32.

16. Wilson, "Is Humanity Suicidal?" p. 29.

17. Ibid., p. 27.

18. For a discussion of welfare economists' efforts to find alternatives to traditional benefit–cost and present-value analyses for deciding biodiversity conservation issues, see Alan Randall, "What Mainstream Economists Have to Say About the Value of Biodiversity," in Wilson, *Biodiversity* pp. 217–223.

19. Bryan G. Norton, "Obligations to Future Generations," in *Encyclopedia of Bioethics* (New York: Macmillan, 1995).

20. See for example, Ernest Partridge, "Nature as a Moral Resource," *Environmental Ethics* (Summer 1984):xx; Holmes Rolston III, *Environmental Ethics: Duties to and Values in the Natural World* (Philadelphia: Temple University Press, 1988); J. Baird Callicott, *In Defense of the Land Ethic* (Albany: State University of New York Press, 1989); Paul Taylor, *Respect for Nature* (Princeton: Princeton University Press, 1986).

21. Edith Brown Weiss, *In Fairness to Future Generations: International Law, Common Patrimony, and Intergenerational Equity* (Tokyo and Dobbs Ferry, N.Y.: United Nations University and Transnational Publishers, 1989), pp. 23–24.

22. Bryan G. Norton, "Intergenerational Equity and Environmental Decisions: A Model Using Rawls' Veil of Ignorance," *Ecological Economics* 1 (1989):137–159.

23. Ibid.

24. Norton, "Obligations," pp. 10–12.

25. Noss and Cooperrider, *Saving Nature's Legacy* p. 18; Defenders of Wildlife, "National Survey on Biodiversity," (July 1993); "Election '94: Voters Want Strong Enviro Laws—Poll," *Greenwire* 4(162) (Dec. 21, 1994):3–4.

26. Stephen M. Meyer, "The Final Act," *New Republic*, Aug. 15, 1994, p. 24; Michael O'Connell, "Response to 'Six Biological Reasons Why the Endangered Species Act Doesn't Work and What to Do About It,'" *Conservation Biology* 6(1) (March 1992):140–143; Richard Tobin, *The Expendable Future: U.S. Politics and the Protection of Biological Diversity* (Durham, N.C.: Duke University Press, 1991), pp. 34–68, 229–270.

27. Oliver A. Houck, "The Endangered Species Act and Its Implementation by the U.S. Departments of Interior and Commerce," *Colorado Law Review* 64 (1993):344.

28. Meyer, "The Final Act," p. 24.

29. Ernst Brandl and Hartwin Bungert, "Constitutional Entrenchment of Environmental Protection: A Comparative Analysis of Experiences Abroad," *Harvard Environmental Law Review* 16(1) (1992):5, 21–23. Brandl and Bungert discuss failed attempts to infer an environmental constitutional right using the First Amendment, Ninth Amendment, and the Due Process Clauses of the Fifth and Fourteenth Amendments. See also A. E. Dick Howard, "State Constitutions and the Environment," *Virginia Law Review* 58 (Feb. 1972):194–196; In addition, a recent Supreme Court case even brings into question the use of the commerce clause by Congress to regulate various private actions. *United States v. Lopez*, 115 S.Ct. 1624 (1995).

30. Oliver A. Houck, "Why Do We Protect Endangered Species and What Does That Say About Whether Restrictions on Private Property to Protect Constitute 'Takings?'" unpublished paper, pp. 17–36; Michael Bean, *The Evolution of National Wildlife Law* (New York: Praeger, 1983), pp. 9–48.

31. Houck, "Why Do We Protect?" p. 18.

32. Defenders of Wildlife, *In Defense of Wildlife: Preserving Communities and Corridors* (Washington, D.C.: Defenders of Wildlife, 1989), p. 68.

33. See, for example, John A. Chiappinelli, "The Right to a Clean and Safe Environment: A Case for a Constitutional Amendement Recognizing Public Rights in Common Resources," *Buffalo Law Review* 40 (1992):599–601.

34. Joseph L. Sax, "The Search for Environmental Rights," *Journal of Land Use and Environmental Law* 6 (1993):103.

35. 112 S. Ct. 2886 (1992).

36. Joseph L. Sax, "Property Rights and the Economy of Nature: Understanding *Lucas v. South Carolina Coastal Council,*" *Stanford Law Review* 45 (1993):1433.

37. Richard J. Lazarus, "Shifting Paradigms of Tort and Property in the Transformation of Natural Resources Law," *Natural Resources Policy and Law: Trends and Directions* (Washington, D.C.: Island Press, 1993), p. 209.

38. A. Dan Tarlock, "Local Government Protection of Biodiversity: What Is Its Niche?" *University of Chicago Law Review* (1993).

39. See, for example, *Lujan v. Defenders of Wildlife,* 112, S.Ct. 2130, 119 L.Ed. 2d 351 (1992).

40. Chiappinelli, "The Right ot a Clean and Safe Environment," p. 605.

41. A. E. Dick Howard, "State Constitutions and the Environment," *Virginia Law Review,* 58(2) (1972):203.

42. Brandl and Bungert, "Constitutional Entrenchment," pp. 4–5.

43. See, for example, J. William Futrell, "Environemntal Rights and the Constitution," in *Blessings of Liberty* (Washington, D.C.: American Law Institute, 1988), pp. 43–61.

44. English translations of foreign constitutional provisions vary. The translations of the Brazilian and Portuguese provisions are from Weiss, *In Fairness,* pp. 298–299 and 312–313. The translation for Turkey is from Brandl and Bungert, "Constitutional Entrenchment," p. 71.

45. Weiss, *In Fairness,* pp. 107, 317–325. The twelve states are California, Florida, Hawaii, Illinois, Massachusetts, Michigan, Montana, New Mexico, New York, Pennsylvania, Rhode Island, and Virginia.

46. 405 U.S. 727 (1972).

47. Garrett Hardin, "Foreword," in Christopher D. Stone, *Should Trees Have Standing? Toward Legal Rights for Natural Objects* (Palo Alto: Tioga, 1988), p. xx.

48. Norton, "Intergenerational Equity," pp. 142–143.

About the Contributors

DINAH BEAR was general counsel of the Council on Environmental Quality, in the Executive Office of the President, from 1983 to 1993, where she had primary responsibility for interpreting and implementing the National Environmental Policy Act. In 1995, she was reappointed general counsel at CEQ.

MOLLIE BEATTIE is director of the U.S. Fish and Wildlife Service, where she is in charge of managing the National Wildlife Refuge System, enforcing the Endangered Species Act, and implementing a wide variety of other wildlife conservation legal authorities. She is former commissioner of Forest, Parks, and Recreation for the state of Vermont.

DAVID R. DOWNES is a senior staff attorney for the Center for International Environmental Law, where he practices biodiversity law, international trade law, and intellectual property rights law. He has written many articles on these topics and is an adjunct professor at American University's Washington College of Law.

CURTIS FISH is an attorney with Milbank, Tweed, Hadley and McCloy in Washington, D.C. Previously, he was a fellow with the U.S. Office of Environmental Policy in the White House, where he provided research and analysis on international environmental issues affecting national and international security.

WILLIAM C. GALLOWAY is a 1995 graduate of the University of Washington School of Law, where he was managing editor of *The Washington Law Review* and worked as an extern to the Sierra Club Legal Defense Fund on salmon recovery and spotted owl litigation.

SCOTT HAJOST is executive director of the World Conservation Union (IUCN) in Washington, D.C., and former international counsel with the Environmental Defense Fund. He has also previously worked at the Environmental Protection Agency and State Department and is a noted authority on international environmental law and negotiations.

SUZANNE IUDICELLO is vice president and general counsel at the Center for Marine Conservation. She is an expert on marine mammal, fisheries, and natural resource conservation issues. She was previously an assistant to the Alaska Commissioner of Fish and Game.

LEESTEFFY JENKINS is an international legal advisor to a number of conservation and animal welfare advocacy groups, including the Humane Society of the United States. She previously clerked for the U.S. Court of International Trade.

PETER JENKINS is a program manager for the Center for Wildlife Law, Institute of Public Law, University of New Mexico Law School. He was policy analyst for the Office of Technology Assessment's *Harmful Non-Indigenous Species in the United States*, published in 1993.

RALPH W. JOHNSON is professor of law at the University of Washington School of Law. He is an expert on water law, the public trust doctrine, and natural resources policy and has previously worked with the U.S. Senate Committee on Interior and Insular Affairs.

WALTER KUHLMANN is a partner with Boardman, Suhr, Curry, and Field in Madison, Wisconsin. He is a leading national forestry litigator, a member of Defenders of Wildlife's Litigation Committee, chairman of its Program Policy Committee, and the author of numerous articles on natural resource conservation. He has taught at the University of Wisconsin Law School.

LINDELL L. MARSH is a partner with the California office of Siemon, Larsen, and Marsh, where he helps public- and private-sector clients develop strategies and programs to address complex or sensitive issues relating to land use or natural resources policy. He is a member of the Board of Councilors of the School of Urban and Regional Planning at the University of Southern California. He is also a frequent writer on these topics.

TODD G. OLSON is founder of Olson Policy Consulting, Inc., where he advises on market-based techniques to implement habitat conservation plans. Current projects include conserving coastal sage scrub and riparian habitats in southern California, where he also helped develop the Natural Communities Conservation Planning process.

JASON PATLIS is an attorney with the National Oceanic and Atmospheric Administration, Department of Commerce, where he handles matters relating to the Endangered Species Act and marine species protection.

JOHN A. PENDERGRASS is a senior attorney with the Environmental Law Institute and director of ELI's Center for State, Local, and Regional Environmental Programs. He has taught at the Chicago–Kent College of Law.

RODGER SCHLICKEISEN has been president of Defenders of Wildlife since 1991. He was previously chief of staff to Senator Max Baucus (D–MT), chief executive officer of the firm Craver, Mathews, Smith, and Company, and associate director for economics and government for the Office of Management and Budget under President Carter. He also was an organizer of the Virginia group of Common Cause, serving as its first elected chairman and helping win enactment of open-government laws.

WILLIAM J. SNAPE III is director of Defenders of Wildlife's Legal Division, where he manages all legal programs and provides legal counsel on all program policy. He has written several articles on international trade, biodiversity protection, and natural resources conservation and has taught at the University of Baltimore School of Law.

DONALD M. WALLER is professor of botany and environmental studies at the University of Wisconsin at Madison. He is a specialist in biodiversity issues and has published numerous articles on the topic. In 1992, he was honored by the U.S. Forest Service for organizing a scientific roundtable on biodiversity.

INDEX

Abandoned Seas: Reversing the Decline of the Oceans (Weber), 129
Abrahamson, Dean E., 240
Adaptability, human, 218
Administration in land regulation, 77
Administrative Procedure Act (APA), 186, 196
Adversarial decision-making, 61
African Convention on the Conservation of Nature and Natural Resources in 1968, 84
Age-class diversity, 23
Agenda 21 (environmental blueprint), 132, 136, 143
Agreement on the Conservation of Polar Bears in 1976, 84
Agricultural practices, global, 150–51, 205–6
Agriculture, U.S. Department of, 58, 109, 147
Alaskan pollock, 122
Allen, Edith B., 240
Allen, Scott, 41
Alligators, 137
Alpha diversity, 23
Alternative dispute resolution (ADR) mechanism, 180–81
Alverson, W. S., 31, 32, 200
Ambiguity of diversity language, 195–96
American Fisheries Society, 113
American Institute of Biological Sciences, 194
Amphibians, 1
Animal Damage Control (ADC) programs, 149–150
Anchovies, 122
Animal and Plant Health Inspection Service (APHIS), 109, 149
Anthropocentrism, 60, 226, 237
Aquatic Research Laws and Treaties: Reference Guide (Buck), 130
Arnold, Ron, 218
Arun River System (Nepal), 137
El-Ashry, Mohamed T., 139, 240
Asia, 120
Assessments, biological, 35

Assumption programs, state, 52
Atmar, W., 31
Atmospheric changes, 128
Audubon Environmental Defense Fund, 143
Authoritarian command and control management, 61–62

Babbitt, Bruce, 14, 34, 36, 37
Badgers, 149
Baker, James, 34
Balancing on the Brink of Extinction: The Endangered Species Act and Lessons for the Future (Kohm), 31, 200
Bale, Ashley, 174
Barber, Charles V., 214
Barbour, M., 240
Barker, R., 200
Barry, Don, 40
Basel Convention on the Control of Transboundary Movements of Hazardous Wastes and Their Disposal, 214
Bean, Michael, 105, 241
Bear, Dinah, 148
Bears, 112–13
Beattie, Mollie, 1–3
Behind the Veil of Economics (Heilbroner), 219
Belsky, M. H., 129
Bennett, William, 219
Berry, Wendell, xix
Best available technology economically achievable (BAT) guidelines, 171
Bill of Rights, 230
Biodiplomacy: Genetic Resources and International Relations (Sanchez & Juma), 216
Biodiversity:
    biogeography, 25–26
    Convention in 1992, 81–86, 89, 108–9, 202–212
    defining, xix, 21–22, 24
    ecosystem management, 16–17
    Endangered Species Act, 18–20
    future prospects for, 30–31

Biodiversity (continued):
    as a goal for conservation efforts, 20–21
    implementing, xii, xiii, 22–24
    indicators of, 149
    marine, 83, 120–28
    measuring, 70–71
    metaphorical references to, xxiii
    obstacles to, xii, 1, 17–18, 45
    political support for, xx
    scale, importance of, 28–29
    science of, xxi–xxii
    static environmental conditions, 26–27
    three levels of, 44
    threshold challenge to, xii, xx
    uncertainty, scientific, 29–30
    see also Constitutional amendment for bio-
        diversity protection, proposed;
        Ecosystem management; Habitat con-
        servation/destruction; various subject
        headings
Biodiversity Prospecting: Using Genetic Resources
    for Sustainable Development (Reid),
    215–16
Biodiversity: Social and Ecological Perspectives
    (Shiva), 215
Biodiversity Treaty, The, 88, 138, 147, 150
Biodiversity (Wilson), 216, 240
Biogeography, 25–26
Biological assessments, 35
Biological basis of land regulation, 77
Biological Journal of the Linnaean Society (Cut-
    ler), 31
Biophilia Hypothesis, The (Kellert & Wilson),
    xxv, 240
Biophilia (love of life), xxiv
Biotechnical revolution, 150, 207
Birds:
    gnatcatcher, California, 36, 50, 59, 69
    habitat conservation/destruction, 22
    Migratory Bird Hunting Stamp Act of 1934,
        17
    production and process method (PPM) mea-
        sures, 94
    warbler, Kirtland's, 19–20
    Wild Bird Conservation Act, 99, 103
Birnie, P. W., 201
Bison, 149
Blackmun, Harry, 236
Blue Ribbon coalitions, 26
Bobcats, 149
Bobertz, Bradley C., 174
Book of Virtues, The (Bennett), 219
Botkin, Dan, 26, 32
Boundary lines in land regulation, 77–78
Boxer, Barbara, 40
Boyle, A. E., 201
Bramble Bush, The (Llewellyn), 213

Brandl, Ernst, 241, 242
Brazil, 85, 235
Breaking the Log Jam: Obstacles to Forest Policy
    Reform in Indonesia and the United States
    (Barber), 214
Brennan, William, 236
Brown, Lester, 219
Browner, Carol, 188
Buber, Martin, 65
Buck, Eugene H., 130
Building Economic Incentives into the Endan-
    gered Species Act
    (Fischer & Hudson), 79
Bungert, Hartwin, 241, 242
Bureau of Land Management (BLM), 50, 58,
    148–49
Bureau of Reclamation, 58, 110
Burke, Edmund, 226
Businesses, regulations on U.S. overseas,
    87–88, 89
Byrne, John A., 65

Caldwell, Lynton, 1
California:
    habitat conservation/destruction, xiii, 36–37
    imports, monitoring, 113
    old-growth forests, 224
    San Bruno Mountain planning process, 63
    water issues, 158
California's Changing Landscapes (Barbour,
    Pavlik, Drysdale, & Lindstrom), 240
Callicott, J. Baird, 241
Canada, 85, 125, 141
Cancer, 205
Capra, Fritjov, 65
Carbon dioxide in coastal waters, 131
Carson, Rachel, xi, 62, 65
Ceballos, Geraldo, 153
Central Valley Project Improvement Act of
    1992 (CVPIA), 55, 58, 152
Challenge of Global Warming, The (Abraham-
    son), 240
Change and environmental principles, xi,
    26–27
Chaos (Gleick), 65
Chequamegon National Forest (Wisconsin), 23
Chestnut blight, 105
Chiappinelli, John A., 241, 242
China, 87, 137
Chinook, winter-run, 58
Chivian, Eric, xxv, 240
Chlorine, 146
Chlorofluorocarbons (CFCs), 132
Christie, E., 201
CITES, see Convention on the International
    Trade in Endangered Species of Wild
    Fauna and Flora Clams, Asian, 83

Clark, Dana, 212
Clean Water Act (CWA), 34, 52, 146, 166–70,
    186
Clearcutting, xiii, 23
Climate change, global, 131–32
Clinton, Bill, 34, 87, 185, 211
Coarse filters protecting ecosystems, 45
Coastal scrub habitat, 36–37
Coastal states and United Nations Convention
    on the Law of the Sea, 124
Coastal Zone Management Act, 41, 52
Cobain, Kurt, xxv
Cobb, John, Jr., 213
Cody, M. L., 31
Colborn, Theo, 239
Collaboration on constituency interests, 63
Command and control mechanisms, 61–62,
    64
Commission on Sustainable Development
    (CSD), UN, 83, 85, 132–37, 142–43,
    153
Committee on Trade and Environment (CTE),
    87
Common law nuisance principles, 38–39, 231,
    232
Competition and and exotic species, 106
Comprehensive Environmental Response,
    Compensation and Liability Act (CER-
    CLA), 146
Confessions of an Eco-Warrior (Foreman), 200
Conflict resolution, 61
Congress, U.S.:
    Biodiversity Convention, 211–12
    business regulations, overseas, 88, 89
    Contract with America, 56
    Council on Environment Quality, 179
    economic impact of biodiversity, 35, 39
    exotic species, 107
    GAP Analysis Program, 147
    God Squad, 152
    House Committee on Merchant Marine and
        Fisheries, 47
    natural preserve approach to biodiversity,
        5
    pollution control, 166–67
    see also Endangered Species Act (ESA)
Conservation Biology, 31, 32
Conservation biology, science of, xxi–xxii, 6,
    30–31
    see also Biodiversity; Ecosystem manage-
        ment; Endangered Species Act (ESA);
        Habitat conservation/destruction; vari-
        ous subject headings
Conservation Biology: The Science of Scarcity and
    Diversity (Sinauer), 118
Conservationists, xxii, 18
Conserving Listed Species, Talk Is Cheaper Than

We Think (Barry & Hoskis), 40
Consortium for Action to Protect the Earth
    (CAPE), 136–37, 143
Constituency interests and conservation plan-
    ning process, 63–64
Constitution, Fifth Amendment to U.S., 38,
    217–18, 232
Constitutional amendment for biodiversity
    protection, proposed, 221
    debate over, 237–38
    environmental provisions found elsewhere,
        235–37
    land ethic, toward a true, 238–39
    language and wording, 233–35
    lawmaking prejudiced against the future,
        229–30
    legal system, limitations of traditional,
        230–33
    society's need/duty to protect living nature,
        222–29
Consultation process and ecosystem manage-
    ment, 35, 40, 51–56
Consultative Group on International Agricul-
    tural Research (CGIAR), 151, 153
Contract with America, 39
Convention on Biological Diversity in 1992
    (CBD), 81–86, 89, 108–9, 198, 202–212
Convention on Nature Protection and Wildlife
    Preservation in the
Western Hemisphere (WHC), 84
Convention on Preservation of Wild Animals,
    Birds, and Fish in Africa in 1900, 84
Convention on the Conservation of Antarctic
    Marine Living Resources in 1982, 84
Convention on the Conservation of Migratory
    Birds in 1916/1936, 84, 89
Convention on the International Trade in
    Endangered Species of Wild Fauna and
    Flora (CITES), 85–86, 99, 100, 125–26,
    206
Convention on Wetlands of International
    Importance in 1975, 85
Cooperrider, Allen Y., 200, 217, 219, 240, 241
Coordinated actions of federal agencies, 54–56
Coral reefs, 128, 131
Corporations, multinational, 86–88
Council on Environment Quality (CEQ), 179,
    183–84, 223
Court system and environmental protections:
    Arnold vs. Mundy (public trust), 158
    Chevron U.S.A. Inc. vs. Natural Resources
        Defense Council Inc. (interpreting stat-
        ues), 168, 172
    Conservation Law Foundation and Town of
        Newington vs. Department of the Air
        Force (environmental impact state-
        ment), 188

Court system and environmental protections
    (*continued*):
  Daubert vs. Merrell Dow Pharmaceuticals
    (false hypotheses), 193
  Defenders of Wildlife vs. Lujan (environmen-
    tal laws), 89, 242
  Dolan vs. Tigard (property rights), 41
  Dosewallips decision (public trust), 162
  ecosystem management, 189–200
  Environmental Defense Fund vs. Massey, 187
  Geer vs. Connecticut (public trust), 163
  Georgia vs. Tennessee Copper (property
    rights), 153
  Gould vs. Greylock Reservation Commission
    (public trust), 163
  Hughes vs. Oklahoma (public trust), 163
  Illinois Central vs. Illinois (public trust), 159,
    162, 163
  *Jefferson County vs. Washington Dept. of Ecol-
    ogy* (public trust), 164
  *Kokechik Fishermen's Ass'n vs. Secretary of
    Commerce* (indirect fish catch), 129
  Lucas vs. South Carolina Coastal Council
    (property rights), 41, 232
  Marks vs. Whitney (public trust), 161
  Mono Lake case (public trust), 158, 159
  National Audubon Society vs. Superior Court
    (public trust), 163
  Orion Corp vs. State (public trust), 163
  *Palia vs. Hawaii Department of Land and Nat-
    ural Resources* (property rights), 40,
    110
  *Penn Central Transportation Co. vs. New York
    City* (takings claims), 40
  Public Citizens vs. USTR (NEPA litigation),
    188
  scientific input, 23–24
  Sierra Club vs. Clark (habitat
    conservation/destruction), 40
  Sierra Club vs. Marita (science standards),
    187, 200, 201
  Sierra Club vs. Morton (legal standing to
    nonhuman nature), 236–37
  Sierra Club vs. Robertson (NEPA litigation),
    188
  species orientation, 48
  Steuart Transportation Co. case (public trust),
    163
  Sweet Home Chapter vs. Interior Department
    (habitat conservation/destruction),
    201
  Sweet Home vs. Babbitt (property rights), 40
  Tennessee Valley Authority vs. Hill (ecosystem
    management), 51, 57, 152
  United States vs. Lopez (commerce), 241
  *United States vs. State Water Resources Control
    Board* (public trust), 163

U.S. vs. Canada (pollution), 88
U.S. vs. Mitchell (dolphin/tuna catches), 89
Washington State Supreme Court, 160
Coyotes, 149
Crisis management and ESA, 34
*Critical Condition: Human Health and the Envi-
    ronment* (Chivian), xxv, 240
Cultural shift needed for biodiversity protec-
    tion, 218–19
Culture reflecting biodiversity, xxiii–xxiv
Cutler, A., 31

Daly, Herman E., 213, 214, 215
Darwin, Charles, xxiv
Decision-making, 61, 118, 227–29
*Declaration of Principles Governing the Sea Bed
    and Floor, and Subsoil Thereof, Beyond the
    Limits of National Jurisdiction,* 65–66
Defenders of Wildlife (environmental organiza-
    tion), xii, xv, 4, 71, 223
Delta smelt, 58
Democracy, 60–61
Denmark, 141
Developed countries, 138, 150, 204
Developing countries, 138, 150, 151, 204
Diamond, J. M., 31
*Discordant Harmonies: A New Ecology for the
    Twenty–First Century* (Botkin), 26, 32
Diversity of Life, The (Wilson), xii
Dixon, John A., 215
Dolphins, 89, 94, 96, 97, 137
Douglas, Marjory S., 62, 65
Douglas, William O., 236
Downes, David R., 83, 150–51, 213–15
Downing, John, 153
Driftnet fishing, 94, 99–100, 127–28
Driftnet Impact Monitoring, Assessment, and
    Control Act of 1987, 127
Drysdale, F., 240
Ducks, 17
Dynamics of Extinction, The (Elliott), 239

Eagles, 18, 149
Earth Day, 62
Earth Summit, 81, 198, 202–212
Earth Transformed by Human Action, The
    (Turner, II), 239
Eastern Tropical Pacific (ETP), dolphins in,
    97
*Ecology of Commerce: A Declaration of Sustain-
    ability* (Hawken), 65
Ecology Diversity and Its Measurement (Magur-
    ran), 31
Ecology, Economics and Ethics (Bormann &
    Kellert), xxv
Ecology and Evolution of Communities (Cody &
    Diamond), 31

Ecology of Invasions by Animals and Plants, The
    (Elton), 240
Economic impact of biodiversity:
    best available technology economically
        achievable guidelines, 171
    Biodiversity Convention, 204
    Commission on Sustainable Development
        (CSD), UN, 137
    Congress, U.S., 35, 39
    conservation value into economic value,
        translating, 71–72
    Endangered Species Act, 13, 34–35, 37–38
    Global Environment Facility, 137–43
    God Squad, 152
    habitat transaction method, 76–77
    incentives, perverse, 68–70
    job loss, 2, 14
    local economics, 207–11
    multinational corporations, 87–88
    Olson's habitat transaction approach, 38
    species protection, xxii
*Economics of Protected Areas: A New Look at
    Benefits and Costs* (Dixon & Sherman),
    215
Ecosystem management, 3–4, 11
    agencies, federal, 16–17
    endangered ecosystems, 223–24
    Endangered Species Act, 13–14, 42–57, 199
    exotic species, 107
    legal system's response to, 189–200, 229–33
    marine environment, 128
    new era in, preparing for, 14–15
    property rights, 12–13
    San Bruno Mountain Habitat Conservation
        Plan, 59–64
Effluent limitations, 168, 170–72
Ehrlich, Ann, 62, 65
Ehrlich, Paul R., 62, 65, 240
Einstein, Albert, 145
*Eleventh Report of the Council on Environmental
    Quality*, 239
Elliott, D. K., 239
Elton, Charles S., 240
Endangered Ecosystems of the United States, 223,
    239
Endangered Species Act (ESA), 222
    challenges to, 230
    coastal sage scrub habitat, 36–37
    D.C. Circuit Court, 40
    economic impacts, 34–35
    ecosystem management, 13–14, 42–57, 199
    Environmental Protection Agency, U.S.,
        167–68
    exotic species, 110
    Fish and Wildlife Service, U.S., 13–15, 50
    funding dilemma, 37–38
    habitat conservation/destruction, xiii, 46

    limitations of, 18–20, 189
    political problems besetting, 33
    property rights, 35
    regulatory/judicial mandates, 43
    San Bruno Mountain Habitat Conservation
        Plan, 59–64
    sanctions, trade, 126
    San Joaquin Delta Estuary, 4
    Sea Turtle Conservation Amendments, 126
    Tellico Dam project (Tennessee), 147–48
    Three Gorges Dam project (China), 87
Environmental conditions, static, 26–27
*Environmental Ethics: Duties to and Values in the
    Natural World* (Rolston, III), 241
Environmental impact statement (EIS), 58,
    109, 182, 185–86, 187, 191
Environmentalism, 218, 231
Environmental Protection Agency, U.S. (EPA):
    discretion, issue of, 168–70
    effluent guidelines, 170–72
    environmental impact statement, 186
    hazardous waste, 172–73
    implementation issues, 173–74
    National Environmental Policy Act of 1970,
        187–88
    new goals, 166–68
Environmental Quality, 223
ESA, see Endangered Species Act
Ethical questions around biodiversity, xxiii,
    218, 225–26, 229
European Community (EC), 96
Everglades, The: River of Grass (Douglas), 65
Evolution of National Wildlife Law, The
    (Bean), 241
Exclusive economic zones (EEZs), 99, 100,
    121
Exotic species, 83
    Animal Damage Control programs, 150
    federal law, 109–10
    harmful, 105–8
    international law, 108–9
    recommendations for dealing with, 113–
        18
    state laws, 110, 113, 115–17
    Wild Bird Conservation Act, 99
*Expendable Future; U.S. Politics and the Protec-
    tion of Biological Diversity* (Tobin), 31,
    241
Experience of Place (Hiss), 65–66
*Extinction: The Causes and Consequences of the
    Disappearance of Species* (Ehrlich &
    Ehrlich), 65

Facilitation in conservation planning process,
    63
Faith in a seed (Thoreau), xxv
Farm Bill, 38, 41

Federal Conservation and Management of Marine Fisheries in the United States (Wise), 129
Federal government:
    agencies influencing biodiversity, 6, 12, 16–17, 35, 51–56
    coordinated actions of agencies, 54–56
    ecosystem management, 12
    exotic species, 109–10
    Memorandum of Understanding on Implementation of the Endangered Species Act, 49, 58
    obstacles to biodiversity, 2
    proper role of, xx
    receptivity of, 3
    salmonid stocks, Pacific, 50
    subsides to public lands, 38
    underutilization of federal statues, 146
Federal Insecticide, Fungicide, and Rodenticide Act (FIFRA), 146
Federal Land Policy and Management Act of 1976 (FLPMA), 34, 148–49
Federal Noxious Weed Act, 109
Ferrets, 149
Fields, Jack, 152
Fifties, The (Halberstam), 220
Fire as indicator of biodiversity, 149
First the Seed (Kloppenburg), 215
Fischer, Hank, 79
Fischman, Robert L., 174
Fish:
    American Fisheries Society, 113
    Central Valley Project Improvement Act, 55
    CITES, 125–26
    driftnets, 99–100, 127–28
    environmental assessment for managing anadromous fish–producing watersheds in eastern Oregon and Washington, 58
    exploiting, 121–23
    habitat conservation/destruction, 17–18
    mare liberum (freedom of the seas), 121–22
    programmatic actions of federal agencies, 52
    regional fishery organizations, 124–25
    salmonid stocks, Pacific, 49–50
    United Nations Convention on the Law of the Sea, 123–24
Fish, Curtis, 83
Fish and Wildlife Coordination Act of 1934, 33
Fish and Wildlife Service, U.S. (FWS):
    assessments, biological, 35
    consultations conducted by, 40
    coordinated actions of federal agencies, 54–56
    darters, snail, 18
    ecosystem management, 13–15, 50
    Endangered Species Act, 34

environmental impact statement, 182
exotic species, 109
GAP Analysis Program, 147
habitat conservation/destruction, 40
Kitland's warbler, 19–20
no-jeopardy mandate of ESA, 51
representative democracy, 61
San Bruno Mountain Habitat Conservation Plan, 63
San Francisco Bay and Delta, 55, 58
species-orientation, 48
Fisherman's Protective Act, 93–94, 100–101, 103, 126
Fleisher, Stephen, 129–30
Florida, xiii, 110
Focused planning, 63
Food Agriculture, Conservation and Trade Act of 1990, 41
Food and Agriculture Organization (FAO), 123, 153
Food Security Act of 1985, 41
Foreign Environmental Practices Act (FEPA), 88
Foreman, D., 200
Forest habitat, 18, 85, 148–49, 223–24
Forest Service, U.S. (USFS):
    age-class diversity, 23
    implementing mechanisms for biodiversity, xiii
    land and resource management plans, 52
    local approach, 190, 197
    Memorandum of Understanding on Implementation of the Endangered Species Act, 50, 58
    National Forest Management Act of 1976, 4
    prairie dogs, 149
For the Common Good (Daly & Cobb), 213
Foucault, Michel, 65
Foxes, 149
Fragmentation, forest, 22, 60, 62, 190–91, 194
Framework Convention on Climate Change, 213
Freedom for the Seas in the 21st Century (Van Dyke, Zaelke, & Hewison), 201
Free market and natural laws of ecology, 38, 151
Friends of the Earth, 143
Futrell, J. William, 242

Gadgil, Madhav, 215
Gamma diversity, 22
Gap Analysis Program (GAP), 147
Gasoline, leaded, 137
GATT, see General Agreement on Tariffs and Trade GEF, see Global Environment Facility Geneen, Harold, 61

General Agreement on Tariffs and Trade
  (GATT), 82, 87, 96–97, 100
  environmental issues, 214
  exotic species, 108
  international environmental agreements,
    103
  local economies ignored by, 208
  plant variety protection, 150
  reforming, 101–3
  tuna, 104
  unilateral trade measures, 127
Genetic diversity within species, 28, 44
Genetic engineering, xxi, 204–5, 207, 210,
    213, 216
Geological Survey, U.S., 147
Georgia, 110
Germany, 84
Ghost Bears (Grumbine), 200
Gillis, Malcolm, xxv
Gilpin, M. E., 118
Gingrich, Newt, 41
Gleick, James, 65
Global Environment Facility (GEF), 83,
    137–43
Global Marine Biological Diversity (Norse), 129
Global 2000 Report to the President, 223, 239
Glowka, Lyle, 213
Gore, Al, 185
Governance of the Environmental Affairs, The:
    Towards Consensus (Yost), 65
Governance structures, historical concepts in
    our, 60–61
Government, see Congress, U.S.; Endangered
    Species Act (ESA);
Federal government; Regulations, government;
    State governments
Ground-disturbing activities, 52
Grumbine, R. E., 200
Guam, 105
Guha, Ramachandra, 215
Guide to the Convention on Biological Diversity, A
    (Glowka), 213
Guinier, Lani, 220
Gustafson, Kristen, 129

Habitat conservation/destruction:
  bears, 112–13
  biodiversity protection at odds with,
    190–91
  conservation plans (HCPs), 36
  Endangered Species Act, xiii, 46
  fish, 18
  Fish and Wildlife Service, U.S., 40
  fragmentation, 22
  habitat transaction method, 72–78
  Natural Community Conservation Plan,
    36–37, 59

Olson's transaction approach, 38
PACFISH strategy, 55
scale, importance of, 28–29
species losses, 17–18
Habitat Conservation Plans (HCP) on San Bruno
    Mountain, San Mateo California: The Fail-
    ure of the First HCPs in the United States,
    40
Hajost, Scott, 83
Halberstam, David, 220
Halprin, Lawrence, 65
Handbook of the Indians of California (Kroeber),
    65
Hardin, Garrett J., 62, 65, 237, 242
Harmful Non-Indigenous Species in the United
    States, 107, 118
Harris, Larry, 26
Hart, Peter D., 151, 240
Hawaii, xiii, 110–11, 113, 119, 236
Hawken, Paul, 65
Hawks, 149
Hazardous waste, 167, 172–73
Health linked to natural diversity, xxiii
Heilbroner, Robert, 219
Hewison, G., 201
Hey, E., 201
Heyman, Ira M., 65
High Seas Driftnet Fisheries Enforcement Act
    of 1992, 94, 99–100
Hippocratic oath, 217
Hiss, Tony, 65–66
History of Public Land Law Development, 64
HIV (human immunodeficiency virus), xxv
Holmes, Oliver W., 152
Hoskis, David, 40
Houseman, Robert, 214
Howard, E. Dick, 234, 241, 242
Hudson, Wendy E., 79
Hybridization and exotic species, 106
Hypotheses, theory of falsifying, 193

I and Thou (Buber), 65
Idaho, 14
Identifying/monitoring natural biological
    resources, 147
Illich, Ivan, 211, 216
Illinois, 236
Ill Winds: Airborne Pollution's Toll on Trees and
    Crops (Mackenzie & El-Ashry), 240
Incentives and private property rights, per-
    verse, 68–70, 78
Incorporating Biodiversity Considerations into the
    Environmental Impact Analysis Under the
    National Environmental Policy Act, 183
Incremental Costs and Financing Policy Issues,
    143
In Defense of the Land Ethic (Callicott), 241

In Defense of Wildlife: Preserving Communities and Corridors, 241
Indian Affairs, Bureau of, 149
Indirect catch in fishing, 122–23
In Fairness to Future Generations: International Law, Common Patrimony, and Intergenerational Equity (Weiss), 241, 242
Infection and exotic species, 106
Intellectual property rights (IPRs), 150–51, 210, 214, 216
Inter-American Tropical Tuna Commission (IATTC), 100, 125
Intergenerational equity, 65, 226–29
Interim Project Cycle, GEF's, 140
Interior Appropriations Act of 1994, 147
Interior Department, U.S., 34, 58, 152
Intermodal Surface Transportation Efficiency Act of 1991, 38
International Agreements to Protect the Environment and Wildlife, 130
International Convention on the Conservation of Atlantic Tunas (ICCAT), 125
International environmental protections:
    CITES, 85–86
    climate change, 131–32
    Commission on Sustainable Development (CSD), UN, 132–37, 142–43
    Convention on Biological Diversity in 1992, 81–82, 202–212
    Convention on Nature Protection and Wildlife Preservation in the Western Hemisphere, 84
    exotic species, 105–18
    implementing, 121
    international environmental agreements (IEAs), 100, 101, 103
    marine biodiversity, 120–28
    multinational corporations, 86–88
    National Environmental Policy Act of 1970, 185
    precautionary principle, 197–99
    trade, 82–83, 93–103
International Law and the Environment (Birnie & Boyle), 201
International Monetary Fund (IMF), 84, 137
International North Pacific Fisheries Commission (INPEC), 125
International Pacific Halibut Commission (IPHC), 125
International Plant Pest Convention (IPPC), 108
International Trade Commission, 130
International Union for Conservation of Nature and Natural Resources (IUCN), 109, 128
International Whaling Commission (IWC), 100

Intertidal zones, 27
Invertebrates, 1
Island biogeography, 26
Israel, 152
Iudicello, Suzanne, 83

Japan, 62, 88, 100
Jefferson, Thomas, 60
Jenkins, Leesteffy, 82
Jenkins, Peter, 83, 119
Jobs *vs.* species protection, 2, 14
John D. and Catherine T. MacArthur Foundation, 141, 212
Johnson, Ralph, 145
Jordan, 152
Jordan, William R., 240
Judicial model of conflict resolution, 61
Juma, C., 216
Justice Department, U.S., 23
Just vs. Marinette County (property rights), 153

Kasich, John, 152
Kellert, Stephen, xxiv, 151, 240
Keystone species, 13–14, 19, 44–45
Kloppenburg, Jack R., Jr., 215
Kohm, K. A., 31, 200
Kroeber, A. L., 65
Krupp, Fred, 176
Kuhlmann, Walter, 31, 148–49, 200
Kuhn, Thomas S., 62, 65

Lacey Act of 1900, 17, 33, 40, 109, 110
Land and Water Conservation Fund (LWCF), 38
Land regulations, 77–78
Landscape approaches, 21
Law reflecting human values, xix–xx
Law of the Sea, The (Sohn & Gustafson), 129
Lawrence, Nathaniel, 194, 200
Lazarus, Richard, 232, 242
Legal system's response to ecosystem management, 189–200, 229–33
Leghold traps, 95–96
Legislative History of the Endangered Species Act of 1973, 57
Leopold, Aldo, xi, 62, 65, 200, 221
    anthropocentric approach, 237
    evolution of his thinking, 11
    intelligent tinkering, xii, xx
    land ethic, 239
    local approach, 190
Lichen, 14
Lindstrom, S., 240
Livestock protection, 149
Llewellyn, Karl, 213
Local ecosystems and the global economy, 207–11

Lousewort, Furbish's, 18, 19
Lovejoy, T. E., 239
Luxembourg, 84

MacArthur, Robert, 25–26, 32
Machiavelli, Niccolo, xxv
MacKenzie, James J., 240
Madison (Wisconsin) Workshop in 1994, 4–5
Magnuson Fishery Conservation and Management Act, 52, 100
Magurran, A. E., 31
Malaysia, xxv, 85
Managing the Commons (Hardin), 65
Maquire, L., 119
Marine biodiversity, 83, 120–28
Marine Mammal Protection Act of 1972 (MMPA), 89, 94, 96–97, 125, 126
Marine mammals, 96–98
Marsh, Lindell, 36
Massachusetts, 236
Mathews, Jessica, 219
McConnell, Moria L., 130
McLaughlin, Richard J., 129
McMillan, M., 31
Measuring conservation value, 72–76
Mech, David, 191
Medicines from nature, xxv, 120, 205, 215
Megafauna, charismatic, 19
Melaleuca (Australian tree), 107
Metapopulation dynamics, 28
Mexico, 96–97, 109
Mexico Conference on Responsible Fishing in 1992, 124
Meyer, Stephen M., 241
Migratory Bird Hunting Stamp Act of 1934, 17
Miller, Brian, 153
Minimum viable population (MVP), 5
Mississippi, 110
Mitigation practices, 28
Monitoring/identifying natural biological resources, 77, 147
Montana, 110, 236
Montreal Guidelines for the Protection of the Marine Environment Against Pollution from Land–Based Sources, 128
Montreal Protocol on Substances That Deplete the Ozone Layer of 1987, 103, 128, 132, 138, 213, 214
Mooney, Harold A., 240
Moral Animal (Wright), 219
Morality and biodiversity protection, xxiii, 218, 225–26, 229
Moriah Fund, 212–13
Mortgaging the Earth (Rich), 142
Mountain lions, 149
Muir, John, 5
Multinational corporations (MNCs), 86–88

Multiple use/sustained yield (MUSY), 3
Murphy, Dennis D., 79, 193, 200
Murrelet, marbled, 18
Mussels, 14, 108

National Biological Service (NBS), 15, 29, 146, 152
National Environmental Policy Act of 1970 (NEPA), 62, 87, 109, 148, 167, 178–88, 191
National Fish and Wildlife Foundation, 147
National Fish and Wildlife Refuge System, 182
National Forest Management Act of 1976 (NFMA), 4, 23, 24, 34, 52, 191
National Marine Fisheries Service (NMFS):
Central Valley Project Improvement Act, 55
chinook, winter–run, 58
consultations conducted by, 40
dolphins, 97
economic impact of biodiversity, 34–35
habitat conservation/destruction, 40
no-jeopardy mandate of ESA, 51
San Francisco Bay and Delta, 58
species protection, 48, 49–50
turtle excluder devices, 98
National Oceanic and Atmospheric Administration (NOAA), 48, 52, 89
National Park Service, 50
National Pollutant Discharge Elimination System (NPDES) permits, 168
National Wildlife Federation, 143
Native Americans, 60
Natural Community Conservation Plan (NCCP), 36–37, 59
Naturalist-preservationist strategy, 5, 227–29
Natural Resources Defense Council, 143
Natural Resources Lawyer 4, 65
Nature Conservancy, The, 21
Neotropical migrant songbird species, 17, 22
NEPA, *see* National Environmental Policy Act of 1970
Nepal, 137
Netherlands, 84
New Rules: Searching for Self–Fulfillment in a World Turned Upside Down (Yankelovich), 65
Nicolet National Forest (Wisconsin), 23
No-jeopardy mandate of ESA, 51
Noncharismatic species, 14, 19, 21
Nongovernmental organizations (NGOs), 134, 141, 143
Noon, Barry, 193, 200
Norse, Elliot, 129
North American Free Trade Area (NAFTA), 100, 108, 109, 208, 214
Northern Rockies Ecosystem Protection Act (NREPA), 5

Northwest Atlantic Fisheries Convention
    (NAFO), 125
Norton, Bryan, 227–29, 237, 240, 241
Noss, Reed, xi, 32, 200, 217, 240, 241
*No Surprise: Assuring Certainty for Private
    Landowners in Endangered Species Act
    Habitat Conservation Planning*, 40
Nugent, G., 119
Nuisance principles, common law, 38–39,
    231, 232

Oak savannas, 28
Oceans, 120–21
    see also Marine *listings*
O'Connell, Michael, 241
O'Connor, Sandra D., 162
Office of Federal Activities (OFA), 186
Office of Technology Assessment (OTA), 105,
    107, 118, 166
Old-growth forests, 18, 223–24
Olson, Todd G., 38, 79
Order of Things, The (Foucault), 65
Our Common Failure, 88
Owls, 18, 50, 58, 149
Ozone-depleting substances, 132, 138

PACFISH (aquatic habitat management strat-
    egy), 55
Packwood, Robert, xxii, xxv
Partridge, Ernest, 240, 241
Patlis, Jason, 33
Patterson, B. D., 31
Pavlik, B., 240
Pelly Amendment to the Fisherman's Protec-
    tive Act, 93–94, 100–101, 103, 126
Pelosi Amendment, 185–86
Pendergrass, John, 146
Pennsylvania, 236
Permit programs, nationwide, 52
Peru, 122
Peters, Robert L., 239, 240
Photosynthesis, marine, 120
Pinchot, Gifford, 5
Pine rocklands, 223
Plant species, 1, 18, 19, 150
Plotkin, Mark J., 240
Plovers, 149
Pollution control:
    Clean Water Act, 167
    coordinating, 146
    effluent guidelines, 170–72
    Environmental Protection Agency, U.S,
        166
    hazardous waste, 172–73
    Montreal Guidelines for the Protection of
        the Marine Environment Against Pol-
        lution from Land–Based Sources, 128

    progress in, 222
    water quality standards, 168–70
Pollution Prevention Act of 1990, 167
Population Bomb, The (Ehrlich), 65
Porpoises, 125
Portugal, 235–36
Prairie dogs, 149
Prairies, tallgrass, 28
Precautionary principle, 103, 197–99
Predators, 1, 106
Present-value discounting techniques, 225–26
Presettlement conditions, 27
Prince, The (Machiavelli), xxv
Prip, Christian, 216
Private property, see Property rights
Privatization, 211
Production and process method (PPM) mea-
    sures, 82, 94, 95, 101–2
Product standards, 94
Programmatic actions of federal agencies,
    51–54
Project Development Facility, GEF's, 140–41
Property rights, xiii
    Bill of Rights, 230
    Commission on Sustainable Development,
        UN, 153
    conservation value into economic value,
        translating, 71–72
    ecosystem management, 12–13
    Endangered Species Act, 35
    enemy, determining the, 67–68
    Fifth Amendment, 217–18, 232
    habitat transaction method, 72–78
    incentives, perverse, 68–70
    intellectual, 150–51, 210, 214, 216
    Lucas vs. South Carolina Coastal Council
        (property rights), 41, 232
    measuring biodiversity, 70–71
    National Biological Service, 152
    nuisance principles, 38–39
    programmatic actions of federal agencies, 53
    public trust for biodiversity, 145–46, 152,
        160
    San Bruno Mountain Habitat Conservation
        Plan, 60
    sui generis system, 150–51
    Supreme Court, U.S., 40
    takings, incidental, 50–51
Public awareness of biological diversity, xii, xx,
    151–52
Public trust for biodiversity, 145–52, 157–63

Quakers, 61

Radicalism of the American Revolution, The
    (Wood), 65
Ramsar Convention of 1975, 85

Randall, Alan, 240
Rawls, John, 226
Reading, Richard, 153
Reagan, Ronald, 223
Record of decision (ROD), 182
*Reducing Risk: Setting Priorities and Strategies for
    Environmental Protection,* 166, 174, 239
Regional fishery organizations, 124–25
Regulations, government, xx
    baseline information needed, 147
    businesses, U.S. overseas, 87–88
    European Community, 96
    genetic engineering, xxi
    land, 77–78
    leghold traps, 96
    nonfederal concerns, intruding on, 2
    standards, 94
    traditional approach to land/sea, 77–78,
        121
Rehnquist, William, 193
Reid, Walter V., 215–16
Renewable Resource (RPA) program, 5
Representative democracy, 60–61
Republican party, 34, 39
Reserve system, cohesive regional, 77
Resource Conservation and Recovery Act
    (RCRA), 146, 166, 172
Respect for Nature (Taylor), 241
Rhode Island, 236
Rich, Bruce, 144
Risk decision square, 227–29
River of the Mother of God and Other Essays
    (Leopold), 11, 200
Rogers, William, 175
Rohlf, D. J., 31
Rolston, Holmes, III, 241
*RSVP Cycles, The: Creative Processes in the
    Human Environment* (Halprin), 65
Ruhl, J. B., 41
Russia, 88, 100

Saal, Frederick S. von, 239
Salmonid stocks, Pacific, 49–50, 55
San Bruno Mountain Habitat Conservation
    Plan (HCP), 59–64
Sanchez, V., 216
Sanctions, trade, 93–94, 100–101, 103,
    126–27
Sand County Almanac, A (Leopold), 11, 65
San Francisco Bay and Delta, 4, 50, 55, 58
San Joaquin Delta Estuary, 4, 50
Santa Clara Law, 65
Satellite imagery, 223
Saving All the Parts (Barker), 200
Saving Nature's Legacy (Cooperrider & Noss),
    200, 219, 240, 241
Sax, Joseph, 160, 163, 232, 242

Scale, importance of, 25, 28–29
Scalia, Antonin, 232
Schlickeisen, Rodger, 219
Science, sensible standards for, 183
Science Advisory Board (SAB), 166, 174, 223
Scientific American, 32
Scientific evidence and legal system's re-
    sponse to biodiversity, 23–24, 191–
    200
Scientific resources from the oceans, 120
Scientific uncertainty, 29–30, 44, 198, 224
Scientist-preachers, xi
Scott, Michael, xi
Seeds, ownership of, 150–51, 205–6
Sen XV, Soshitsu, 65
Shendon, Philip, xxv
Sherman, Paul B., 215
Shiva, Vandana, 215
*Should Trees Have Standing? Toward Legal Rights
    for Natural Objects* (Stone), 65, 237, 242
Sierra Club, 5, 143
    see also under Court system and environ-
        mental protections
Silent Spring (Carson), 65, 146
Simberloff, D., 31, 239
Simon, Julian L., 224, 240
Single species orientation, 18–19, 22, 24, 48,
    121, 194
Site-specific actions, 53–54
Small Grants Program, GEF's, 141
Snails, 14
Snakes, 105
Social tensions over biodiversity protection,
    218
Society of Conservation Biology, 194
Sohn, Louis B., 129
Songbirds, 17
Soto, Ana M., 239
Soulé, M. E., 118
South Dakota, 110
Species protection:
    coarse filters, 45
    court system, 48
    critics of, xxii
    ecosystem management, 191
    free market influencing, 38
    healthy environment needed for, xxi
    jobs *vs.,* 2, 14
    keystone species, 13–14
    National Marine Fisheries Service, 48,
        49–50
    obstacles to biodiversity, 17
    programmatic actions of federal agencies, 53
    scientific methods, 223
    species–by–species, 18–19, 22, 24, 48, 121,
        194
Sponges, sea, 120

Standards, water quality, 168–70
Standards in international trade, 94, 126
State governments:
  assumption programs, 52
  constitutional environmental provisions, 236
  Endangered Species Act, 37
  environmental policy acts (SEPAs), 109
  exotic species, 110, 113, 115–17
  instream flow requirements, 162
  police powers, 2
  successful conservation efforts, 17
  water issues, 146, 169
State of the World (Brown), 219
Static environmental conditions, 26–27
Stockholm Declaration, 88
Stone, Christopher, 65, 237
Structure of Scientific Revolutions, The (Kuhn), 65
Subsides to public lands, government, 38
Subsidiary Body on Scientific, Technical, and Technological
  Advice (SBSTTA), 84, 204
Subsistence economy, 216
Sui generis (its own kind) system and property rights, 150–51
Supreme Court, U.S., 39, 40, 51, 175
  see also Court system and environmental protections
Sustainable development, 65, 83, 85, 88, 205–6, 209–12
Sustainable dynamic areas (SDA), 5
Switzerland, 84
Swordfish, 122

Taiwan, 103
Takings, 50–51
  see also Property rights
Tao of Physics (Capra), 65
Tarlock, Dan, 232, 242
Taxol (anticancer drug), 205
Taylor, Paul, 241
Tea Life, Teachers Mind (Sen XV), 65
Technical support in conservation planning process, 63
Technologies to Maintain Biological Diversity, 175
Tellico Dam project (Tennessee), 147–48, 152, 153
Texas, 110
Theory, relevance of, 25–28
Theory of Island Biogeography, The (MacArthur & Wilson), 32
This Fissured Land: An Ecological History of India (Gadgil & Guha), 215
Thomas, Jack W., 5
Thoreau, Henry D., xxiii
Thorton, Robert D., 79

Three Gorges Dam project (China), 87, 137
Tigers, 137
Tilman, David, 153
Timber industry, xiii, 23, 85, 108, 187
Tobin, Richard, 31, 241
Tongass National Forest (Alaska), xiii
Total maximum daily load (TMDL), 169
Toward a History of Needs (Illich), 216
Townsend, Kenneth N., 214
Toxic Substance Control Act (TSCA), 146
Trade, international:
  Biodiversity Convention, 206–7
  environment vs., 86–87, 94
  exotic species, 83, 108, 113
  GATT, 82, 101–3
  implementation of trade measures, 95–101
  intellectual property rights, 150–51
  sanctions and standards, 93–95, 126–27
Trade Related Intellectual Property Rights (TRIPS), 150
Transnational and Contemporary Problems, 130
Treaty for the Preservation and Protection of Fur Seals of 1911, 84
Tuna, 89, 94, 103, 104, 125, 126
Turkey (country), 236
Turner, B. L., II, 239
Turning Point (Capra), 65
Turtle excluder devices (TEDS), 98
Turtles, sea, 97–98, 126
Tyranny of the Majority (Guinier), 220

Udall, Stewart, 229
Umbrella species, 45
Uncertainty, scientific, 29–30, 44, 198, 224
Understanding on the Interim Guidance on the Implementation of the GEF Project/Program Cycle, 144
Unilateral trade measures, 87, 95, 100–101, 126–27
Unions for the Protections of New Varieties of Plants (UPOV), 153
United Kingdom, 88
United Nations:
  Code on Conduct of Transnational Corporations, 87
  Commission on Sustainable Development (CSD), 83, 85, 132–37, 142–43, 153
  Conference on Environment and Development in 1992, 202–206
  Conference on Highly Migratory and Straddling Stocks in 1993, 124
  Convention on the Law of the Sea (UNCLOS), 84, 123–24, 127
  driftnet fishing, 99–100, 127
  Earth Summit, 81
  Environment Program (UNEP), 128, 130, 135, 185

Food and Agriculture Organization, 123, 153
intergenerational equity, 65
Stockholm Declaration, 88
World Charter for Nature, 88
Upland areas and public trusts, 161
Use of Trade Measures in Selected Multilateral Environmental Agreements (Houseman), 214
Utah, 110
Utilitarianism, concept of, 225–26

Valuing the Earth: Economics, Ecology, Ethics, 214
Van Dyke, J. M., 201
Venezuela, 97
Vienna Convention for the Protection of the Ozone Layer in 1985, 128

Waller, Donald, 1, 4, 31, 200
Washington State Supreme Court, 160
Water issues:
aquifer use, 14
Arun River System (Nepal), 137
California Water Board, 158
Central Valley Project Improvement Act, 55
Consortium for Action to Protect the Earth, 136
coral reefs, 131
effluent guidelines, 168, 170–72
Federal Ecosystem Directorate and Water Policy Council of California, 58
instream flow requirements, 162
intertidal zones, 27
Mono Lake decision, 159
pollution control, 167
programmatic actions of federal agencies, 52
quality standards, 168–70
San Joaquin Delta Estuary, 4, 50
security of nations tied to, 152
state governments, 146
Tellico Dam project (Tennessee), 147–48, 152, 153

Water Quality Act of 1987, 170
Weber, Peter, 129
Weintraub, B. A., 201
Weiss, Edith B., 65, 235, 241, 242
Westman, Walter E., 240
West Virginia, 110
Wetlands, midwestern, 223
Wilcove, D. S., 31
Wildavsky, Aaron, 224, 240
Wild Bird Conservation Act of 1992, 99, 103
Wild Earth, 32
Wild Forests: Conservation Biology and Public-Policy (Alverson, Kuhlmann & Waller), 31, 200
Wildlands Project, 5
Wilson, Edward O., xi, xii, xxiv, 26, 31, 32, 216, 225, 240
Wilson, Pete, 4
Winckler, S., 200
Winston, K. C., 31
Wisconsin National Forests, 190–91
Wisdom of the Spotted Owl: Policy Lessons for a New Century (Yaffee), 31
Wise, John P., 129
Wise use coalitions, 5, 26
Wold, Chris, 213, 215
Wolves, 71, 149, 190–91
Wood, Gorton, 65
World Bank, 83, 142
World Development Report 1992: Development and the Environment, 130
World Heritage Convention of 1975, 85
World Trade Commission, 65
World Trade Organization (WTO), 82, 87, 151, 212
World War II, 61
Wright, Robert, 218, 219
Yankelovich, Daniel, 65

Yost, Nicholas, 65

Zaelke, D., 201